⩕ SAT® MASTERY
READING

MasteryPrep

Inquiries concerning this publication should be mailed to:

MasteryPrep
7117 Florida Blvd.
Baton Rouge, LA 70806

MasteryPrep is a trade name and/or trademark of Ring Publications LLC.

10 9 8 7 6 5 4 3 2 1

ISBN-13: 978-1-948846-77-6

Table of Contents

1 Chapter

Reading Introduction

LEARNING TARGETS

1. Identify pacing techniques that help improve Time Mastery.

2. Implement the basic approach for quantitative information questions.

3. Apply strategies for active reading and avoiding trap answers to Reading questions.

Warm-Up | Do not answer these questions. Skip to page 4.

Questions 1–3 are based on the following passage and supplementary material.

This passage is adapted from Alicia Diefendorf, "The Who and What of Gentrification." (c)2018 by MasteryPrep. Diefendorf is a journalist who focuses on cities and their economies. Gentrification is a phenomenon characterized by the redevelopment of urban neighborhoods primarily for the wealthy.

We are not observing the steady decay of all urban neighborhoods, or a redevelopment of inner-city areas by the wealthy all at once. The 2010 American
Line Community Survey (ACS) did not definitively provide
5 evidence of an overwhelming upper-income takeover of the nation's cities over the past decade. The findings were ambiguous: Many of the larger cities on the East Coast lost low-income residents to the upper class, sometimes in large numbers. Urban areas in the Midwest, including
10 Minneapolis, lost fewer low-income residents to neighborhood gentrification. The cities that showed the least displacement of low-income populations to the wealthy were in the South and Southwest. But when it comes to calculating the wealthy takeover of low-
15 income urban areas, raw ACS numbers are an inexact measuring tool. A closer look at the survey's findings reveals that the gentrification of low-income, inner-city areas between 2000-2010 was primarily driven by the movement of people under 45 into urban areas (45,000
20 of them to Portland alone) and the increasing consumer preference for urbanity, often of those who were raised far from any downtown area.

Gentrified urban areas that gained these younger residents in the first half of the decade preserved those
25 numbers during the recession from 2007 to 2009. These neighborhoods also, according to a 2015 study by *Governing*, experienced somewhat less unemployment than areas not undergoing gentrification. Few young professionals invested in gentrifying neighborhoods
30 during the recession because most did not have sufficient capital to do so. But there is increasing evidence that the investment trends initiated before the economic bust will resume now that the crisis is over. It is essential to remember that evidence of increasing numbers of
35 upper-class residents in a given area is not a marker of gentrification; the wealthy population can rise in urban areas that already house predominantly upper-class residents, in those whose demographics are mixed, and even in those experiencing a modest decline in upper-
40 class population.

Upper-Class Population by Gentrification Size/Rate

Chart 1

2018 Upper-Class Population Shares by
Amount of Gentrification in Urban Areas (%)

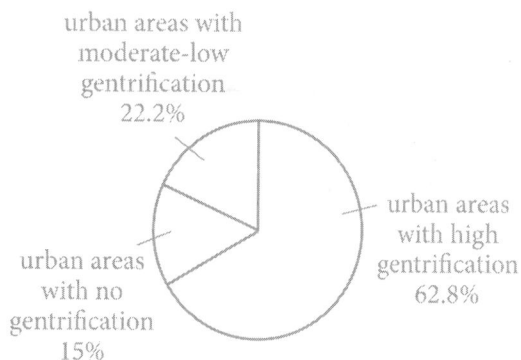

urban areas with moderate-low gentrification
22.2%

urban areas with high gentrification
62.8%

urban areas with no gentrification
15%

Chart 2

2018 Upper-Class Population Growth Rate
by Neighborhood Gentrification

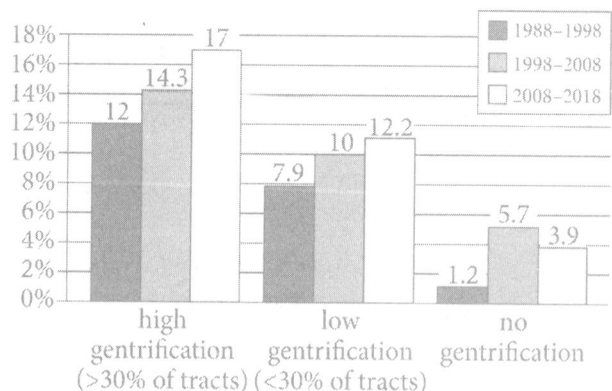

Legend: 1988–1998, 1998–2008, 2008–2018

high gentrification (>30% of tracts): 12, 14.3, 17
low gentrification (<30% of tracts): 7.9, 10, 12.2
no gentrification: 1.2, 5.7, 3.9

Adapted from Clarissa J. Dey, "Gentrification Growth from the Upper Class Since 1990: Positioning the Invasive 2010s on the Map." © 2019 by MasteryPrep

Warm-Up

1

The main purpose of the passage is to

A) explain the problems with gentrification.

B) show gentrification trends over time.

C) propose a potential solution to gentrification.

D) challenge the idea that gentrification is worsening over time.

2

Where does the author indicate that the fewest low-income residents have been lost?

A) The Pacific Northwest

B) Midwest

C) Southwest

D) The East Coast

3

The author of the passage would most likely consider the information in chart 1 to be

A) excellent evidence for the arguments made in the passage.

B) possibly accurate but too crude to be truly informative.

C) compelling but lacking in historical information.

D) representative of a perspective with which the author disagrees.

Foundation

Answer the following question as your teacher leads the discussion.

1. Why is the SAT important?

_____

_____

_____

Refer to these graphs as your teacher discusses the importance of going to college.

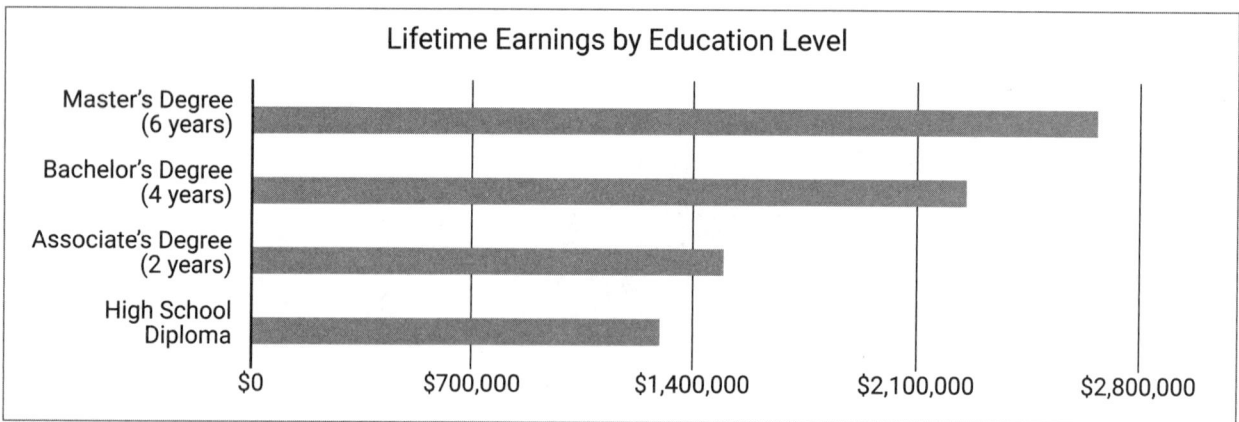

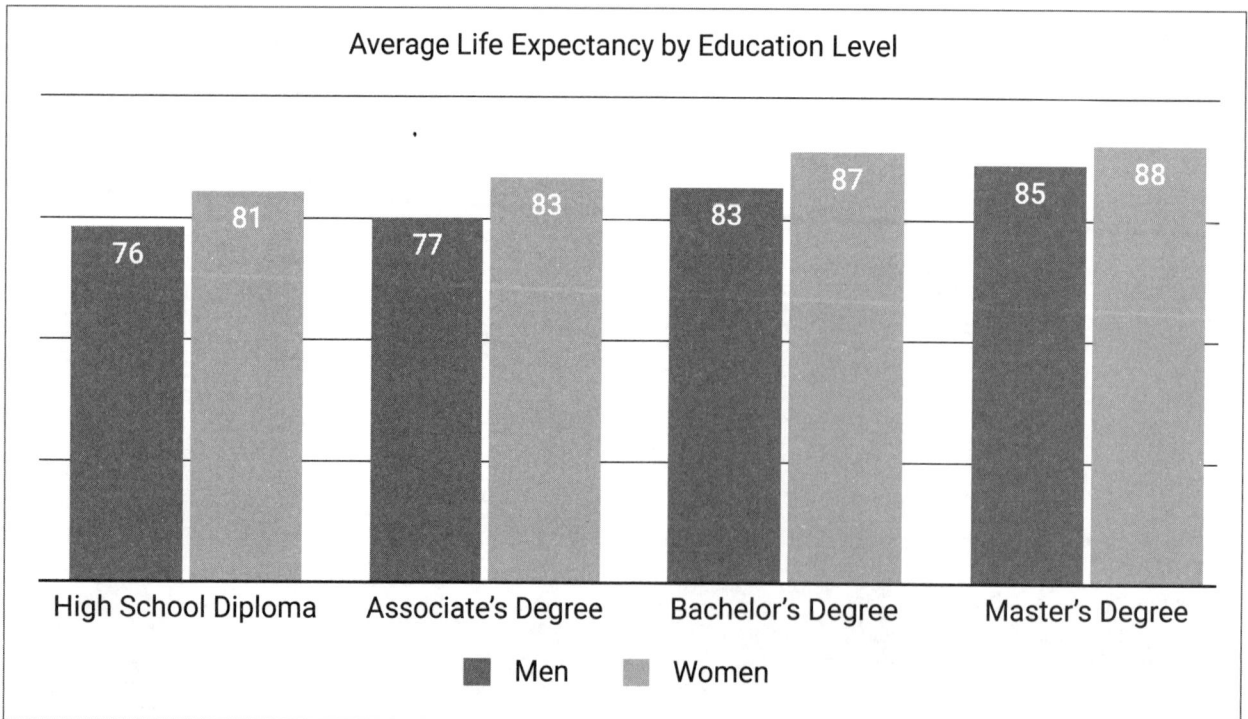

Lifetime Earnings by Education Level

Education Level	
Master's Degree (6 years)	
Bachelor's Degree (4 years)	
Associate's Degree (2 years)	
High School Diploma	

$0 $700,000 $1,400,000 $2,100,000 $2,800,000

Average Life Expectancy by Education Level

	High School Diploma	Associate's Degree	Bachelor's Degree	Master's Degree
Men	76	77	83	85
Women	81	83	87	88

■ Men   ■ Women

Foundation

Write a response to questions 2–4 in the space provided.

2. How will a better SAT score help you?

_____

_____

_____

3. How will a better SAT score help your family?

_____

_____

_____

4. What dreams do you have? How will college help you achieve those dreams?

_____

_____

_____

Fill in the number of points each section of the SAT is worth as your teacher discusses SAT scoring.

Writing and Language

_____

+

Math   **Reading**

_____   _____

1600

5.   About how many points is each question worth? _____

Raw Score: the total number of questions answered correctly.

Foundation

Review the following conversion table with your teacher.

SAT Conversion Table

Raw Score (# of correct answers)	Math Section Score	Reading Test Score	Writing and Language Test Score	Raw Score (# of correct answers)	Math Section Score	Reading Test Score	Writing and Language Test Score
0	200	10	10	31	530	27	29
1	200	10	10	32	540	27	30
2	210	10	10	33	550	28	31
3	230	10	10	34	550	28	31
4	240	11	11	35	560	29	32
5	260	11	12	36	570	29	33
6	270	12	12	37	580	29	33
7	290	13	13	38	590	30	34
8	300	14	14	39	590	30	35
9	320	14	15	40	600	31	36
10	330	15	15	41	610	31	36
11	340	16	16	42	620	32	37
12	350	16	17	43	630	33	39
13	360	17	18	44	640	33	40
14	380	17	18	45	650	34	
15	390	18	19	46	660	35	
16	400	18	19	47	670	35	
17	410	19	20	48	680	36	
18	420	20	21	49	680	37	
19	430	20	22	50	690	37	
20	440	21	22	51	700	39	
21	450	21	23	52	720	40	
22	460	22	24	53	730		
23	470	23	24	54	740		
24	480	23	25	55	760		
25	490	24	25	56	770		
26	500	24	26	57	790		
27	510	25	27	58	800		
28	510	25	27				
29	520	26	28				
30	530	26	29				

Use the conversion table to answer these questions 6–8.

6. If you get a raw score of 32, how many questions did you get correct? _____

7. If you get a raw score of 32, what is your Reading score? _____

8. If you get a raw score of 32, how many Reading points will you earn? _____

Foundation

Answer questions 9–12 to calculate the number of questions you can miss and still reach your goal score.

9. What is your goal score? _____

10. How many Reading points will you need to earn?

    goal score ÷ 4 = _____

    rounded to nearest ten: _____

11. How many Reading questions do you need to get right? Use the conversion table.

    _____ **This is your goal raw score.**

12. How many questions can you afford to miss?

    52 − goal raw score = _____

Foundation

Label each part of the Mastery Pyramid.

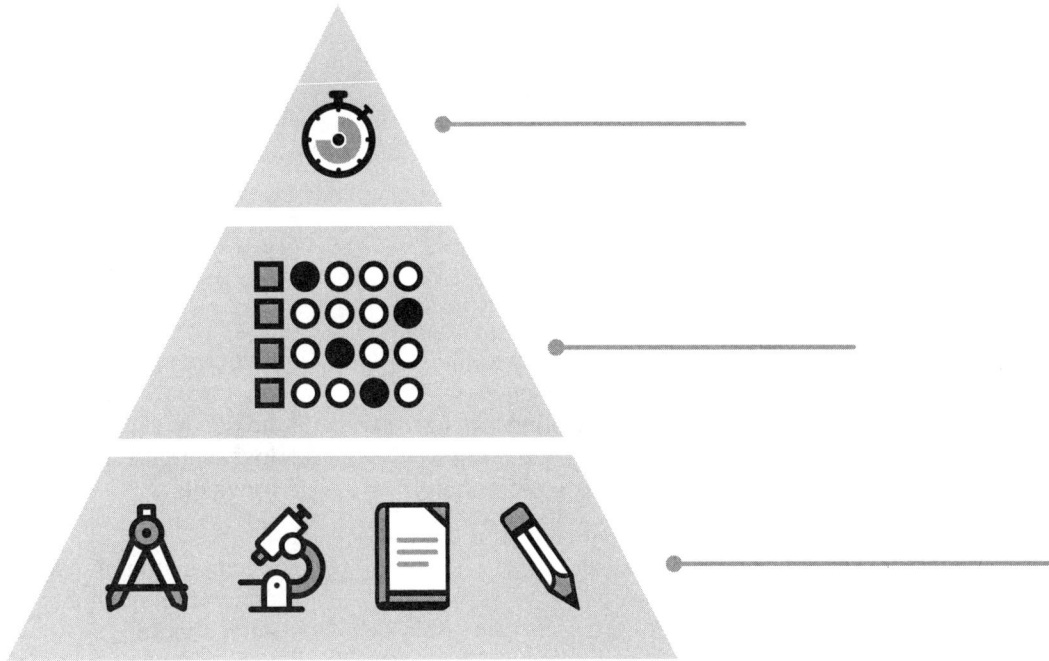

Refer to the following information as your teacher leads the discussion.

Stamina	Pace	Time Management
• Reading is the 1st test section, so it sets the tone for the rest of your experience with the SAT. • **Stamina** is the ability to maintain a high energy level and to focus over a sustained period. • You can improve stamina by practicing lots of questions.	• **Pace** is your average, consistent speed through the test. • The best way to hit a pace on a test is by answering lots of practice questions at that pace beforehand.	• **Time Management** is how well you budget your time answering each question. • If you've spent 30 seconds on a question and there's no end in sight, cut your losses. Make a guess and move on. • Practice time management during the mini-tests in each chapter.

Fill in the pacing plan with your teacher.

Time Limit	# of Passages	Time Spent on Passages	Minutes per Passage	Time Remaining
65 minutes	5	_____ minutes	_____	_____ minutes

Foundation

Review the following graph as you discuss pacing with your teacher.

Reading Difficulty

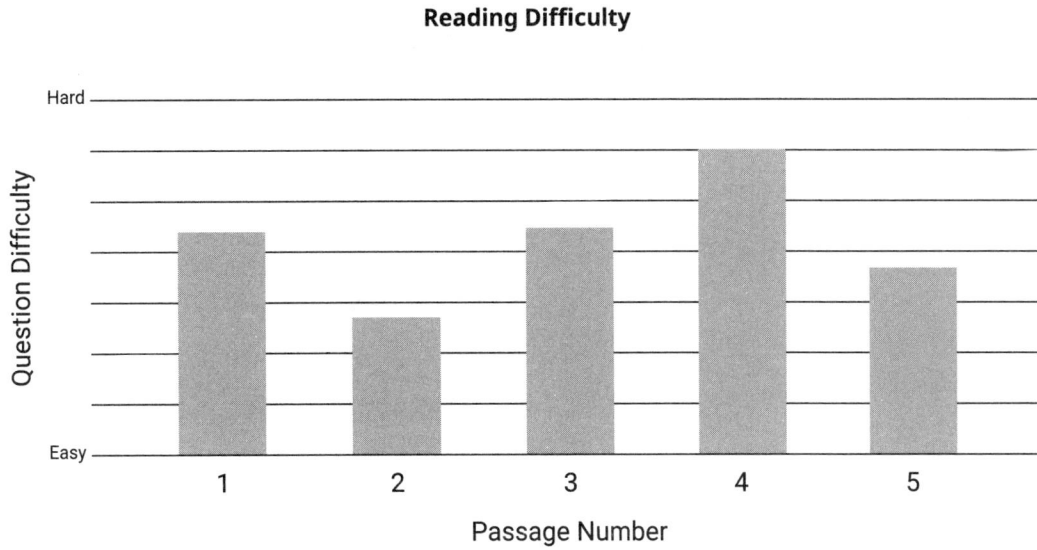

Reading Test Pacing Strategy

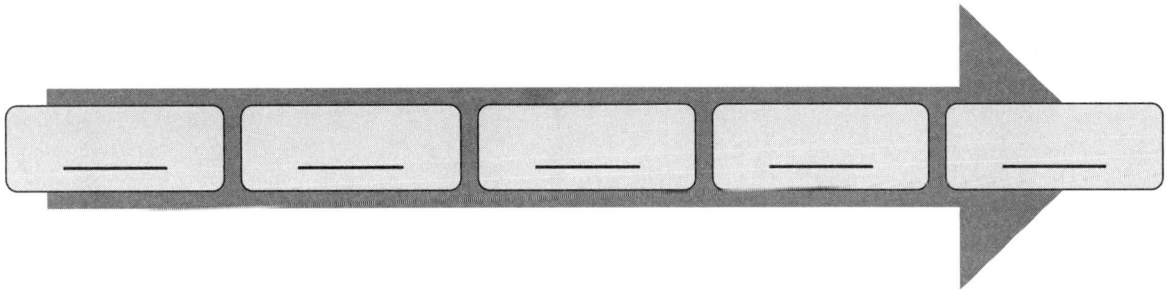

Foundation

If you set your watch to noon exactly, at what time will you begin each new passage or task? Fill in each blank.

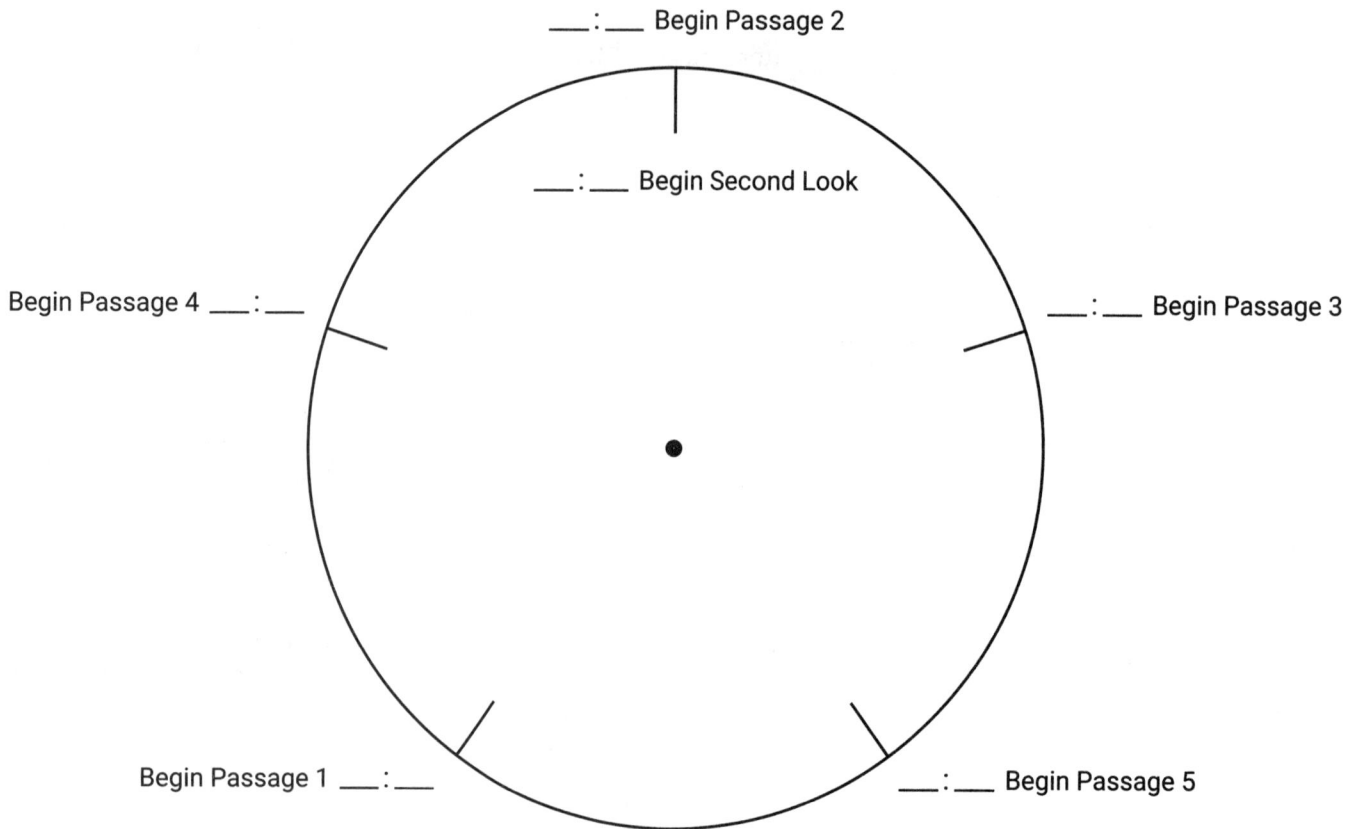

___ : ___ Begin Passage 2

___ : ___ Begin Second Look

Begin Passage 4 ___ : ___

___ : ___ Begin Passage 3

Begin Passage 1 ___ : ___

___ : ___ Begin Passage 5

Reading Passage Pacing Plan	

Time Limit:
 	
_____
	1. Active Reading
	  - Engage with the text.
	  - Falling behind? Read the first and last sentence of each paragraph.

Time Limit:
 	
_____
	2. Answer Questions
	  - Line numbers first.
	  - First question last (unless it's a line number question).

Time Limit:
 	
_____
	3. Second Look and Cleanup
	  - Check your answers.
	  - Bubble in answers on your answer sheet.
	  - Don't skip this step!

2

The passage indicates that the hypothesis made by the archeologists in lines 34–38 may be

A) irrelevant.

B) biased.

C) false.

D) verifiable.

5

Which choice provides the best evidence for the answer to the previous question?

A) Lines 8–12 ("Students have … school")

B) Lines 15–16 ("People … realize")

C) Lines 18–23 ("The impact … down")

D) Lines 24–26 ("Venturing … those efforts")

This page intentionally left blank

Foundation

Answer the questions or fill in the blanks as your teacher leads the discussion.

13. What is a black hole question?

_____

14. Skipping means skipping the work, not skipping _____.

15. On the Reading test, if you're wondering if you're taking even slightly too long on a question, what should you do?

_____

Foundation

Review the following chart as your teacher leads the discussion.

Within-Passage Difficulty Curve

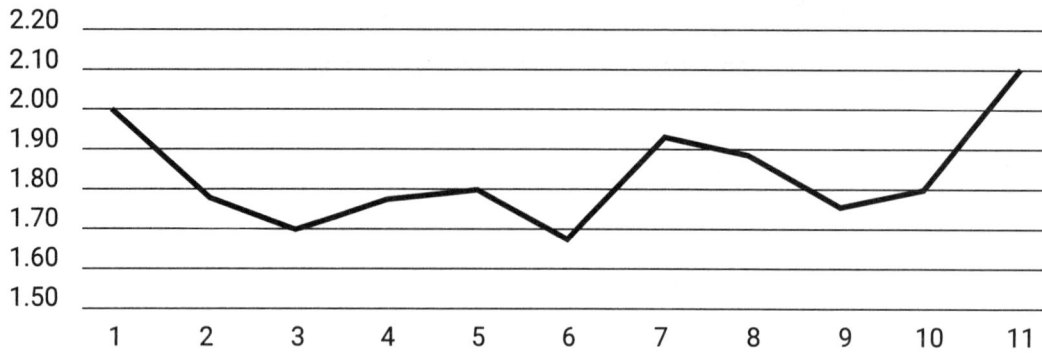

Review the following as your teacher leads the discussion.

Information and Ideas	Rhetoric	Synthesis
✓ Reading Closely • Determining explicit meanings • Determining implicit meanings • Using analogical reasoning ✓ Citing Textual Evidence ✓ Determining Central Ideas and Themes ✓ Summarizing ✓ Understanding Relationships ✓ Interpreting Words and Phrases in Context	✓ Analyzing Word Choice ✓ Analyzing Text Structure • Analyzing overall text structure • Analyzing part-whole relationships ✓ Analyzing Point of View ✓ Analyzing Purpose ✓ Analyzing Arguments • Analyzing claims and counterclaims • Assessing reasoning • Analyzing evidence	✓ Analyzing Quantitative Information ✓ Analyzing Multiple Texts

SAT Mastery Chapter Map

Introduction — Warm-Up → Foundation — Practice Set 1 → Approach — Practice Set 2 → Strategies — Practice Set 3 → Mini-Test — Wrap-Up

Review the following information with your teacher.

Passage 1
U.S. and World Literature

Focus on ...
- Story Arc: what happens in the beginning, middle, and end
- Characters: motivation, actions, relationships, and emotions

Passages 2 and 4
History and Social Studies

Focus on ...
- Passage Main Idea: usually found in the first or last paragraph
- Evidence: any data or support the author gives for a claim
- Opinions: of both the author and any other people mentioned
- Purpose or Takeaway: why the author is writing this (usually in the first or last paragraph)

Passages 3 and 5
Science

Focus on ...
- Passage Main Idea: usually found in the first or last paragraph
- Evidence: any data or support the author gives for a claim
- Technical Terms: use them as signposts

Paired Passages

As you read, look for ...
- the main idea of each passage
- supporting arguments for each claim
- the relationship and references between the passages
- shared traits between the passages

This page intentionally left blank

Practice Set 1 | Do not answer these questions. Skip to page 22.

Questions 1–11 are based on the following passage and supplementary material.

This passage is adapted from Justine Martino, "Advancements in Wind Turbine Technology." © 2018 by MasteryPrep.

Wind turbine installations are ongoing, although the manufacturing industry is a bit troubled because the demand for wind turbines greatly outstrips supply.
Line This difficult marketplace might be hampering growth,
5 but innovations continue; based on the excitement this month at the AWEA Clean Power Expo in Denver, Colorado, specialists in the wind turbine industry are excited about the future.

One advancement that's thrilled many people is the
10 creation of large wind turbine rotors. A few years ago, wind turbines cost $2.40 a watt, and Keith Longtin, wind products manager at General Electric and a leading wind turbine expert, hypothesized that the cost would never drop below $2 a watt. However, he recently stated,
15 "Today, the cost is $1.60 a watt, and it's possible it will continue to decrease."

The Office of Energy Efficiency & Renewable Energy has set a target of reaching less than $1.50 per watt—not just for wind turbines, but for entire power systems—by
20 2025. Longtin believes the wind power market might reach that goal before then. If achieved, the entire cost of wind power could be approximately 70 cents per kilowatt-hour, much less expensive than the projected average price for electricity generated by new coal-fired
25 power plants.

Every division of the wind turbine manufacturing industry has been seeking methods to reduce costs and improve the electric output of wind turbines, which has resulted in continual price reductions. To
30 illustrate, Longtin gives the example of turbines that use curved blades to capture greater wind speeds: Longtin's department built a blade in the 2000s that resulted in new advancements for wind turbines—advancements that are unmatched to this day. At the time, his team had
35 to use costly manufacturing techniques to create a mold for casting the enormous blade. But recent innovations have made it possible to use advanced printing technology to create even sleeker curves. New research has found that 3-D printing machines can produce
40 blades that generate power up to five times faster than traditional blades.

At the same time, engineers at the Berkeley National Laboratory (BNL) have created floating marine platforms using a type of fiberglass from
45 Pittsburgh Plate Glass called Advantex, which is light but durable. Floating turbine platforms may reduce the cost of building wind turbines, making wind energy less expensive. BNL's floating platform—a spar-buoy system—is currently the only competitor to anchored
50 platforms with regard to mass production.

One of Longtin's former co-workers, Robert Yost, CEO of Yost Wind Turbine Development, stated this month that his company is building a new commercial line of jet engine-style mini wind turbines that can be
55 used on wind farms. The general idea, which is not new, is that the wind would flow between rows of smaller turbines. This technology is especially efficient because the wind turbines are placed close together, increasing energy output. Whereas a traditional wind turbine might
60 generate 240 watts of power, a wall of mini turbines can create up to 440 watts of power. He anticipates that the mini turbines will create 20 to 30 percent more energy over the long term.

In coming years, Longtin has high hopes for artificial
65 intelligence, expecting to profit from the large reductions in expenses that artificial intelligence (AI) has created in other industries. He aims to improve wind turbine efficiency by combining AI with traditional turbine technology, allowing blades to respond more quickly
70 to varying wind speeds. Longtin projects that using AI could raise efficiency from approximately 33 percent to 45 percent. Further, incorporating additional service notifications for maintenance workers could raise wind power efficiency as much as 48 percent, which would
75 reduce by a third the number of wind turbines needed on a wind farm. Longtin is hopeful that, despite the challenges inherent in working with a constantly moving object, the ability to use AI with wind turbines will soon be available.

Figure 1

Current Energy Efficiency per
Megawatt-Hour in 2019

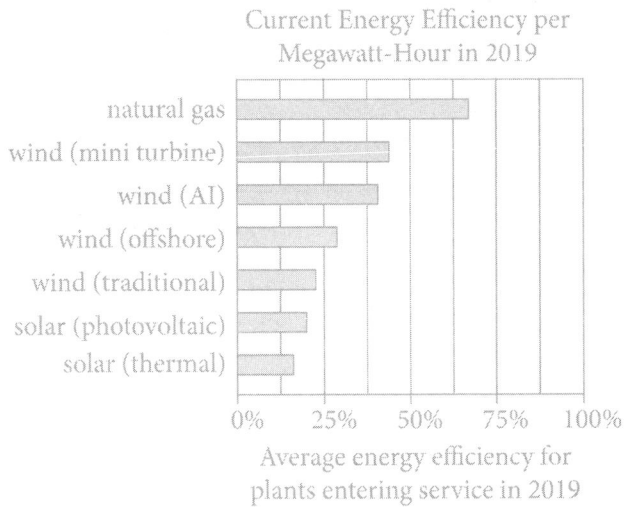

Average energy efficiency for
plants entering service in 2019

Adapted from Meghan Liederman,
"Competitive Energy Sources Widen the
Field." © 2019 by MasteryPrep.

Figure 2

Wind Turbine Efficiency per Megawatt-Hour (MWh)
(Projected beyond 2015)

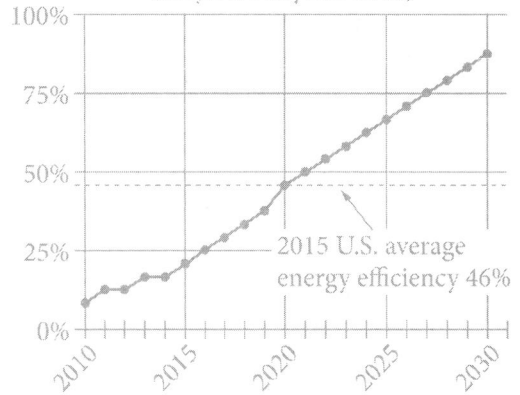

2015 U.S. average
energy efficiency 46%

Adapted from Atsu Gamal, "Tall, Sleek,
Powerful: Is Energy's Future in Wind
Turbines?" © 2019 by MasteryPrep.

1

This passage is written from the point of view of a

A) consumer evaluating various options.

B) scientist comparing multiple research projects.

C) journalist explaining innovations in a field.

D) hobbyist expanding upon earlier theories.

2

As used in line 4, "difficult" most nearly means

A) unstable.

B) arduous.

C) demanding.

D) inconvenient.

3

It can be inferred from the passage that most people
in the wind power industry believe that

A) the public has been too slow to adopt wind
power.

B) wind turbines have weaknesses that have yet to
be discovered.

C) the electric output compared to the cost of wind
power technology can be improved.

D) Advantex is too costly for widespread adoption.

Approach

Review the following as your teacher leads the discussion on the three steps of the Approach.

Each step on the Approach begins with an E.

Entrance

Central ideas and claims questions can be identified by these terms:

- main idea
- central idea
- central claim
- central problem

The Entrance gives you the information you can use to identify the question type.

Entrance > Evidence and Elimination > Exit

Approach

Review the following as your teacher leads the discussion on the three steps of the Approach.

Reading has an extra step: finding **evidence** in the passage.

Evidence and Elimination

To answer a central ideas and themes question, follow these steps:

1. Reread the introduction and conclusion.
2. Come up with a loose interpretation of the central idea.
3. Eliminate answer choices that don't agree with the central idea.
4. Eliminate answer choices that give details instead of central ideas.

The process focuses on eliminating wrong answers, rather than finding right ones.

Entrance   **Evidence and Elimination**   Exit

Approach

Review the following as your teacher leads the discussion on the three steps of the Approach.

Exit
If you've found the answer ... Compare your answer to the details of the paragraph or passage to ensure they all support this central idea. Mark your answer and keep moving.
If you're stuck between two choices ... Select the choice that is most closely related to the conclusion.
If you have no idea what the answer is ... Select the choice that reflects the claim or topic suggested by the title.

Depending on how confident you feel about answering the question, you can Exit in one of three ways.

The following questions refer to the passage on page 20. Review questions 7 and 8. Work with your teacher to choose the correct answer from the remaining choices.

You'll get two chances to practice Exit.

Entrance 〉 Evidence and Elimination 〉 Exit

This page intentionally left blank

Entrance
Quantitative information questions can be identified by these terms: • chart • table • graph • figure • infographic

Questions 4–6 refer to the passage on pages 20–21. Review question 4 with your teacher. Do not answer the question.

Entrance 〉 Evidence and Elimination 〉 Exit

4

Which of the following statements is supported by Figure 1?

A) Mini turbines are about twice as efficient as traditional turbines.

B) Offshore wind platforms are the least energy efficient form of wind energy.

C) Natural gas output exceeds wind energy utilizing AI by at least 50%.

D) Traditional wind turbines are as efficient as offshore wind platforms.

Approach

Review questions 5 and 6 on your own. Circle the part of the question that identifies it as a quantitative information question.

5

According to Figure 2, in what year is the average efficiency of wind turbine power projected to be equal to the 2015 U.S. average energy efficiency?

A) 2015

B) 2020

C) 2024

D) 2030

6

According to Figure 1, in 2019, the efficiency of which of the following power sources was projected to be closest to the 2015 U.S. average energy efficiency shown in Figure 2?

A) Wind (AI)

B) Wind (offshore)

C) Wind (traditional)

D) Wind (mini turbine)

Questions 1–11 are based on the following passage and supplementary material.

This passage is adapted from Justine Martino, "Advancements in Wind Turbine Technology." © 2018 by MasteryPrep.

Wind turbine installations are ongoing, although the manufacturing industry is a bit troubled because the demand for wind turbines greatly outstrips supply.
Line This difficult marketplace might be hampering growth,
5 but innovations continue; based on the excitement this month at the AWEA Clean Power Expo in Denver, Colorado, specialists in the wind turbine industry are excited about the future.

One advancement that's thrilled many people is the
10 creation of large wind turbine rotors. A few years ago, wind turbines cost $2.40 a watt, and Keith Longtin, wind products manager at General Electric and a leading wind turbine expert, hypothesized that the cost would never drop below $2 a watt. However, he recently stated,
15 "Today, the cost is $1.60 a watt, and it's possible it will continue to decrease."

The Office of Energy Efficiency & Renewable Energy has set a target of reaching less than $1.50 per watt—not just for wind turbines, but for entire power systems—by
20 2025. Longtin believes the wind power market might reach that goal before then. If achieved, the entire cost of wind power could be approximately 70 cents per kilowatt-hour, much less expensive than the projected average price for electricity generated by new coal-fired
25 power plants.

Every division of the wind turbine manufacturing industry has been seeking methods to reduce costs and improve the electric output of wind turbines, which has resulted in continual price reductions. To
30 illustrate, Longtin gives the example of turbines that use curved blades to capture greater wind speeds: Longtin's department built a blade in the 2000s that resulted in new advancements for wind turbines—advancements that are unmatched to this day. At the time, his team had
35 to use costly manufacturing techniques to create a mold for casting the enormous blade. But recent innovations have made it possible to use advanced printing technology to create even sleeker curves. New research has found that 3-D printing machines can produce
40 blades that generate power up to five times faster than traditional blades.

At the same time, engineers at the Berkeley National Laboratory (BNL) have created floating marine platforms using a type of fiberglass from
45 Pittsburgh Plate Glass called Advantex, which is light but durable. Floating turbine platforms may reduce the costs of building wind turbines, making wind energy less expensive. BNL's floating platform—a spar-buoy system—is currently the only competitor to anchored
50 platforms with regard to mass production.

One of Longtin's former co-workers, Robert Yost, CEO of Yost Wind Turbine Development, stated this month that his company is building a new commercial line of jet engine-style mini wind turbines that can be
55 used on wind farms. The general idea, which is not new, is that the wind would flow between rows of smaller turbines. This technology is especially efficient because the wind turbines are placed close together, increasing energy output. Whereas a traditional wind turbine might
60 generate 240 watts of power, a wall of mini turbines can create up to 440 watts of power. He anticipates that the mini turbines will create 20 to 30 percent more energy over the long term.

In coming years, Longtin has high hopes for artificial
65 intelligence, expecting to profit from the large reductions in expenses that AI has created in other industries. He aims to improve wind turbine efficiency by combining AI with traditional turbine technology, allowing blades to respond more quickly to varying wind speeds.
70 Longtin projects that using AI could raise efficiency from approximately 33 percent to 45 percent. Further, incorporating additional service notifications for maintenance workers could raise wind power efficiency as much as 48 percent, which would reduce by a third
75 the number of wind turbines needed on a wind farm. Longtin is hopeful that, despite the challenges inherent in working with a constantly moving object, the ability to use AI with wind turbines will soon be available.

Approach

Figure 1

Current Energy Efficiency per
Megawatt-Hour in 2019

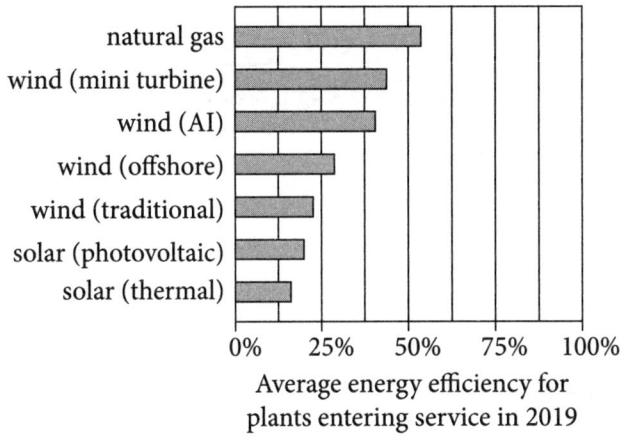

Average energy efficiency for
plants entering service in 2019

Adapted from Meghan Liederman, "Competitive Energy
Sources Widen the Field." © 2019 by MasteryPrep.

Figure 2

Wind Turbine Efficiency per Megawatt-Hour (MWh)
(Projected beyond 2015)

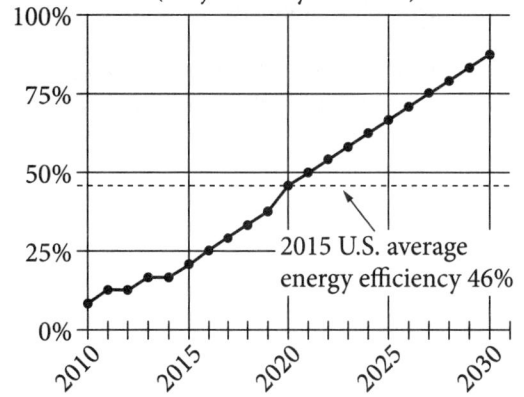

2015 U.S. average
energy efficiency 46%

Adapted from Atsu Gamal, "Tall, Sleek, Powerful: Is Energy's
Future in Wind Turbines?" © 2019 by MasteryPrep.

Evidence and Elimination

To answer a quantitative information question, follow these steps:

1. Read the graphic's labels and examine its data.
2. Fact check each choice against data from the graph. If a choice makes multiple claims, fact check each one.

Questions 4–6 refer to the passage on pages 28–29. Answer question 4 with your teacher.

Entrance **Evidence and Elimination** Exit

4

Which of the following statements is supported by Figure 1?

A) Mini turbines are about twice as efficient as traditional turbines.

B) Offshore wind platforms are the least energy efficient form of wind energy.

C) Natural gas output exceeds wind energy utilizing AI by at least 50%.

D) Traditional wind turbines are as efficient as offshore wind platforms.

Approach

Answer questions 5 and 6 on your own. Focus on eliminating incorrect answers.

5

According to Figure 2, in what year is the average efficiency of wind turbine power projected to be equal to the 2015 U.S. average energy efficiency?

A) 2015

B) 2020

C) 2024

D) 2030

6

According to Figure 1, in 2019, the efficiency of which of the following power sources is projected to be closest to the 2015 U.S. average energy efficiency shown in Figure 2?

A) Wind (AI)

B) Wind (offshore)

C) Wind (traditional)

D) Wind (mini turbine)

Approach

Exit
If you've found the answer ... Double-check that the facts in the answer choice match the information in the graphic.
If you're stuck between two choices ... Get technical. Eliminate the choice that doesn't exactly state what is represented in the graphic or discussed in the passage.
If you have no idea what the answer is ... Guess a choice that has strong similarities to at least one other choice.

Questions 7 and 8 refer to the passage on pages 28–29. Review questions 7 and 8. Work with your teacher to choose the correct answer from the remaining choices.

Entrance 〉 Evidence and Elimination 〉 **Exit**

7

Which choice is supported by the data in Figure 2?

A) Wind turbine efficiency was stable between 2013 and 2014.

B) Wind turbine efficiency rose at a steady rate between 2010 and 2015.

C) Wind turbine efficiency is projected to reach 75% by 2025.

D) Wind turbine efficiency is expected to increase through 2050.

8

Which statement is best supported by the data presented in Figure 1?

A) Natural gas is more efficient than all other forms of energy.

B) Wind turbines utilizing AI are less efficient than offshore wind platforms.

C) Offshore wind platforms are more efficient than all other forms of energy.

D) Thermal energy is more efficient than photovoltaic energy.

This page intentionally left blank

Practice Set 2 | Do not answer these questions. Skip to page 36.

Questions 1-11 are based on the following passage and supplementary material.

This passage is adapted from Justine Martino, "Advancements in Wind Turbine Technology." © 2018 by MasteryPrep.

Wind turbine installations are ongoing, although the manufacturing industry is a bit troubled because the demand for wind turbines greatly outstrips supply.
Line This difficult marketplace might be hampering growth,
5 but innovations continue; based on the excitement this month at the AWEA Clean Power Expo in Denver, Colorado, specialists in the wind turbine industry are excited about the future.

One advancement that's thrilled many people is the
10 creation of large wind turbine rotors. A few years ago, wind turbines cost $2.40 a watt, and Keith Longtin, wind products manager at General Electric and a leading wind turbine expert, hypothesized that the cost would never drop below $2 a watt. However, he recently stated,
15 "Today, the cost is $1.60 a watt, and it's possible it will continue to decrease."

The Office of Energy Efficiency & Renewable Energy has set a target of reaching less than $1.50 per watt—not just for wind turbines, but for entire power systems—by
20 2025. Longtin believes the wind power market might reach that goal before then. If achieved, the entire cost of wind power could be approximately 70 cents per kilowatt-hour, much less expensive than the projected average price for electricity generated by new coal-fired
25 power plants.

Every division of the wind turbine manufacturing industry has been seeking methods to reduce costs and improve the electric output of wind turbines, which has resulted in continual price reductions. To
30 illustrate, Longtin gives the example of turbines that use curved blades to capture greater wind speeds: Longtin's department built a blade in the 2000s that resulted in new advancements for wind turbines—advancements that are unmatched to this day. At the time, his team had
35 to use costly manufacturing techniques to create a mold for casting the enormous blade. But recent innovations have made it possible to use advanced printing technology to create even sleeker curves. New research has found that 3-D printing machines can produce
40 blades that generate power up to five times faster than traditional blades.

At the same time, engineers at the Berkeley National Laboratory (BNL) have created floating marine platforms using a type of fiberglass from
45 Pittsburgh Plate Glass called Advantex, which is light but durable. Floating turbine platforms may reduce the costs of building wind turbines, making wind energy less expensive. BNL's floating platform—a spar-buoy system—is currently the only competitor to anchored
50 platforms with regard to mass production.

One of Longtin's former co-workers, Robert Yost, CEO of Yost Wind Turbine Development, stated this month that his company is building a new commercial line of jet engine-style mini wind turbines that can be
55 used on wind farms. The general idea, which is not new, is that the wind would flow between rows of smaller turbines. This technology is especially efficient because the wind turbines are placed close together, increasing energy output. Whereas a traditional wind turbine might
60 generate 240 watts of power, a wall of mini turbines can create up to 440 watts of power. He anticipates that the mini turbines will create 20 to 30 percent more energy over the long term.

In coming years, Longtin has high hopes for artificial
65 intelligence, expecting to profit from the large reductions in expenses that AI has created in other industries. He aims to improve wind turbine efficiency by combining artificial intelligence with traditional turbine technology, allowing blades to respond more quickly to varying wind
70 speeds. Longtin projects that using artificial intelligence could raise efficiency from approximately 33 percent to 45 percent. Further, incorporating additional service notifications for maintenance workers could raise wind power efficiency as much as 48 percent, which would
75 reduce by a third the number of wind turbines needed on a wind farm. Longtin is hopeful that, despite the challenges inherent in working with a constantly moving object, the ability to use AI with wind turbines will soon be available.

Figure 1

Current Energy Efficiency per
Megawatt-Hour in 2019

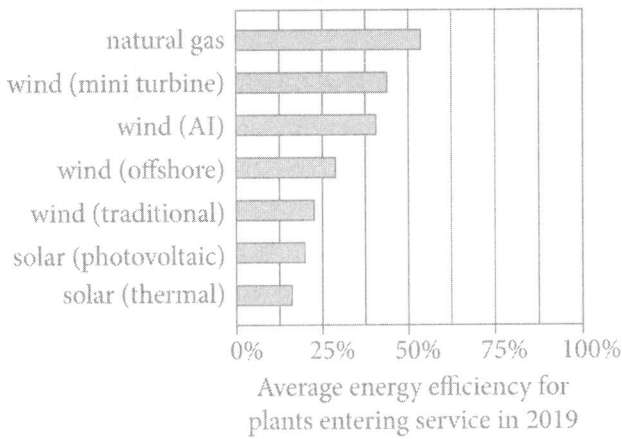

Average energy efficiency for
plants entering service in 2019

Adapted from Meghan Liederman, "Competitive Energy
Sources Widen the Field." © 2019 by MasteryPrep.

Figure 2

Wind Turbine Efficiency per Megawatt-Hour (MWh)
(Projected beyond 2015)

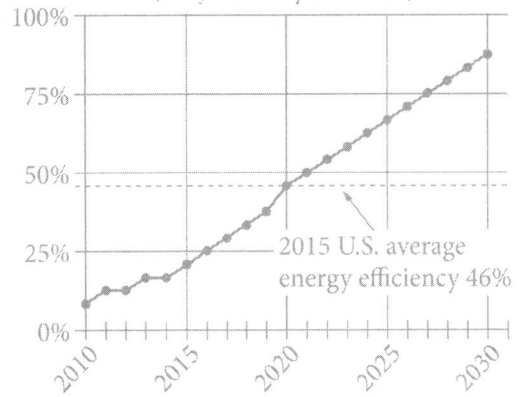

2015 U.S. average
energy efficiency 46%

Adapted from Atsu Gamal, "Tall, Sleek, Powerful: Is Energy's
Future in Wind Turbines?" © 2019 by MasteryPrep.

9

According to the passage, mini turbines will increase efficiency by

A) harnessing wind through tightly spaced turbines.

B) reducing the weight load of wind turbines.

C) utilizing less square footage to operate.

D) costing less to manufacture than other turbines.

10

Which sentence provides the best evidence for the previous question?

A) Lines 36–38 ("But … curves")

B) Lines 55–57 ("The general … turbines")

C) Lines 57–59 ("This technology … output")

D) Lines 61–63 ("He anticipates … term")

11

As it is used in lines 64, "high hopes" most nearly means

A) pleasant feelings.

B) lofty ideas.

C) elevated costs.

D) optimistic expectations.

Strategy

Questions 12–20 are based on the following passage and supplementary material.

This passage is adapted from Lena Baranowski et al., "Volcanoes and Economical Disaster Three Thousand Years Ago in Western Europe." ©2015 by MasteryPrep.

Roughly 3200 years ago, a large volcano erupted somewhere in the world, triggering a lengthy period of civilizational disaster known as the Bronze Age Collapse. Determining precisely which volcano caused it has been
Line difficult.

5 Scientists know a volcano erupted somewhere on Earth sometime during the Late Bronze Age because of evidence that is etched in Scottish stalagmites showing layers of thorium deposits and miniscule grains of volcanic rocks. These stalagmites show that the amount
10 of carbon the unknown volcano sprayed into the atmosphere places it on the list of the most powerful climate-disrupting eruptions of the ancient age, a period from 3000 B.C.E. to 476 C.E. Specifically, the carbon from the volcano cooled Earth by blocking solar rays
15 from reaching the ground.

In 1993, a group of scientists led by dendrologist Darragh Baillie discovered evidence compounding the connection between the unknown eruption and the beginning of the Bronze Age Collapse. They analyzed
20 preserved tree rings from underneath the peat bogs in Ireland, as well as juniper tree ring data from Turkey, to conclude that climate deterioration and the influx of cold weather began suddenly between 1120 and 1150 B.C.E. (and was particularly intense between 1110 and
25 1135 B.C.E.). Such a drastic change suggests that an enormous volcanic eruption discharged carbon into the atmosphere and triggered the cooling. Afterward, further volcanic eruptions and carbon settling, along with the resulting cycling of water and heat, could have
30 caused cooling through 1000 B.C.E.

Geologist Jón Eiríksson and other scientists now think they have found the mystery volcano: Iceland's Hekla 3. Based on archeological data and the remains of ancient civilizations throughout Egypt and ancient
35 Greece, the scientists concluded that Hekla 3 erupted suddenly before the end of the 12th century B.C.E. What resulted was the decline of ancient cities—including the capital of the Assyrian empire, Troy—because of massive drought and famines caused by environmental change.
40 The scientists then began to analyze the appearance of tephra markers (pieces of volcanic rock) around the volcano. They took 112 ice core samples from the Icelandic shelf, revealing layers of benthic material— remnants of sea creatures—and other evidence. The
45 amount of tephra released and the estimated amount of

lava released ($0.5k^3$ meters) suggest the eruption would be classified as a 6 on the volcanic explosivity index (which goes from 1 to 8)—one of the largest during the Bronze Age.
50 The group also completed UV microscopic analyses of the layers of rock remains within the ice cores to establish the time period of the eruption. The blast did not, they found, happen before 1100 B.C.E. and almost certainly occurred in the 12th century B.C.E.
55 The scientists weren't surprised that an Icelandic volcano could have triggered the Collapse, Eiríksson explains. "Arctic volcanos are common sources of environmental change." Also, according to Eiríksson, with tephra evidence throughout the Arctic—in
60 Greenland and Iceland—there is a "definite likelihood" that its source was in the north.

Yet another possibility—given the rock data and geography—is Italy's Santorini, which is thought to have erupted between 1600 and 1627 B.C.E. But analyses by
65 Eiríksson's researchers showed that the size of Santorini's explosion was not big enough to cause significant climate change, whereas Hekla 3's explosion impacted the global climate. This finding supports the theory that Hekla 3 was the cause of the Bronze Age Collapse
70 around 1100 B.C.E.

Estimated Temperature in the Eastern Mediterranean
3300 B.C.E. to 100 B.C.E.

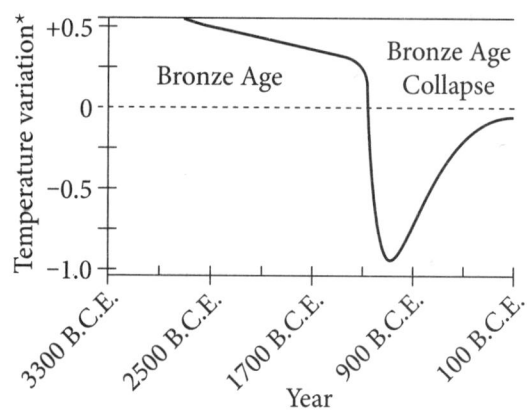

*Variation from the Holocene average temperature, in °C, represented at 0. Adapted from Cedric Melbourne Temperature Record Series, originally published in 2015.

Strategy

Avoiding Trap Answers

The SAT likes to make questions more challenging by offering up appealing but incorrect answer choices. Avoid falling for trap answers using these tips …

1. Outliers: ignore outliers. Only pick them if you've eliminated the other three choices.

2. Recycled Words: get technical. Eliminate the choice that just repeats words from the passage and doesn't exactly state what is represented in the graphic or discussed in the passage.

3. Distractors: take it easy. Avoid choices that require too much reasoning to make it work.

Questions 12–14 refer to the passage on page 36. Use these tips to answer the question as a class.

12

The author of the passage refers to Santorini primarily to convey that the volcano's eruption

A) was insignificant on the volcanic explosivity index.

B) was ruled out as the cause of the Bronze Age Collapse.

C) occurred between 1600 and 1627 B.C.E.

D) resulted in volcanic glass deposits similar to those of Hekla 3.

Strategy

Refer to the passage on page 36. Work with your teacher to answer questions 13 and 14.

13

The passage and the figure are in agreement that the onset of the Bronze Age Collapse began

A) around 1600 B.C.E.

B) around 1100 B.C.E.

C) just before 3200 B.C.E.

D) around 112 B.C.E.

14

What statement is best supported by the data presented in the figure?

A) The greatest temperature drop during the Bronze Age Collapse occurred centuries after the warmest temperatures of the Bronze Age.

B) The sharp drop in temperature supports the theory that an Icelandic volcano erupted during the Bronze Age.

C) Climate change from volcano activity continued for hundreds of years after Hekla 3 exploded.

D) Tephra marker analysis is the best method scientists have for measuring temperature changes after volcano activity.

Active Reading

The most important skill you'll need for the Reading test is the ability to read each passage effectively and in a way that prepares you for the questions to come. Use these tips …

1 As you read, find the main idea or topic of each paragraph. Draw a box around it.

2 Annotate the passage as you read using +, –, and ! symbols.

3 Find what's interesting. Read to learn, not to pass a test.

Question 15 refers to the passage on page 36. Use the elimination tips to answer the question as a class.

15

Which choice best illustrates the claim that Santorini was not to blame for the Bronze Age Collapse?

A) Lines 10–16 ("These stalagmites … ground")

B) Lines 26–28 ("Such … cooling")

C) Lines 41–43 ("The scientists … volcano")

D) Lines 65–69 ("But analyses … climate")

Strategy

Questions 16 and 17 refer to the passage on page 36. Do not answer the questions.

16

The phrase "Yet another possibility" in line 63 implies that

A) massive volcano eruptions occur regularly.

B) the effects of volcanic eruptions endure for decades.

C) scientists are aware of other volcanic eruptions that occurred during the Bronze Age.

D) other volcanos have created huge craters.

17

Where does the author indicate that the Bronze Age volcanic eruption was most likely located?

A) in Italy

B) in the Arctic region

C) in the Antarctic region

D) near the equator, in South America

This page intentionally left blank

Practice Set 3 | Do not answer these questions. Skip to page 44.

Questions 12-20 are based on the following passage and supplementary material.

This passage is adapted from Lena Baranowski et al., "Volcanoes and Economical Disaster Three Thousand Years Ago in Western Europe." ©2015 by MasteryPrep.

Roughly 3200 years ago, a large volcano erupted somewhere in the world, triggering a lengthy period of civilizational disaster known as the Bronze Age Collapse.
Line Determining precisely which volcano caused it has been
5 difficult.

Scientists know a volcano erupted somewhere on Earth sometime during the Late Bronze Age because of evidence that is etched in Scottish stalagmites showing layers of thorium deposits and miniscule grains of
10 volcanic rocks. These stalagmites show that the amount of carbon the unknown volcano sprayed into the atmosphere places it on the list of the most powerful climate-disrupting eruptions of the ancient age, a period from 3000 B.C.E. to 476 C.E. Specifically, the carbon
15 from the volcano cooled Earth by blocking solar rays from reaching the ground.

In 1993, a group of scientists led by dendrologist Darragh Baillie discovered evidence compounding the connection between the unknown eruption and the
20 beginning of the Bronze Age Collapse. They analyzed preserved tree rings from underneath the peat bogs in Ireland, as well as juniper tree ring data from Turkey, to conclude that climate deterioration and the influx of cold weather began suddenly between 1120 and 1150
25 B.C.E. (and was particularly intense between 1110 and 1135 B.C.E.). Such a drastic change suggests that an enormous volcanic eruption discharged carbon into the atmosphere and triggered the cooling. Afterward, further volcanic eruptions and carbon settling, along
30 with the resulting cycling of water and heat, could have caused cooling through 1000 B.C.E.

Geologist Jón Eiríksson and other scientists now think they have found the mystery volcano: Iceland's Hekla 3. Based on archeological data and the remains
35 of ancient civilizations throughout Egypt and ancient Greece, the scientists concluded that Hekla 3 erupted suddenly before the end of the 12th century B.C.E. What resulted was the decline of ancient cities—including the capital of the Assyrian empire, Troy—because of massive
40 drought and famines caused by environmental change.

The scientists then began to analyze the appearance of tephra markers (pieces of volcanic rock) around the volcano. They took 112 ice core samples from the Icelandic shelf, revealing layers of benthic material—
45 remnants of sea creatures—and other evidence. The amount of tephra released and the estimated amount of lava released (0.5k³ meters) suggest the eruption would be classified as a 6 on the volcanic explosivity index (which goes from 1 to 8)—one of the largest during the
50 Bronze Age.

The group also completed UV microscopic analyses of the layers of rock remains within the ice cores to establish the time period of the eruption. The blast did not, they found, happen before 1100 B.C.E. and almost
55 certainly occurred in the 12th century B.C.E.

The scientists weren't surprised that an Icelandic volcano could have triggered the Collapse, Eirksson explains. "Arctic volcanos are common sources of environmental change." Also, according to Eiríksson,
60 with tephra evidence throughout the Arctic—in Greenland and Iceland—there is a "definite likelihood" that its source was in the north.

Yet another possibility—given the rock data and geography—is Italy's Santorini, which is thought to have
65 erupted between 1600 and 1627 B.C.E. But analyses by Eiríksson's researchers showed that the size of Santorini's explosion was not big enough to cause significant climate change, whereas Hekla 3's explosion impacted the global climate. This finding supports the theory
70 that Hekla 3 was the cause of the Bronze Age Collapse around 1100 B.C.E.

Estimated Temperature in the Eastern Mediterranean
3300 B.C.E. to 100 B.C.E.

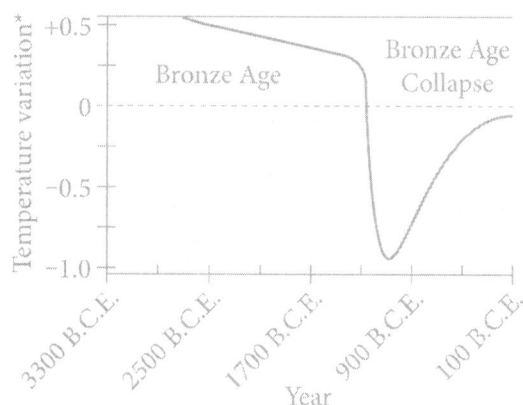

*Variation from the Holocene average temperature, in °C, represented at 0. Adapted from Cedric Melbourne Temperature Record Series, originally published in 2015.

18

The main purpose of the passage is to

A) describe changes in Earth's ancient geologic history.

B) explain how scientists utilize tree ring data.

C) describe evidence that links Hekla 3 to the Bronze Age Collapse.

D) explain how carbon from volcanic eruptions can cool Earth.

19

Over the course of the passage, the author's focus shifts from

A) a critique of a scientific method to a new hypothesis.

B) an explanation of an event to its probable cause.

C) the use of juniper tree ring data to a new method of carbon dating.

D) the use of tephra markers to examining the composition of ice core samples.

20

The author likely uses the phrase "etched in" (line 8) in order to

A) demonstrate the artistic nature of the scientists' work.

B) highlight that ancient societies etched information on stone.

C) underscore the care with which scientists handle data.

D) reinforce that the evidence is valid and permanent.

Mini-Test

Complete the mini-test. When you have finished, double-check your work.

Use the following guide as your teacher discusses the purpose of mini-tests.

Mini-Tests for Reading

Time Limit	# of Passages	# of Questions	# of Questions on the Chapter Topic	Pace
12 minutes	1	10–11	6	About 30 seconds per question

Fill in the blank.

Practice makes _____.

1   1

Questions 11–21 are based on the following passage and supplementary material.

This passage is adapted from Samuel I. Jacobs and Sandra Lise, "Does Empathy Help Leaders Make Good Decisions?" ©2020 by MasteryPrep.

Day in and day out, thousands of people in supervisory roles—in a wide range of occupations—set out to make effective decisions. They are frequently
Line called upon to make choices on behalf of their
5 employees, which can include everything from addressing safety concerns to mediating conflicts to developing new policies. The wide range of factors guiding such daily decisions can call up ambivalent feelings among managers about the role of empathy in
10 decision-making. Many people in supervisory positions lead with empathy in hopes of making the best choices on their employees' behalf. At the same time, some try to minimize a reliance on empathy; they worry that if they overidentify with staff members on a personal level, they
15 may not make the best choices on a professional level.

Sociologists describe empathy as a powerful tool, serving various societal, psychological, and political functions. Occupational psychologists, however, are not so sure. According to Bloom (2016), empathic leadership
20 in business may not lead to the best outcomes. People who are highly in tune with the feelings of others tend to mirror their emotions, both good and bad (a state known as "affective empathy"). Essentially, some leaders, consciously or subconsciously, tend to make decisions
25 that will inflict the least amount of psychological pain or discomfort on their employees. Unfortunately, affective empathy on the part of those in management may not lead to effective results in business. This finding is not shocking to occupational psychologists. Studies have
30 shown that some leaders too often let empathy drive their professional decisions—and their motivations are subject to hypersensitivity, social projection, and bias.

What is surprising is that most people in supervisory roles recognize that, while practicing empathy is
35 important, leading with a focus on emotion does not always result in productive outcomes for employees, employers, or business as a whole. In this article, we present psychological insight to explain this paradox— i.e., that some equate empathy with effective leadership
40 (the belief that the more they relate to employees on a personal level, the better their business will function). Although a correlation between empathy and sound decision-making might seem intuitive to administrators, this presupposition may be unfounded. Rather, we argue

45 that effective employer-employee outcomes are less reliant on empathy from leaders than people assume.

Why do supervisors assume that empathy is closely linked to effective decision-making on behalf of employees? Perhaps those in managerial roles think
50 that leading with a sensitivity to others' personal circumstances conveys a stronger sense of support. According to a study by Businessolver, many business executives believe that cultivating empathy with employees will ultimately lead to higher staff retention,
55 productivity, and, as a result, revenue. For this reason, some company cultures are defined by a sense of "family" in order to motivate workers. As for employees, many do not see the value of empathic leadership when it comes to high-level decisions in the workplace.

60 The notion that leading with empathy might not be "good for business" may seem strange because people are often encouraged to "walk a mile in another's shoes." However, despite good intentions, some supervisors struggle to strike a balance between relating to
65 employees personally and maintaining a professional distance. Some of those in managerial positions either overinvest or underinvest in the use of empathic leadership. At the same time, employee perceptions on the value of empathy in the workplace may depend on
70 industry and circumstance.

Managers' Perceived and Employees'
Actual View of Empathic Leadership

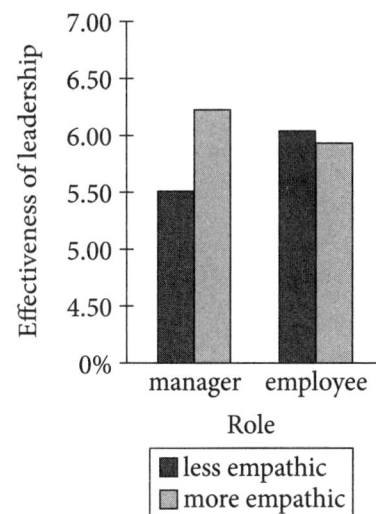

11

The authors most likely use the examples in lines 5–7 of the passage ("which … policies") to highlight the

A) variety of decisions managers have to make.

B) recent changes in the kinds of issues managers address.

C) anxiety decision-making causes for managers.

D) legal ramifications of some high-level decisions.

12

In line 13, the word "minimize" most nearly means

A) discount.

B) downplay.

C) shrink.

D) restrict.

13

The authors indicate that some managers value empathic decision-making because they feel it

A) functions as a powerful political tool.

B) is a simple way to demonstrate compassion.

C) encourages employees to reciprocate.

D) can help them make the best decisions for others.

14

Which choice provides the best evidence for the answer to the previous question?

A) Lines 10–12 ("Many … behalf")

B) Lines 16–18 ("Sociologists … functions")

C) Lines 23–26 ("Essentially … employees")

D) Lines 29–32 ("Studies … bias")

15

The "occupational psychologists" mentioned in lines 18 and 29 would likely describe the "affective empathy" phenomenon as

A) predictable.

B) controversial.

C) alarming.

D) remarkable.

1

1

16

The passage indicates that the assumption made by those in supervisory roles in lines 37–41 may be viewed by others in the workplace as

A) hypocritical.

B) biased.

C) mistaken.

D) corroborated.

17

Which choice provides the best evidence for the answer to the previous question?

A) Lines 49–51 ("Perhaps … support")

B) Lines 52–55 ("According … revenue")

C) Lines 57–59 ("As for … workplace")

D) Lines 63–66 ("However … distance")

18

As it is used in line 38, "paradox" most nearly means

A) error.

B) mystery.

C) reversal.

D) contradiction.

19

The authors refer to a study by Businessolver (line 52) in order to

A) offer an explanation.

B) introduce a debate.

C) question a hypothesis.

D) support a conclusion.

20

The graph following the passage offers evidence that some managers base their predictions of how effective their decisions will be on

A) acceptance from employees.

B) their level of empathy.

C) employee motivation.

D) relationships with employees.

21

The authors would likely attribute some managers' misperceptions about the effectiveness of empathic leadership as represented in the graph to

A) an unintentional desire to avoid inflicting pain.

B) an increasingly personal work culture.

C) a growing opposition to relationship building.

D) a misunderstanding of personal intentions.

STOP

**If you finish before time is called, you may check your work on this section only.
Do not turn to any other section.**

Wrap-Up

Refer to pages 48 and 49 as your teacher leads the discussion. Do not answer the questions.

Questions 4–6 are based on the following passage and supplementary material.

This passage is adapted from Alicia Diefendorf, "The Who and What of Gentrification." (c)2018 by MasteryPrep. Diefendorf is a journalist who focuses on cities and their economies. Gentrification is a phenomenon characterized by the redevelopment of urban neighborhoods primarily for the wealthy.

We are not observing the steady decay of all urban neighborhoods, or a redevelopment of inner-city areas by the wealthy all at once. The 2010 American
Line Community Survey (ACS) did not definitively provide
5 evidence of an overwhelming upper-income takeover of the nation's cities over the past decade. The findings were ambiguous: Many of the larger cities on the East Coast lost low-income residents to the upper class, sometimes in large numbers. Urban areas in the Midwest, including
10 Minneapolis, lost fewer low-income residents to neighborhood gentrification. The cities that showed the least displacement of low-income populations to the wealthy were in the South and Southwest. But when it comes to calculating the wealthy takeover of low-
15 income urban areas, raw ACS numbers are an inexact measuring tool. A closer look at the survey's findings reveals that the gentrification of low-income, inner-city areas between 2000-2010 was primarily driven by the movement of people under 45 into urban areas (45,000
20 of them to Portland alone) and the increasing consumer preference for urbanity, often of those who were raised far from any downtown area.

Gentrified urban areas that gained these younger residents in the first half of the decade preserved those
25 numbers during the recession from 2007 to 2009. These neighborhoods also, according to a 2015 study by *Governing*, experienced somewhat less unemployment than areas not undergoing gentrification. Few young professionals invested in gentrifying neighborhoods
30 during the recession because most did not have sufficient capital to do so. But there is increasing evidence that the investment trends initiated before the economic bust will resume now that the crisis is over. It is essential to remember that evidence of increasing numbers of
35 upper-class residents in a given area is not a marker of gentrification; the wealthy population can rise in urban areas that already house predominately upper-class residents, in those whose demographics are mixed, and even in those experiencing a modest decline in upper-
40 class population.

Upper-Class Population by Gentrification Size/Rate

Chart 1

2018 Upper-Class Population Shares by Amount of Gentrification in Urban Areas (%)

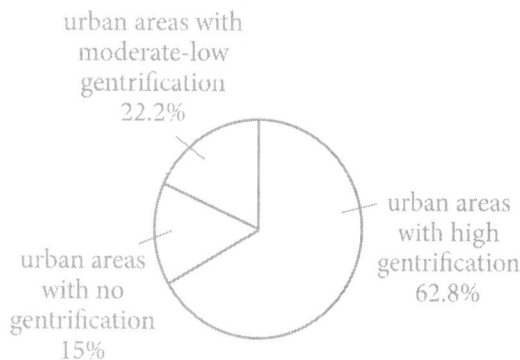

urban areas with moderate-low gentrification 22.2%

urban areas with no gentrification 15%

urban areas with high gentrification 62.8%

Chart 2

2018 Upper-Class Population Growth Rate by Neighborhood Gentrification

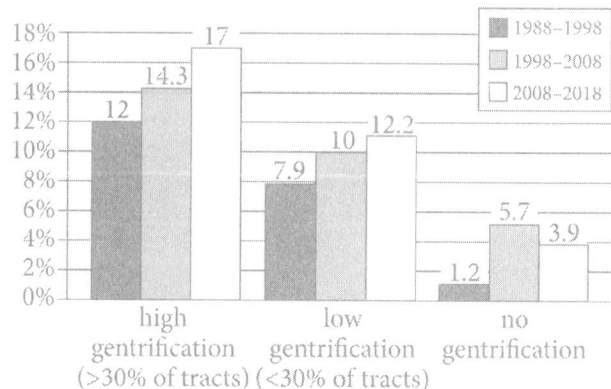

Legend: 1988–1998, 1998–2008, 2008–2018

high gentrification (>30% of tracts): 12, 14.3, 17
low gentrification (<30% of tracts): 7.9, 10, 12.2
no gentrification: 1.2, 5.7, 3.9

Adapted from Clarissa J. Dey, "Gentrification Growth from the Upper Class Since 1990: Positioning the Invasive 2010s on the Map." © 2019 by MasteryPrep

4

Over the course of the passage, the focus shifts from

A) defining gentrification to explaining the issues related to it.

B) explaining the problems with gentrification to suggesting a potential solution.

C) presenting alternatives to gentrification to resignation about it continuing.

D) explaining gentrification trends across regions to trends across time.

5

As used in line 19, "driven" most nearly means

A) fueled by.

B) moved with.

C) rode around.

D) skipped over.

6

According to Figure 2, the years 2008–2018 were characterized by

A) more growth in upper-class populations in all neighborhood areas than had taken place from 1988 to 1998.

B) more growth of upper-class populations in non-gentrifying areas than in high gentrification areas.

C) a significant increase in upper-class populations in non-gentrified areas compared to the years from 1998 to 2008.

D) roughly equal growth in high gentrification areas and non-gentrified areas.

Review

Quantitative information questions can be identified by these terms:

- chart
- table
- graph
- figure
- infographic

To answer a quantitative information question, follow these steps:

1. Read the graphic's labels and examine its data.
2. Fact check each choice against data from the graph. If a choice makes multiple claims, fact check each one.

If you've found the answer ...

Double-check that the facts in the answer choice match the information in the graphic.

If you're stuck between two choices ...

Get technical. Eliminate the choice that doesn't exactly state what is represented in the graphic or discussed in the passage.

If you have no idea what the answer is ...

Guess the choice that has strong similarities to at least one other choice.

2
Chapter

Reading Closely

LEARNING TARGETS

1. Draw reasonable inferences and make logical conclusions from information and ideas explicitly stated in the text.

2. Implement the basic approach for reading closely questions.

3. Apply the *Predict the Future* strategy and utilize pacing and keywords to improve scanning techniques on reading closely questions.

Warm-Up | Complete the warm-up. When you have finished, double-check your work.

Questions 1–3 are based on the following passage.

This passage is adapted from Robert Fitschen, "Organic Food Woes: Why Organic Agriculture May Not Be the Solution." ©2016 by MasteryPrep.

When it comes to food, everyone wants it to be cost-efficient. Keeping food affordable gives families the ability to buy more with their available income,
Line which is great for the economy and (hopefully) good
5 for families' health as well. Furthermore, with growing world populations and income inequalities, the only sustainable way to continue is to keep essential goods like food affordable for everyone.

Modern industrial agriculture has resulted in the
10 ability of farms to yield high volumes of food. Thanks to genetic engineering, pesticides, and artificial fertilizers, today's average American farm feeds approximately 200 people. Additionally, modern farmers are able to increase food production using less land and fewer
15 resources. For instance, a farm in Ohio can produce over 150 bushels of wheat per acre, which translates to great quantities of less expensive food for consumers. Considering that most of the world lives in poverty, struggling to consume enough calories to begin with,
20 finding ways to offer more food that costs less would seem like a smart choice for the world's health.

Evidently, that's not what all nutritionists think. Many believe that organic produce is better for the body—more nutritious and tastier, too—than produce
25 grown using modern farming techniques. Nutritionists generally do not approve of methods used to grow larger and pest-resistant crops. By contrast, organic farmers, by avoiding genetic modifications and artificial growth enhancements, are believed to grow healthier foods.
30 The general public appears to be catching on as well. American consumers bought 8.9% more organic food in 2015 than the previous year—collectively spending $32 billion—and they are buying it for their health as much as for its taste.
35 However, a recent study in *Health* did the math and came to a troubling realization: organic foods are 65% more expensive on average than genetically modified foods. Because more money is needed to purchase organic foods, they may not be as good for the world's population as many had hoped.

1

According to the passage, a major impact of genetically modifying food is that it

A) raises the cost of organically grown produce.

B) allows farmers to grow more crops with fewer resources.

C) causes dietary problems among the world's poorest populations.

D) improves the nutritional value found in common foods.

2

It can most reasonably be inferred from the passage that experts in the agriculture industry believe that

A) shoppers don't understand what genetically modified food means.

B) genetically modified foods have risks that have not yet been verified.

C) the high cost of organic foods is a barrier to its accessibility.

D) organic produce is too expensive to be marketable.

3

The author indicates that people value organic produce because they feel it

A) supports a more natural environment.

B) is an inexpensive way to eat healthy food.

C) balances out the cons of genetically modified foods.

D) is better for their overall health.

This page intentionally left blank

Foundation

Work with your group to read the following passage and identify three suspects. Write the suspects, evidence of guilt, and evidence of innocence under Part One on the following page.

The Case of the Missing Sandwich

José grimaced as he felt his stomach grumbling; he couldn't wait for lunch time. When the bell rang, he went to his locker and pulled out his lunch bag. It felt oddly light, but he didn't think much of it until he got to the cafeteria and opened it. The turkey-bacon-cheese club sandwich that he had so carefully made that morning was missing!

José poked his best friend, Carl, hard in the arm.

"My sandwich is missing," he said.

"So?" shrugged Carl, chowing down on cafeteria pizza.

Carl was always hungry and would eat anything he could get his hands on. José scowled and went to go find the thief. Even though Carl knew his locker combination, he didn't think his best friend would steal his lunch.

José decided to start where he'd last seen his lunch: his locker. But, when he got there, he noticed the start of a crumb path leading down the hallway, so he decided to follow it. The crumb trail disappeared behind the door to the gym. He poked his head inside and scanned the basketball court. It was empty except for Sandra, who was practicing her free throws. He and Sandra were always arguing.

"Sandra, did you steal my sandwich?"

She rolled her eyes, said "I'm a vegetarian," and kept practicing.

Defeated, José went back to the cafeteria and slumped down in his seat. His eyes widened when he saw, from across the room, Mike eating a tasty-looking turkey sandwich.

José stalked over, "Mike, did you steal my sandwich?"

"No way," said Mike. "Did your sandwich have tomatoes on it? Because this one has tomatoes on it."

José had to admit his sandwich had been tomato-less. But other than that, it looked a lot like his sandwich.

"Where were you last period?" he asked Mike.

"Um, in biology class, duh," Mike said.

"But you left early to go to the bathroom, remember?" his girlfriend added. Mike nodded in agreement.

José couldn't figure it out. Who had taken his sandwich?

Key Terms

Inference: a conclusion based on evidence and reason.

Part One

List each of the suspects. For each, describe the evidence that supports their guilt or innocence.

Suspect 1: _____Carl_____

Evidence of Guilt

Always hungry, Knows his locker combination

Evidence of Innocence

He's his best friend

Suspect 2: _____Sandra_____

Evidence of Guilt

Always arguing

Evidence of Innocence

Vegetarian

Suspect 3: _____Mike_____

Evidence of Guilt

Eating similar looking sandwich, left class early

Evidence of Innocence

tomatoes on sandwich

Part Two

With your group, identify the most likely suspect and make an inference as to what their motivation may have been.

Who is the most likely suspect? _____Mike_____

How do you know? Make an inference as to what their motive may have been.

He suspiciously left early the previous class. Rob was just hungry

Practice Set 1 | Complete the practice set. When you have finished, double-check your work.

Questions 1–11 are based on the following passage.

This passage is adapted from Dylan Hale, "Exercise Caution with Online Reviews." ©2019 by MasteryPrep.

"Word of mouth" has typically been a trusted way to find recommendations. Looking for a babysitter? Ask your neighbor. Online reviews from trusted sites can
Line also help to inform our choices, but new research shows
5 that web-based ratings don't necessarily help consumers make the best decisions. A recent controlled study of online consumers indicated that user-generated reviews and ratings are highly vulnerable to "groupthink"—and that the "group" in question can be manipulated.

10 This may not be true in all cases. Although common sense dictates that people may be better off seeking some recommendations through personal channels, the quality of some products and services can indeed be verified through substantial quantities of reviews.
15 Restaurant reviews, for example, usually reflect a valid general consensus if made up of a large number of user comments and ratings.

But how do these types of reviews reflect upon other products and services across the board? According to
20 some, the larger the sample size, the more accurate the overall rating will be. Statisticians, however, are quick to point out that this is not always the case due to uncontrolled variables. Crowdsourced and anonymous reviews are prone to implicit biases, and these can
25 influence the opinions of later reviewers and result in skewed outcomes. To accurately test this notion, researchers would need to conduct a large group study, incorporate artificial reviews, and analyze the reviews' impact on the group's opinions.

30 Rachel Adriano, a sociologist at the University of Illinois at Urbana-Champagne, sought to do just that. Adriano has been working behind the scenes with a well-known video streaming website. The site encourages users to write short reviews of each video
35 and to rate other reviews with a positive or negative vote. The reviews are arranged in chronological order and include the vote count (videos on the site receive about twenty reviews and five votes per review, on average). Previously, Adriano had studied the elasticity
40 of music preferences among adults; in particular, she examined the effect that individual critics could have on a community of listeners. This time, however, she wanted to know how much a community of reviewers could impact an individual, and to what degree this impact could be manipulated by third parties.

45 For one year, every review posted by a user on the website received a random "up" vote (favorable), a "down" vote (unfavorable), or to serve as a control, no vote whatsoever. Adriano's team then studied how subsequent users rated those reviews. More than 15,000
50 reviews were seen over 4 million times—and voted on by approximately 100,000 users.

The results showed that when it comes to video reviews, "groupthink" can take hold rather quickly. Reviews that received false "up" votes were 41% more
55 likely to receive additional "up" votes than the reviews in the control group, Adriano reports. Additionally, these reviews were no more likely than those in the control group to be down-voted. At the conclusion of the experiment, reviews boosted by false "up" votes were
60 30% more popular on average. However, the same was not true for reviews weakened by a false "down" vote. The reviews that received "down" votes were quickly canceled out by other (authentic) "up" votes.

"The study wasn't designed to explain the rationale
65 behind people's opinions," Adriano says, "only to capture what people are doing. Since this kind of reviewing is a social activity, social rules apply; thus, people are more inclined to perceive favorable reactions to a review as genuine, rather than unfavorable reactions, which are
70 sometimes viewed as behaviors known as 'trolling.'"

Maureen Esses, a marketing analyst, sees no reason to disagree with this interpretation, saying that "peer-generated reviews should be taken with a grain of salt." She explains that the purpose of an online video
75 can have a significant impact on the degree to which reviewers can be influenced. "You would think that people would respond similarly to a movie trailer and a TV show trailer, but movie trailers elicit stronger emotional responses from viewers (nearly 40% stronger)
80 than TV show trailers do." Why is that? Before we apply these findings, we need to answer these sorts of questions.

So, will popular online video makers begin tipping favorable viewer comments in their direction to boost
85 their ratings? "I'm sure it's tempting," Esses says. However, if users begin to suspect that video ratings and reviews are being manipulated by the producers, they may not use the website at all.

1

The author of the passage suggests that large quantities of online reviews may be more effective at

A) building a sense of hype than generating real interest in a product.

B) generating a wide variety of discussions than exploring a single topic in-depth.

C) providing reliable recommendations for some products and services than for others.

D) promoting large companies rather than small businesses.

2

Which choice does the author explicitly cite as an example of a product or service that receives accurate ratings from a large quantity of reviews?

A) Action movies

B) Babysitters

C) Restaurants

D) Entertainment

3

The author indicates that if video producers manipulate online reviews, they may

A) make people uninterested in leaving their own reviews.

B) deter people from using the website.

C) make it difficult to obtain accurate market data.

D) boost peoples' confidence in the video's content.

Approach

Entrance

Reading closely questions can be identified by this feature:

- a question that asks for specific information from the passage

... or the following terms:

- indicate
- identify
- cite
- state
- suggest
- according to the passage/author

The following questions refer to the passage on page 56. Review question 4 with your teacher. Do not answer the question.

Entrance ⟩ Evidence and Elimination ⟩ Exit

4

According to the passage, crowdsourced and anonymous online reviews can collectively

A) manipulate an individual into making poor decisions.

B) sway the opinions of individuals.

C) concisely represent the opinions of a large group of people.

D) provide accurate market data despite control variable errors.

Review questions 5 and 6 on your own. Circle the part of the question that identifies it as a reading closely question. Do not answer the questions.

5

The passage indicates that people tend to respond emotionally to videos that

A) include humorous advertisements.

B) highlight their favored musical artists.

C) promote well-known streaming sites.

D) feature previews of upcoming motion pictures.

6

According to the author, some believe that product reviews are more accurate if they

A) are generated in-person versus online.

B) are drawn from a random sample of consumers.

C) are part of a large sample of reviews.

D) are verified as authentic and unbiased.

Questions 1–11 are based on the following passage.

This passage is adapted from Dylan Hale, "Exercise Caution with Online Reviews." ©2019 by MasteryPrep.

"Word of mouth" has typically been a trusted way to find recommendations. Looking for a babysitter? Ask your neighbor. Online reviews from trusted sites can
Line also help to inform our choices, but new research shows
5 that web-based ratings don't necessarily help consumers make the best decisions. A recent controlled study of online consumers indicated that user-generated reviews and ratings are highly vulnerable to "groupthink"—and that the "group" in question can be manipulated.

10 This may not be true in all cases. Although common sense dictates that people may be better off seeking some recommendations through personal channels, the quality of some products and services can indeed be verified through substantial quantities of reviews.
15 Restaurant reviews, for example, usually reflect a valid general consensus if made up of a large number of user comments and ratings.

But how do these types of reviews reflect upon other products and services across the board? According to
20 some, the larger the sample size, the more accurate the overall rating will be. Statisticians, however, are quick to point out that this is not always the case due to uncontrolled variables. Crowdsourced and anonymous reviews are prone to implicit biases, and these can
25 influence the opinions of later reviewers and result in skewed outcomes. To accurately test this notion, researchers would need to conduct a large group study, incorporate artificial reviews, and analyze the reviews' impact on the group's opinions.

30 Rachel Adriano, a sociologist at the University of Illinois at Urbana-Champagne, sought to do just that. Adriano has been working behind the scenes with a well-known video streaming website. The site encourages users to write short reviews of each video
35 and to rate other reviews with a positive or negative vote. The reviews are arranged in chronological order and include the vote count (videos on the site receive about twenty reviews and five votes per review, on average). Previously, Adriano had studied the elasticity
40 of music preferences among adults; in particular, she examined the effect that individual critics could have on a community of listeners. This time, however, she wanted to know how much a community of reviewers could impact an individual, and to what degree this impact could be manipulated by third parties.

45 For one year, every review posted by a user on the website received a random "up" vote (favorable), a "down" vote (unfavorable), or to serve as a control, no vote whatsoever. Adriano's team then studied how subsequent users rated those reviews. More than 15,000
50 reviews were seen over 4 million times—and voted on by approximately 100,000 users.

The results showed that when it comes to video reviews, "groupthink" can take hold rather quickly. Reviews that received false "up" votes were 41% more
55 likely to receive additional "up" votes than the reviews in the control group, Adriano reports. Additionally, these reviews were no more likely than those in the control group to be down-voted. At the conclusion of the experiment, reviews boosted by false "up" votes were
60 30% more popular on average. However, the same was not true for reviews weakened by a false "down" vote. The reviews that received "down" votes were quickly canceled out by other (authentic) "up" votes.

"The study wasn't designed to explain the rationale
65 behind people's opinions," Adriano says, "only to capture what people are doing. Since this kind of reviewing is a social activity, social rules apply; thus, people are more inclined to perceive favorable reactions to a review as genuine, rather than unfavorable reactions, which are
70 sometimes viewed as behaviors known as 'trolling.'"

Maureen Esses, a marketing analyst, sees no reason to disagree with this interpretation, saying that "peer-generated reviews should be taken with a grain of salt." She explains that the purpose of an online video
75 can have a significant impact on the degree to which reviewers can be influenced. "You would think that people would respond similarly to a movie trailer and a TV show trailer, but movie trailers elicit stronger emotional responses from viewers (nearly 40% stronger)
80 than TV show trailers do." Why is that? Before we apply these findings, we need to answer these sorts of questions.

So, will popular online video makers begin tipping favorable viewer comments in their direction to boost
85 their ratings? "I'm sure it's tempting," Esses says. However, if users begin to suspect that video ratings and reviews are being manipulated by the producers, they may not use the website at all.

Approach

Evidence and Elimination

To answer a reading closely question, follow these steps:

❶ Identify the keywords in the question.

❷ Scan the passage for related keywords.

❸ Eliminate answer choices not supported by evidence from the passage.

Answer question 4 with your teacher.

Entrance | **Evidence and Elimination** | Exit

4

According to the passage, crowdsourced and anonymous online reviews can collectively

A) manipulate an individual into making poor decisions.

B) sway the opinions of individuals.

C) concisely represent the opinions of a large group of people.

D) provide accurate market data despite control variable errors.

Approach

The following questions refer to the passage on page 60. Answer questions 5 and 6 on your own. Focus on eliminating incorrect answers.

5

The passage indicates that people tend to respond emotionally to videos that

A) include humorous advertisements.

B) highlight their favored musical artists.

C) promote well-known streaming sites.

D) feature previews of upcoming motion pictures.

6

According to the author, some believe that product reviews are more accurate if they

A) are generated in-person versus online.

B) are drawn from a random sample of consumers.

C) are part of a large sample of reviews.

D) are verified as authentic and unbiased.

Approach

Exit

If you've found the answer ...

Check to make sure that the answer matches the details of the passage. Mark your answer and continue to the next question.

If you're stuck between two choices ...

Break the remaining answer choices into pieces and compare them to find the essential difference. Test each piece against the passage for accuracy.

If you have no idea what the answer is ...

Pick the answer that is either the longest or the shortest of all the answers.

Review questions 7 and 8. Work with your teacher to choose the correct answer from the remaining choices.

Entrance 〉 Evidence and Elimination 〉 Exit

7

Which question was Adriano's study of online reviews primarily intended to answer?

A) What products and services benefit the most from online crowd-ranked customer reviews?

B) ~~Are rating and review systems fair and objective in determining the best product or service on the market?~~

C) To what degree can a group of stated opinions influence the subsequent opinions of other individuals?

D) ~~What are the most effective marketing techniques to convince consumers to return and post product reviews online?~~

8

According to the passage, Adriano's findings regarding "groupthink" in online reviews are significant because they

A) ~~support the claims made from previous data.~~

B) ~~question the validity of a popular viewpoint.~~

C) demonstrate the potency of a social phenomenon.

D) contradict a long-held belief.

Practice Set 2

Complete the practice set. When you have finished, double-check your work.

Questions 1–11 are based on the following passage.

This passage is adapted from Dylan Hale, "Exercise Caution with Online Reviews." ©2019 by MasteryPrep.

"Word of mouth" has typically been a trusted way to find recommendations. Looking for a babysitter? Ask your neighbor. Online reviews from trusted sites can
Line also help to inform our choices, but new research shows
5 that web-based ratings don't necessarily help consumers make the best decisions. A recent controlled study of online consumers indicated that user-generated reviews and ratings are highly vulnerable to "groupthink"—and that the "group" in question can be manipulated.
10 This may not be true in all cases. Although common sense dictates that people may be better off seeking some recommendations through personal channels, the quality of some products and services can indeed be verified through substantial quantities of reviews.
15 Restaurant reviews, for example, usually reflect a valid general consensus if made up of a large number of user comments and ratings.

But how do these types of reviews reflect upon other products and services across the board? According to
20 some, the larger the sample size, the more accurate the overall rating will be. Statisticians, however, are quick to point out that this is not always the case due to uncontrolled variables. Crowdsourced and anonymous reviews are prone to implicit biases, and these can
25 influence the opinions of later reviewers and result in skewed outcomes. To accurately test this notion, researchers would need to conduct a large group study, incorporate artificial reviews, and analyze the reviews' impact on the group's opinions.
30 Rachel Adriano, a sociologist at the University of Illinois at Urbana-Champagne, sought to do just that. Adriano has been working behind the scenes with a well-known video streaming website. The site encourages users to write short reviews of each video
35 and to rate other reviews with a positive or negative vote. The reviews are arranged in chronological order and include the vote count (videos on the site receive about twenty reviews and five votes per review, on average). Previously, Adriano had studied the elasticity
40 of music preferences among adults; in particular, she examined the effect that individual critics could have on a community of listeners. This time, however, she wanted to know how much a community of reviewers could impact an individual, and to what degree this impact could be manipulated by third parties.

45 For one year, every review posted by a user on the website received a random "up" vote (favorable), a "down" vote (unfavorable), or to serve as a control, no vote whatsoever. Adriano's team then studied how subsequent users rated those reviews. More than 15,000
50 reviews were seen over 4 million times—and voted on by approximately 100,000 users.

The results showed that when it comes to video reviews, "groupthink" can take hold rather quickly. Reviews that received false "up" votes were 41% more
55 likely to receive additional "up" votes than the reviews in the control group, Adriano reports. Additionally, these reviews were no more likely than those in the control group to be down-voted. At the conclusion of the experiment, reviews boosted by false "up" votes were
60 30% more popular on average. However, the same was not true for reviews weakened by a false "down" vote. The reviews that received "down" votes were quickly canceled out by other (authentic) "up" votes.

"The study wasn't designed to explain the rationale
65 behind people's opinions," Adriano says, "only to capture what people are doing. Since this kind of reviewing is a social activity, social rules apply; thus, people are more inclined to perceive favorable reactions to a review as genuine, rather than unfavorable reactions, which are
70 sometimes viewed as behaviors known as 'trolling.'"

Maureen Esses, a marketing analyst, sees no reason to disagree with this interpretation, saying that "peer-generated reviews should be taken with a grain of salt." She explains that the purpose of an online video
75 can have a significant impact on the degree to which reviewers can be influenced. "You would think that people would respond similarly to a movie trailer and a TV show trailer, but movie trailers elicit stronger emotional responses from viewers (nearly 40% stronger)
80 than TV show trailers do." Why is that? Before we apply these findings, we need to answer these sorts of questions.

So, will popular online video makers begin tipping favorable viewer comments in their direction to boost
85 their ratings? "I'm sure it's tempting," Esses says. However, if users begin to suspect that video ratings and reviews are being manipulated by the producers, they may not use the website at all.

9

The author indicates that people are likely to

A) rely on reviews of movies rather than television shows.

B) assume that most reviews are fake.

C) perceive "thumbs up" reactions to a review as genuine.

D) write a positive review rather than a negative one.

10

What does the author suggest about the "word of mouth" method of verifying information?

A) It is reliable only when limited to a small number of peers.

B) It is still the recommended method of verifying certain services.

C) It became outdated when online product-review platforms gained popularity.

D) It is most useful for sources of entertainment such as restaurants.

11

The passage most strongly suggests that "groupthink" is

A) a powerful phenomenon.

B) influenced by businesses.

C) generally slow to evolve.

D) not yet fully understood.

Strategy

Questions 12–20 are based on the following passage.

This passage is adapted from Noah Gallant, "Brace for Impact." ©2019 by MasteryPrep.

About 4.5 billion years ago, Earth's moon began to form, creating a celestial body that has influenced human societies throughout history. Understanding the origin of the moon, though, has been difficult.

That a natural satellite formed in Earth's orbit sometime after Earth came into existence is noted in the atmosphere and composition of the moon in the form of metals and other elements. These characteristics suggest that during the Hadean eon, which took place about 20 to 100 million years after the solar system was formed, debris was released into space that collided with the young Earth and accreted to form an enormous, natural satellite.

In 2010, scientists at the Planetary Science Institute developed the Giant Impact Theory by calculating the growth rate of the second- and third-largest celestial bodies in the general vicinity of Earth. Based on radiometric dating of lead in uranium-rich minerals, they also calculated the potential velocity and direction of a debris blast to determine if enough material could be generated by an impact to form a new moon. The scientists deduced that such an impact would result in the formation of numerous moonlets that would eventually aggregate into the moon itself. Continued, regular accretion of these moonlets, as well as other interstellar gas and dust (left behind by a nebula that collapsed into the sun 4.6 billion years ago) contributed to the relatively massive moon we have today.

Astrophysicist Alessandra Mastrobuono-Battisti and her team now think they've pinpointed the object that collided with Earth: a Mars-sized object known as Theia. A particular point of geological interest, she observes, is the lunar crust. The highly igneous composition of lunar rocks collected during the Apollo moon landing suggests that a large portion of the moon had melted at some point, creating a magma ocean, and that thermal energy became trapped due to accretion.

The scientists worked to simulate collisions between young protoplanets and planetesimals (smaller bodies in space) in the early solar system. They analyzed thousands of possible collisions, taking place one astronomical unit—the distance between the sun and Earth—from the sun. The composition and the number of planets produced (three to four rocky planets) demonstrated that a new planet is likely to take on the composition of the most recent celestial body it collided

with. In fact, it is ten times more likely to do so than researchers previously estimated.

The scientists also analyzed the composition of lunar rocks and the water in lunar magma in comparison to Earth rocks to confirm the similarity of their isotopic signatures; the moon could not, they deduced, have formed elsewhere in the solar system.

"We're not shocked that an early collision with Earth might have caused the formation of the moon," Mastrobuono-Battisti says. "Their similar compositions support an impact." And, she adds, because isotopes differ by a few parts in a million—including highly siderophilic tungsten—there is wide agreement that the the Giant Impact Theory is plausible.

Another proposed explanation, which accounts for both the moon's size and orbit, is the Capture Theory. It states that Earth's gravity snagged a passing body that had formed elsewhere in the solar system. But when Mastrobuono-Battisti's team studied the shape and orbit of the moon, they found that the moon is spherical and aligns evenly with Earth, while captured orbiters are often oddly shaped and randomly positioned. This, the team suggests, reinforces the case that the moon formed when Theia collided with Earth 4.5 billion years ago.

Predict the Future

When you're struggling to find evidence, the Predict the Future strategy is an excellent way to guide you toward a correct answer.

1. Cover the answers.

2. Read the question and come up with your own answer.

3. Select the answer that best matches your prediction.

Review question 12 with your teacher. Use the Predict the Future strategy to answer the question as a class.

12

After scientists calculated the growth rate of bodies near Earth to develop the Giant Impact Theory (line 15), they

A) concluded the moon was probably captured by Earth's gravitational pull.

B) compared igneous compositions to determine why the moon's crust no longer matched Earth's.

C) verified that an impact with Earth created enough debris to form the moon.

D) determined that debris from an impact with Earth easily escaped the solar system.

Strategy

The following questions refer to the passage on page 66. Work on your own using the Predict the Future strategy to answer questions 13 and 14.

13

According to the passage, Theia most likely caused the formation of the moon by

A) combining several planetesimals orbiting Earth.

B) colliding with the Earth.

C) capturing interstellar dust from a collapsed nebula.

D) adjusting a protoplanet's orbit to revolve around Earth.

14

The author indicates that scientists referenced the Apollo moon landing because they

A) used the mission's data as a basis for an experiment.

B) calculated the moon's growth rate since the landing.

C) did not know if the astronauts had found any magma pools.

D) studied the lunar rocks collected during the mission.

Strategy

Scanning for Evidence

Answer reading closely questions more accurately and quickly by improving your ability to find evidence in the passage.

1. Scan at the right pace: faster than reading, slower than skipping.

2. Focus on keywords in the question, but be open to using keywords in the answer choices when you need them.

3. Scan for synonyms and concepts, not just exact word matches.

4. Find hard evidence.

Review question 15 with your teacher. Use the tips to answer the question as a class.

15

The passage identifies which of the following as components of the material that fused together to create the moon?

A) Metals and isotopes

B) Interstellar gas and dust

C) Uranium-rich minerals

D) Satellites orbiting Mars

Strategy

The following questions refer to the passage on page 66. Work on your own to use the tips to answer questions 16 and 17.

16

It can most reasonably be inferred from the passage that the composition of planets formed via the collision of protoplanets and planetesimals

A) was likely altered by intense heat.

B) was hard to analyze through simulation.

C) varied depending on the speed of the collision.

D) had been misunderstood by scientists.

17

According to the passage, what does the author claim is a noted feature of geological interest?

A) The lunar rocks collected previously

B) The creation of the magma ocean

C) The trapped thermal energy

D) The lunar crust

This page intentionally left blank

Practice Set 3 | Complete the practice set. When you have finished, double-check your work.

Questions 12–20 are based on the following passage.

This passage is adapted from Noah Gallant, "Brace for Impact." ©2019 by MasteryPrep.

About 4.5 billion years ago, Earth's moon began to form, creating a celestial body that has influenced human societies throughout history. Understanding the
Line origin of the moon, though, has been difficult.
5   That a natural satellite formed in Earth's orbit sometime after Earth came into existence is noted in the atmosphere and composition of the moon in the form of metals and other elements. These characteristics suggest that during the Hadean eon, which took place about 20
10   to 100 million years after the solar system was formed, debris was released into space that collided with the young Earth and accreted to form an enormous, natural satellite.

In 2010, scientists at the Planetary Science Institute
15   developed the Giant Impact Theory by calculating the growth rate of the second- and third-largest celestial bodies in the general vicinity of Earth. Based on radiometric dating of lead in uranium-rich minerals, they also calculated the potential velocity and direction
20   of a debris blast to determine if enough material could be generated by an impact to form a new moon. The scientists deduced that such an impact would result in the formation of numerous moonlets that would eventually aggregate into the moon itself. Continued,
25   regular accretion of these moonlets, as well as other interstellar gas and dust (left behind by a nebula that collapsed into the sun 4.6 billion years ago) contributed to the relatively massive moon we have today.

Astrophysicist Alessandra Mastrobuono-Battisti and
30   her team now think they've pinpointed the object that collided with Earth: a Mars-sized object known as Theia. A particular point of geological interest, she observes, is the lunar crust. The highly igneous composition of lunar rocks collected during the Apollo moon landing suggests
35   that a large portion of the moon had melted at some point, creating a magma ocean, and that thermal energy became trapped due to accretion.

The scientists worked to simulate collisions between young protoplanets and planetesimals (smaller bodies
40   in space) in the early solar system. They analyzed thousands of possible collisions, taking place one astronomical unit—the distance between the sun and Earth—from the sun. The composition and the number of planets produced (three to four rocky planets)
45   demonstrated that a new planet is likely to take on the composition of the most recent celestial body it collided

with. In fact, it is ten times more likely to do so than researchers previously estimated.

The scientists also analyzed the composition of lunar
50   rocks and the water in lunar magma in comparison to Earth rocks to confirm the similarity of their isotopic signatures; the moon could not, they deduced, have formed elsewhere in the solar system.

"We're not shocked that an early collision with
55   Earth might have caused the formation of the moon," Mastrobuono-Battisti says. "Their similar compositions support an impact." And, she adds, because isotopes differ by a few parts in a million—including highly siderophilic tungsten—there is wide agreement that the
60   the Giant Impact Theory is plausible.

Another proposed explanation, which accounts for both the moon's size and orbit, is the Capture Theory. It states that Earth's gravity snagged a passing body that had formed elsewhere in the solar system. But when
65   Mastrobuono-Battisti's team studied the shape and orbit of the moon, they found that the moon is spherical and aligns evenly with Earth, while captured orbiters are often oddly shaped and randomly positioned. This, the team suggests, reinforces the case that the moon formed
70   when Theia collided with Earth 4.5 billion years ago.

18

When does the author indicate the moon was most likely formed?

A) About 4.5 billion years ago

B) Approximately 20 million years ago

C) Approximately 100 million years ago

D) About 7 billion years ago

19

As used in line 61, the phrase "Another proposed explanation" suggests that

A) large body collisions in space occur regularly.

B) the debris from planetary collisions can reform over millenniums.

C) scientists have formed other theories that explain the moon's origin.

D) other natural satellites have formed from similar collisions in the past.

20

The author refers to the Capture Theory primarily to suggest that scientists

A) do not agree with Mastrobuono-Battisti's research findings.

B) have analyzed other hypotheses suggesting how the moon was formed.

C) have become quite knowledgeable about astrophysics.

D) can't explain the moon's orbiting pattern.

Mini-Test

Complete the mini-test. When you have finished, double-check your work.

Questions 11–21 are based on the following passage.

This passage is adapted from Alan Delmas, "The Future of the American Homestead." ©2019 by MasteryPrep.

Contrary to the beliefs of some, we are not experiencing an exodus from our hometowns, or a permanent movement of adults away from their parents. *The Washington Post* conducted an analysis that did not
[5] yield widespread evidence of a long-term migration away from one's roots. The study results varied by region: Most adults in the Rocky Mountain states tend to live farther away from their hometowns, an average of 40 miles. Those in the South, including Alabama, Tennessee, and
[10] Kentucky, tend to live an average of six miles from their parents. The average distance between adults and their hometowns nationwide is a mere 18 miles. And when it comes to overall proximity, less than 25% of American adults live more than a few hours' drive from their
[15] parents. A closer look at this pattern shows that remote adults are most likely to return to their extended families during a "settling down period" (often 10–15 years after high school graduation) during which their lives are marked by marriage, homeownership, and the start of a
[20] family. The percentage of adults who re-established roots in their hometowns rose during the recession years from 2007–2009. Many did so, according to a 2015 meta-analysis by urbanologist Pearce Jennings, because their hometowns were more cost-efficient than many other
[25] areas of the country. Likewise, fewer young families settled into popular urban areas during the recession years due to cost. But there is no evidence to show that the demographic trend of the time has reversed itself now that the economic recession has abated. Indeed,
[30] the decision to relocate "closer to home" is not solely based on finances; many adults are returning to their childhood locales to be close to family and to reintegrate into a familiar, tight-knit community.

America's adults face a series of crossroads,
[35] particularly those individuals who relocate from small communities to larger cities after college graduation. Some, including highly successful professionals, find that the urban lifestyle they found exciting as young singles loses its appeal once they decide to marry and start a
[40] family. How these adults arrive at this conclusion, I do not know. What I do know is that financial success is not the main predictor of where young families choose to settle.

[45] The notion that "the best and the brightest" young adults migrate out of insular communities and settle away from their parents is simply not a reality. As a society, we need to rethink the negative stigma associated with living in small towns and rural areas.

[50] Some of the research on adults who settle in close proximity to their hometowns, after having relocated elsewhere, comes from a study conducted by Arizona State University researchers Jennifer DiGeso and Jared Hudson. It was DiGeso and Hudson who identified the
[55] defining characteristics of "return migrants"; they are well-educated, more financially successful than those who remain in their hometowns after high school, and finally, they tend to be parents of young children.

The researchers have arrived at the most common
[60] reason why adults choose to relocate close to where they grew up: they want to be near family. Approximately 90% of return migrants have relatives in their hometown, including parents and siblings; some have a need to care for ailing parents; some return to help with a family
[65] business; but most have a strong desire to live and work close to their roots for the sake of their own children. As young families move back to their hometowns, they cite advantages such as proximity to grandparents, emotional ties, and a built-in support network to assist with
[70] childcare. Many express a desire to raise their children where they already know people, and they rely on those relationships. Such parents benefit from personal connections with teachers and school administrators.

But in some instances, depending on location, a
[75] return to one's roots comes with sacrifice. There are return migrants who achieve financial prosperity, but there are others who take cuts in pay to return to small towns or rural areas. Most report that the trade-off is worth the sacrifice. Small communities, which
[80] are sometimes perceived as "the birthplace of sound values," are increasingly the locales of choice for those who grew up nearby. Many adults are not returning to their hometowns temporarily; they are re-establishing roots where they intend to raise the next generation of
[85] families.

1

11

Which choice best summarizes the first paragraph of the passage (lines 1–33)?

A) *The Washington Post* analysis demonstrated a notable growth in the number of adults moving away from their hometowns.

B) *The Washington Post* did not provide reliable evidence for analyzing demographic trends of adults in American cities.

C) Research shows that, nationwide, most adults are choosing to reside close to their hometowns.

D) Fewer adults are living in close proximity to their hometowns since roughly 2000, while more adults are living in large cities.

12

According to the passage, adults in which region are most likely to reside the farthest distance from where they grew up?

A) The South

B) Urban areas in the Northeast

C) Alabama, Tennessee, and Kentucky

D) Rocky Mountain states

13

In line 19, "marked" is closest in meaning to

A) characterized.

B) written.

C) significant.

D) stained.

14

According to the passage, which choice best describes many adults' perception about living in a city?

A) Downtown housing is less affordable than suburban housing.

B) Urban areas lose their appeal once adults decide to marry and begin a family.

C) Inner city neighborhoods offer a keen sense of identity.

D) Metropolitan areas offer inadequate access to quality education.

15

Which choice does the author explicitly cite as an advantage of returning to one's hometown?

A) Improved health

B) Convenience

C) Childcare assistance

D) Lifestyle

16

The passage implies that small towns or rural areas

A) are experiencing an exodus of many residents to larger cities.

B) have a reputation for providing excellence in education.

C) are characterized by an unfair stereotype.

D) offer fewer modern amenities than urban areas.

1   **1**

17

Which choice provides the best evidence for the answer to the previous question?

A) Lines 25–27 ("Likewise … cost")

B) Lines 47–49 ("As a society … areas")

C) Lines 59–61 ("The researchers … family")

D) Lines 72–73 ("Such … administrators")

18

As used in line 2, "exodus" is closest in meaning to

A) departure.

B) retirement.

C) retreat.

D) alienation.

19

DiGeso and Hudson claim that which of the following is a defining characteristic of return migrants?

A) They have ailing parents.

B) They are financially stable.

C) They have grown children.

D) They are well-educated.

20

Which statement about return migrants can most reasonably be inferred from the passage?

A) They return home because they have attained financial success.

B) They are more likely to reside in urban areas now that the economy is stable.

C) They demand academic excellence from their children.

D) They are most likely to be between their late 20s and early 30s.

21

What does the author imply about those who make financial sacrifices to return to their hometown?

A) They have less educational achievement upon returning than do other return migrants.

B) They have to care for ailing parents, unlike other return migrants.

C) They believe the drawbacks are outweighed by the same benefits valued by other return migrants.

D) They were hit harder by the recession than were other return migrants.

STOP

If you finish before time is called, you may check your work on this section only.
Do not turn to any other section.

This page intentionally left blank

Wrap-Up

Complete the wrap-up. When you have finished, double-check your work.

Questions 4–6 are based on the following passage.

This passage is adapted from Dominique Ricarte, "GMO and Organic Food: Pros and Cons." ©2016 by MasteryPrep.

In the article published by *Health*, researchers from Oregon State University conducted a meta-analysis comparing the nutritional values of genetically modified and organic foods across 46 different kinds of produce,
Line from vegetables to fruits to grains. They concluded that
5 genetically modified food was less nutritious across the board, though it varied for each crop type. For instance, genetically modified bread crops (like wheat) and cereal grains (like barley) provided less nutrition than organic bread crops by only 15%. Yet, for plant crops like
10 vegetables and fruits, as well as some nuts, organic foods contained 55% more nutritional value than those that were genetically modified.

Pest resistance is a critical factor in growing ample crops. Genetically modified foods are engineered to
15 resist pests, whereas foods grown organically are often prone to infestation and disease. Research has also shown that genetically modified fruits and vegetables often grow larger than their organic counterparts. So, when agriculturalists talk about "growing more food,"
20 they are actually talking about growing foods that are not only resilient, but also larger in size.

But genetic modifications in farming are becoming the norm; in fact, most crops grown today are genetically modified, rendering "natural" produce almost extinct.
25 Some health experts suggest that we are consuming more genetically modified foods than our bodies can properly digest. In addition, genetically modified foods are allegedly linked to an increase in food allergies, which is counter to the idea that a diet rich in fruits,
30 vegetables, nuts, and grains sustains health.

According to the study's authors, an ideal worldwide food system would integrate the production of both genetically modified and organic foods, as Michael Crowley of Oregon State University explained:
35

The final conclusion? A two-pronged approach. Where nutrition is concerned, it's probably best to grow fruits and vegetables organically. But for providing calories in bulk (especially through bread crops), genetic modifications are too
40 advantageous to ignore.

Moving forward, Crowley believes we should seek to develop an innovative, sustainable food system that strikes a balance between the nutritional benefits of organic foods and the growing capabilities of genetically
45 modified foods. We must strongly evaluate the complex factors that will preserve the health and well-being of our world population for generations to come.

4

According to the passage, genetically engineered crops are designed to

A) require less water to grow.

B) resist pest infestations.

C) be reasonably simple to cultivate.

D) mature more quickly.

5

What can reasonably be inferred about the nutritional researchers cited in the passage?

A) Their research enables the growing techniques used by modern farmers to yield larger fruits.

B) They have discovered the cause of food allergies.

C) They use their findings to promote the popularity of genetically modified foods.

D) They believe that both genetically modified and organic foods can be beneficial to society.

6

The passage indicates that the problem with consuming too many genetically modified foods is that

A) people may be more prone to developing food allergies.

B) people may be unable to digest natural foods.

C) people may neglect to supplement their nutritional needs.

D) new and innovative farming techniques will be ignored.

This page intentionally left blank

Review

Entrance

Reading closely questions can be identified by this feature:

- a question that asks for specific information from the passage

... or the following terms:

- indicate
- identify
- cite
- state
- suggest
- according to the passage/author

Evidence and Elimination

To answer a reading closely question, follow these steps:

1. Identify the keywords in the question.
2. Scan the passage for related keywords.
3. Eliminate answer choices not supported by evidence from the passage.

Exit

If you've found the answer ...

Check to make sure that the answer matches the details of the passage. Mark your answer and continue to the next question.

If you're stuck between two choices ...

Break the remaining answer choices into pieces and compare them to find the essential difference. Test each piece against the passage for accuracy.

If you have no idea what the answer is ...

Pick the answer that is either the longest or the shortest of all the answers.

Chapter

Citing Textual Evidence

LEARNING TARGETS

1. Cite the textual evidence that best supports a claim or point.

2. Implement the basic approach for citing textual evidence questions.

3. Apply the *Cut and Paste* and *Working Backward* strategies to citing textual evidence questions.

Warm-Up

Complete the warm-up. When you have finished, double-check your work.

Questions 1–4 are based on the following passage.

This passage is adapted from Zamir Saxena, *The Gut and Gene Therapy*. ©2019 by MasteryPrep.

When scientists first discovered how to alter the genetics of microbes, they began to take stock of the discovery's potentially far-reaching applications
Line for both science and medicine. While the ability to
5 engineer genetics for applied use in medicine was a mere theoretical notion just decades ago, some of today's scientists are aspiring to engineer synthetic microbes that can treat disease. One business is currently achieving this goal. We have entered a world where the
10 human microbiome and synthetic biology meet, through which genetic engineering creates living medicine.

Many of the microbes that naturally live in our gut keep us healthy. Our guts' own bacteria, fungi, and other microorganisms are used to manage metabolism,
15 inflammation, autoimmune conditions, and the production of vitamins within our bodies. The problem is that it's difficult to identify and study these microbes outside of their hosts, and, as a consequence, patients have not been able to benefit from lab-created microbes.
20 The Human Microbiome Project, however, is working to fully identify the microflora of the human gut; if scientists could match a specific microbe to a health problem, they could engineer microbes in the gut to treat dozens of health disorders.

25 Genetic studies conducted in the 1980s and 1990s revealed evidence of the potential for synthetic microbes, as scientists began altering genetic traits in microbes using a technique called microinjection. Initially, this work was limited to academic, lab-
30 based experiments that only interested scientists. Everything changed when SynB, a drug created by the Massachusetts biotech company Synlogic, came onto the scene. SynB is a strain of *Escherichia coli Nissle (E. coli)*, a probiotic that can be used to treat life-threatening levels
35 of protein in the bloodstream. The bacteria housed in our gut play an important role in moving excess proteins out of the body. But about 1 in 10,000 babies are born with a genetic disorder that prevents their bodies from expelling these proteins, resulting in a buildup of toxic
40 protein levels that could lead to fatality. Synthetic *E. coli* may reduce these risks, and Synlogic resolved to create the probiotic using genetically engineered microbes.

To manufacture the microbes, Synlogic used microinjection, the same method previously studied for
45 its potential use in the creation of treatments for celiac disease and type 1 diabetes. Scientists isolated a gene from a different microbe that could act as a transporter for protein and inserted it into the probiotic. Next, they partnered the *E. coli* with a promoter (a sequence of
50 DNA that manages gene activity) that is present during protein digestion. Finally, mice were injected with the modified probiotic; when they were fed protein, the promoter activated, and their guts reproduced the probiotic. Scientists were encouraged by the results.
55 SynB went on to undergo clinical trials in 2018, becoming the world's first gene therapy used to treat the rare genetic disorder in children. Eventually, scientists hope to use microinjection techniques to treat other rare diseases.

1

According to the author, the ability to fully identify the human microbiome is significant primarily because

A) it will allow researchers to analyze conditions such as inflammation.

B) it will allow scientists to conduct academic, lab-based experiments.

C) the study of microbes will enable scientists to improve microinjection techniques.

D) the study of these microbes could contribute to the development of synthetic microbes to treat a variety of physical illnesses.

2

Which choice provides the best evidence for the answer to the previous question?

A) Lines 1–4 ("When … medicine")

B) Lines 13–16 ("Our guts' … bodies")

C) Lines 20–24 ("The Human … disorders")

D) Lines 29–30 ("Initially … scientists")

Warm-Up

3

Which of the following does the author explicitly state as a function of the gut's microbiome?

A) Regulating the heart

B) Excreting hormones

C) Producing vitamins

D) Lowering cholesterol

4

Which choice provides the best evidence for the answer to the previous question?

A) Lines 12–13 ("Many … healthy")

B) Lines 13–16 ("Our guts' … bodies")

C) Lines 16–19 ("The problem … microbes")

D) Lines 20–24 ("The Human … disorders")

Foundation

Good evidence is:

A) about the same topic as the claim.

B) consistent with the claim

Work with your teacher to circle the quote that best supports the claim in question 1. Write down the reason why it is the best choice.

1. **Claim:** My best friend, Sandra, has seen the band Ruby Loo 15 times.

   A. "I love Ruby Loo." —Sandra

   B. "Sandra always goes to see Ruby Loo when they're in town." —Sandra's mom

   C. "Ruby Loo is the most popular band in the United States." —*Music Insider* magazine

   D. "I've seen Ruby Loo with Sandra over a dozen times. This time, however, was by far the best." —Sandra's friend, Alexa

   Why? _____

   _____

Key Terms

Claim: a statement that is asserted to be true.

Foundation

For questions 2 and 3, work on your own to circle the quote that best supports the claim. Write down the reason why it is the best choice.

2. **Claim:** Even though hoagies remain popular, paninis are the best-selling sandwiches in Pittsburgh.

    A. "Every child in Pittsburgh grows up eating hoagies, also known as submarine sandwiches, all the time."
    — Pittsburgh resident

    B. "Many sandwich shop owners in Pittsburgh tell us they are selling two paninis for every hoagie these days."
    —TV news reporter

    C. "The panini was introduced into the Pittsburgh culinary scene by Italian immigrants who arrived in the 20th century." —University of Pittsburgh Historical Society

    D. "While hoagies are an important part of the culture of Pittsburgh, younger people tend to favor crunchy, warm paninis." —Mrs. Sandra, sandwich shop owner

    Why? _____

    _____

3. **Claim:** The superhero Camila the Comet can fly from New York to Los Angeles in under 10 minutes.

    A. "I saw Camila the Comet fly over my rooftop 10 minutes ago!" —a New York City resident

    B. "Camila the Comet can be seen flying all over the United States, from New York to Los Angeles." —*Average News* report

    C. "We have concluded that Camila the Comet can reach a top speed of 19,000 MPH, meaning she can travel from California to New York in only six minutes." —Superhero scientist Dr. Z

    D. "I have been practicing my flying skills every night."   Camila the Comet

    Why? _____

    _____

Foundation

Work with your teacher to write the number of the sentence that is most relevant to the claim in A. Then, complete B, C, and D on your own.

[1] For many teenagers in the United States, getting a driver's license is a rite of passage. [2] Passing the driving test is a symbol that a teenager is ready to have more independence. [3] After all, in most parts of the country, it is difficult to get around without a car. [4] However, in European countries, teenagers typically don't get their driver's license until much later in life, if at all. [5] Does this mean European teenagers are less independent than their American peers? [6] Not necessarily. [7] Public transportation is more accessible in Europe. [8] Even if you live in a rural or suburban area, it is usually possible to take a train or bus to the city. [9] That means European teenagers can get around on their own to meet up with their friends, get to school, or go out—even without a driver's license. [10] If you ask a European teenager if they wish they had a driver's license like an American teen, though, you might be surprised by the response. [11] They have grown up seeing American teenagers driving in the movies—and they want in. [12] "I think it is so cool that American kids can have their own cars," says Theo, 17, of Austria. [13] "I don't know anyone with a car. [14] I wish my parents would buy me one!" [15] If European teens want cars so badly, why don't they just buy them for themselves? [16] Well, only 20% of European teenagers work, compared to 50% of American teenagers, so many don't have the money to do so. [17] That's yet another difference between teenage life in the United States and in Europe.

A. European teens are inspired by American Hollywood films.

_____

B. Many places in the United States have limited public transit options.

_____

C. More American teenagers work than European teenagers.

_____

D. For many American teenagers, a driver's license is a sign that they are growing up.

_____

This page intentionally left blank

Practice Set 1 | Complete the practice set. When you have finished, double-check your work.

Questions 1–14 are based on the following passage.

The passage is adapted from Samantha Collins, Jeremy Corrigan, and Mark Usborne, "The Authority of the Media." ©2020 by MasteryPrep.

Information that is obtained through reading online and print media, as well as watching television news, is a kind of public knowledge. In contrast to
Line private information (such as the affairs of one's family
5 and friends; the enjoyment of certain hobbies; covert personal relationships), public knowledge gains credibility the more widely it is shared. A debate about the implementation of a proposed law; the outcome of local, state, and national elections; recent military
10 activity in a war zone; the repercussions of a global health crisis—these are examples of public knowledge of which "informed citizens" are generally expected to be aware. Public information, as we perceive it, is circulated to all members of society, even to those who might not
15 be interested, as opposed to private information, which each individual can choose to seek out or disregard. In short, people generally view public knowledge, such as what is portrayed via news organizations, as a universal good that cannot be solely driven by demand.
20 Public information is produced, disseminated, and received via a highly sophisticated and complex process. Although the widely-held belief is that public information should be accurate and reliable, there is sometimes less agreement about what the general
25 population needs to know, who is best qualified to share and explain the information, and how such authoritative influences should be selected and evaluated.
Traditionally, media outlets such as major cable news networks and prominent, national newspapers have been
30 widely assumed to be authoritative sources of reliable information and conventional wisdom. They have exemplified *Merriam-Webster Dictionary*'s definition of authority as "the power to influence or command the thought, opinion, or behavior of others." In recent
35 years, however, a reluctance to blindly accept these conventional sources of public knowledge has not only emerged, but also surged. As a result, there has been a greater demand for authorities to be straightforward and transparent about the values that shape their decisions.
40 Our study shows that the press across all platforms has not been exempt from this expectation. Increasingly, the public demands that members of the media present neutral, transparent information that is standard across news sources. Not surprisingly, some journalists
45 are uneasy about the current debate regarding their

authority to share public information in ways they see fit:

Standardizing, or leveling, television news could result in the oversimplification of information and misguided popularity contests for featured stories
50 (online news editor, 2015).

Decisions about which stories matter to audiences are increasingly made by editors who refer to the "most read" lists on popular websites. As a result, readers and viewers—who used to know their
55 places—are being called upon to act as journalistic referees, scrutinizing our integrity (broadcast journalist, 2016).

These journalists go beyond simply defending their own professions. By equating the standardization of
60 news with an oversimplification of information, as well as stating that readers and viewers "used to know their places," these newspeople are vying for a specific and exclusive form of public knowledge: one that is exempt from popular influence, framed by experts,
65 and circulated to an aware but generally unengaged society. This declaration by industry professionals rejects the populace's opportunity to be involved in creating public knowledge. Because skepticism about the long-established authority of the media now exists at
70 almost every level, the journalists mentioned above are unsettled. Several of our study participants expressed that the job of broadcast, online, and print journalists is to "convey information in its raw form without interjecting personal bias"; they should "inform rather
75 than dictate"; and the general public should be given "comprehensive information" on which "we can form our own opinions."
At the heart of this debate are two distinct interpretations of authority. The members of the
80 media cited above resist challenges to their authority to share public information objectively. They oppose standardization of news: the demands by some for straightforward, objective information rather than crafted narratives; the driving force of website analytics
85 (whereby editors choose stories based on the number of clicks they receive online); the balance of popular culture with "serious" news.

1

The authors indicate that the public has grown to prefer that the news media disclose

A) potential biases about the events covered.

B) fewer details than are absolutely required.

C) explanations from reliable sources on the stories they share.

D) information that people might wish to keep private.

2

Which choice provides the best evidence for the answer to the previous question?

A) Lines 13–16 ("Public … disregard")

B) Lines 31–34 ("They have … others")

C) Lines 37–39 ("As a result … decisions")

D) Lines 44–46 ("Not surprisingly … fit")

3

According to the passage, which expectation do many people have for journalists today?

A) They should be driven by private economic decisions.

B) They should be impartial in reporting information.

C) They should be mindful of the difference between public and private information.

D) They should be truthful about their professional qualifications.

4

Which choice provides the best evidence for the answer to the previous question?

A) Lines 3–7 ("In contrast … shared")

B) Lines 22–27 ("Although … evaluated")

C) Lines 51–53 ("Decisions … websites")

D) Lines 71–74 ("Several … bias")

Approach

Entrance

Citing textual evidence questions can be identified by these features:

- All answer choices are line numbers followed by a set of parentheses.
- The question includes the words *best evidence* and *previous question*.

The following questions refer to the passage on page 88. Review questions 5 and 6 with your teacher. Do not answer the questions.

Entrance ⟩ Evidence and Elimination ⟩ Exit

5

The authors indicate that public information provided by the media

A) is an assumed societal commodity.

B) is received with confidence.

C) pertains to insignificant subjects.

D) goes beyond what the public demands.

6

Which choice provides the best evidence for the answer to the previous question?

A) Lines 16–19 ("In short … demand")

B) Lines 20–22 ("Public … process")

C) Lines 66–68 ("This declaration … knowledge")

D) Lines 78–79 ("At the heart … authority")

Review questions 7 and 8 on your own. Circle the citing textual evidence question. Do not answer the questions.

7

The passage indicates that the assumption made about the media in lines 28–31 may be

A) hypocritical.

B) irrational.

C) questionable.

D) confirmed.

8

Which choice provides the best evidence for the answer to the previous question?

A) Lines 7–13 ("A debate … aware")

B) Lines 34–37 ("In recent … surged")

C) Lines 59–66 ("By equating … society")

D) Lines 71–74 ("Several … bias")

Questions 1–14 are based on the following passage.

The passage is adapted from Samantha Collins, Jeremy Corrigan, and Mark Usborne, "The Authority of the Media." ©2020 by MasteryPrep.

Information that is obtained through reading online and print media, as well as watching television news, is a kind of public knowledge. In contrast to
Line private information (such as the affairs of one's family
5 and friends; the enjoyment of certain hobbies; covert personal relationships), public knowledge gains credibility the more widely it is shared. A debate about the implementation of a proposed law; the outcome of local, state, and national elections; recent military
10 activity in a war zone; the repercussions of a global health crisis—these are examples of public knowledge of which "informed citizens" are generally expected to be aware. Public information, as we perceive it, is circulated to all members of society, even to those who might not
15 be interested, as opposed to private information, which each individual can choose to seek out or disregard. In short, people generally view public knowledge, such as what is portrayed via news organizations, as a universal good that cannot be solely driven by demand.
20 Public information is produced, disseminated, and received via a highly sophisticated and complex process. Although the widely-held belief is that public information should be accurate and reliable, there is sometimes less agreement about what the general
25 population needs to know, who is best qualified to share and explain the information, and how such authoritative influences should be selected and evaluated.

Traditionally, media outlets such as major cable news networks and prominent, national newspapers have been
30 widely assumed to be authoritative sources of reliable information and conventional wisdom. They have exemplified *Merriam-Webster Dictionary*'s definition of authority as "the power to influence or command the thought, opinion, or behavior of others." In recent
35 years, however, a reluctance to blindly accept these conventional sources of public knowledge has not only emerged, but also surged. As a result, there has been a greater demand for authorities to be straightforward and transparent about the values that shape their decisions.
40 Our study shows that the press across all platforms has not been exempt from this expectation. Increasingly, the public demands that members of the media present neutral, transparent information that is standard across news sources. Not surprisingly, some journalists
45 are uneasy about the current debate regarding their authority to share public information in ways they see fit:

Standardizing, or leveling, television news could result in the oversimplification of information and misguided popularity contests for featured stories
50 (online news editor, 2015).

Decisions about which stories matter to audiences are increasingly made by editors who refer to the "most read" lists on popular websites. As a result, readers and viewers—who used to know their
55 places—are being called upon to act as journalistic referees, scrutinizing our integrity (broadcast journalist, 2016).

These journalists go beyond simply defending their own professions. By equating the standardization of
60 news with an oversimplification of information, as well as stating that readers and viewers "used to know their places," these newspeople are vying for a specific and exclusive form of public knowledge: one that is exempt from popular influence, framed by experts,
65 and circulated to an aware but generally unengaged society. This declaration by industry professionals rejects the populace's opportunity to be involved in creating public knowledge. Because skepticism about the long-established authority of the media now exists at
70 almost every level, the journalists mentioned above are unsettled. Several of our study participants expressed that the job of broadcast, online, and print journalists is to "convey information in its raw form without interjecting personal bias"; they should "inform rather
75 than dictate"; and the general public should be given "comprehensive information" on which "we can form our own opinions."

At the heart of this debate are two distinct interpretations of authority. The members of the
80 media cited above resist challenges to their authority to share public information objectively. They oppose standardization of news: the demands by some for straightforward, objective information rather than crafted narratives; the driving force of website analytics
85 (whereby editors choose stories based on the number of clicks they receive online); the balance of popular culture with "serious" news.

Approach

Evidence and Elimination

To answer a citing textual evidence question, follow these steps:

1. Bracket the referenced lines.
2. Use the bracketed lines to answer the previous question.
3. Eliminate choices not used to answer the previous question.

Answer questions 5 and 6 with your teacher.

Entrance   Evidence and Elimination   Exit

5

The authors indicate that public information provided by the media

A) is an assumed societal commodity.

B) is received with confidence.

C) pertains to insignificant subjects.

D) goes beyond what the public demands.

6

Which choice provides the best evidence for the answer to the previous question?

A) Lines 16–19 ("In short … demand")

B) Lines 20–22 ("Public … process")

C) Lines 66–68 ("This declaration … knowledge")

D) Lines 78–79 ("At the heart … authority")

Approach

The following questions refer to the passage on page 92. Answer questions 7 and 8 on your own. Focus on eliminating incorrect answers.

7

The passage indicates that the assumption made about the media in lines 28–31 may be

A) hypocritical.

B) irrational.

C) questionable.

D) confirmed.

8

Which choice provides the best evidence for the answer to the previous question?

A) Lines 7–13 ("A debate … aware")

B) Lines 34–37 ("In recent … surged")

C) Lines 59–66 ("By equating … society")

D) Lines 71–74 ("Several … bias")

Approach

	Exit

If you've found the answer …

Make sure that the bracketed lines in your answer choice directly support the answer to the previous question. If so, mark your answer and continue to the next question.

If you're stuck between two choices …

Mix and match your bracketed lines and the remaining choices to the previous question. Select the choices that best connect an answer to its support.

If you have no idea what the answer is …

Select the choice that contains the most synonyms of words found in the previous question's answer.

Review questions 9 and 10. Work with your teacher to choose the correct answer from the remaining choices.

Entrance ⟩ Evidence and Elimination ⟩ **Exit**

9

What can reasonably be inferred about the standardization of news from the passage?

A) ~~It has led to a distrust of the news media.~~

B) It caused a change in the public's critique of the media.

C) ~~It is a cause of political polarization.~~

D) It is unsupported by journalists.

10

Which choice provides the best evidence for the answer to the previous question?

A) ~~Lines 40–41 ("Our study … expectation")~~

B) Lines 47–49 ("Standardizing … stories")

C) Lines 51–53 ("Decisions … websites")

D) ~~Lines 58–59 ("These … professions")~~

Practice Set 2 | Complete the practice set. When you have finished, double-check your work.

Questions 1–14 are based on the following passage.

The passage is adapted from Samantha Collins, Jeremy Corrigan, and Mark Usborne, "The Authority of the Media." ©2020 by MasteryPrep.

Information that is obtained through reading online and print media, as well as watching television news, is a kind of public knowledge. In contrast to
Line private information (such as the affairs of one's family
5 and friends; the enjoyment of certain hobbies; covert personal relationships), public knowledge gains credibility the more widely it is shared. A debate about the implementation of a proposed law; the outcome of local, state, and national elections; recent military
10 activity in a war zone; the repercussions of a global health crisis—these are examples of public knowledge of which "informed citizens" are generally expected to be aware. Public information, as we perceive it, is circulated to all members of society, even to those who might not
15 be interested, as opposed to private information, which each individual can choose to seek out or disregard. In short, people generally view public knowledge, such as what is portrayed via news organizations, as a universal good that cannot be solely driven by demand.
20   Public information is produced, disseminated, and received via a highly sophisticated and complex process. Although the widely-held belief is that public information should be accurate and reliable, there is sometimes less agreement about what the general
25 population needs to know, who is best qualified to share and explain the information, and how such authoritative influences should be selected and evaluated.
    Traditionally, media outlets such as major cable news networks and prominent, national newspapers have been
30 widely assumed to be authoritative sources of reliable information and conventional wisdom. They have exemplified *Merriam-Webster Dictionary*'s definition of authority as "the power to influence or command the thought, opinion, or behavior of others." In recent
35 years, however, a reluctance to blindly accept these conventional sources of public knowledge has not only emerged, but also surged. As a result, there has been a greater demand for authorities to be straightforward and transparent about the values that shape their decisions.
40 Our study shows that the press across all platforms has not been exempt from this expectation. Increasingly, the public demands that members of the media present neutral, transparent information that is standard across news sources. Not surprisingly, some journalists
45 are uneasy about the current debate regarding their authority to share public information in ways they see fit:

    Standardizing, or leveling, television news could result in the oversimplification of information and misguided popularity contests for featured stories
50   (online news editor, 2015).

    Decisions about which stories matter to audiences are increasingly made by editors who refer to the "most read" lists on popular websites. As a result, readers and viewers—who used to know their
55   places—are being called upon to act as journalistic referees, scrutinizing our integrity (broadcast journalist, 2016).

    These journalists go beyond simply defending their own professions. By equating the standardization of
60 news with an oversimplification of information, as well as stating that readers and viewers "used to know their places," these newspeople are vying for a specific and exclusive form of public knowledge: one that is exempt from popular influence, framed by experts,
65 and circulated to an aware but generally unengaged society. This declaration by industry professionals rejects the populace's opportunity to be involved in creating public knowledge. Because skepticism about the long-established authority of the media now exists at
70 almost every level, the journalists mentioned above are unsettled. Several of our study participants expressed that the job of broadcast, online, and print journalists is to "convey information in its raw form without interjecting personal bias"; they should "inform rather
75 than dictate"; and the general public should be given "comprehensive information" on which "we can form our own opinions."
    At the heart of this debate are two distinct interpretations of authority. The members of the
80 media cited above resist challenges to their authority to share public information objectively. They oppose standardization of news: the demands by some for straightforward, objective information rather than crafted narratives; the driving force of website analytics
85 (whereby editors choose stories based on the number of clicks they receive online); the balance of popular culture with "serious" news.

11

The authors make which point about the views of the public relative to the views of the media?

A) The public believes it should be involved in generating public knowledge, but the media believes the public is largely uneducated.

B) The public has become skeptical of the media, but the media is resistant to scrutiny.

C) The public wants the media to decide what information is newsworthy, but the media wants public involvement.

D) The public thinks that private information should be protected, but the media thinks all information should be public.

12

Which choice provides the best evidence for the answer to the previous question?

A) Lines 3–7 ("In contrast … shared")

B) Lines 22–27 ("Although … evaluated")

C) Lines 59–66 ("By equating … society")

D) Lines 68–71 ("Because … unsettled")

13

The authors make which point about the kind of audience some members of the media would like to serve?

A) Some members of the media want an audience that reads many kinds of news stories.

B) Some members of the media value an audience that is aware but generally not invested in the news.

C) Some members of the media seek an audience that will form its own opinions.

D) Some members of the media prefer an audience that is diverse.

14

Which choice provides the best evidence for the answer to the previous question?

A) Lines 13–16 ("Public … disregard")

B) Lines 53–56 ("As a result … integrity")

C) Lines 59–66 ("By equating … society")

D) Lines 79–87 ("The members … news")

Strategy

Questions 15–26 are based on the following passages.

Passage 1 is adapted from Thomas Roy, "Ocean Mining: The Next Gold Rush?" ©2019 by MasteryPrep. Passage 2 is from the editors of MasteryPrep, "Regulating Seafloor Expedition." ©2019 by MasteryPrep.

Passage 1

Chase down profits and you will end up on the ocean floor. That's the word from an exclusive conference on mining the seafloor.

Line 5 Hosted in Jamaica by the International Seabed Authority (ISA), the gathering assembled international scholars, experts from the legal and scientific communities, and government and industry representatives who are all driven to explore the ocean floor.

10 The conference took place right after the 2018 issuance of 29 exploration licenses to government-sponsored companies. Nautilus Minerals of Australia says that it will debut its first underwater exploration probes within five years, while Japan Oil, Gas, and

15 Metals National Corporation has already begun prospecting. Another international company, UK Seabed Resources, hopes to be harvesting deep-sea minerals in the near future, including rare, precious metals.

Within a few years, these companies might be able

20 to exploit the abundance of marine resources in order to satisfy the growing demand for rare earth elements and minerals, such as copper. Like the scientists who transformed the world through their discovery of electricity, unearthed resources could transform

25 the global economy. The revenue from rare earth minerals and precious metals could potentially lead to unprecedented economic growth and improved quality of life.

With this in mind, the ISA and the various

30 governments involved would ensure the participation of developing states. "In this world, what is better: a country whose citizens struggle or a country where people are given the chance to prosper?" asks Diedre McDorman of the International Seabed Authority.

35 "Poverty helps no one. Prosperity helps us all."

Revenue generated from mineral extraction would be evenly distributed to developing countries directly from the ISA or from the mining companies. Redistributing the profits in this way allows for greater investment in

40 infrastructure, so that investments in mining operations benefit locals.

Developing countries are open to ocean mining if it boosts job growth, negotiating power, and exports, which could easily improve local economies. Others

45 hope to use the investment to improve training for engineers and other mining professionals.

Passage 2

The interest in deep-sea exploration is moving from scientific investigation to big business. We have recently seen an expansion in the number of licenses offered to

50 government-sponsored companies to mine the seafloor. This will certainly enrich a few investors, but all of humanity may benefit: a sustainable supply of critical minerals could help us all.

However, prior to government-backed companies

55 embarking on ocean mining, we ought to consider several issues. Initially, seabed mining does not appear to impact some environmental factors; there is (probably) very little life at such depths, and therefore few ecosystems to worry about disrupting. But other

60 potential consequences—both on the ocean floor and on the ground above—are worthy of consideration.

This is partially about ethics. Some have argued that the ocean's riches should not be exploited, that we know too little about life on the seafloor to risk disturbing it.

65 Others have declared that we should stop degrading the earth in order to sustain our consumer lifestyles.

History shows that such concerns are often overridden, and the public may not be interested in protecting a deep-sea ecosystem that they see as devoid

70 of life. Ultimately, the world on the ocean floor is hidden, and few people are likely to value what they can't see over their everyday needs and wants.

We must also consider international economic competition. The resources that are found in the ocean

75 are coveted by nations around the globe. Issues regarding their governance have scarcely been addressed—and the applicable laws and regulations are incomplete and piecemeal, to say the least.

Ocean prospectors, like their Old West predecessors,

80 are frequently averse to addressing these issues. One businessman at the recent ISA conference in Jamaica entreated his peers to lobby against additional regulations. Yet companies stand to profit from clear and fair oversight of the extraction of sea minerals. In the

85 absence of any clear framework, claims will be contested, funding insecure, and profits made uncertain. It is in the best interest of all of humanity to settle these issues before diving in.

Citing Textual Evidence

Strategy

Cut and Paste

Use this strategy on citing textual evidence questions when you don't know the answer to the previous question.

1. "Cut" the previous question.
2. "Paste" it in place of the second question.
3. Select the lines that answer the first question.

Review questions 15 and 16 with your teacher. Use the Cut and Paste strategy to answer the questions as a class.

15

The author of Passage 1 notes that ocean mining could have which positive effect?

A) It could satisfy the demand for rare and precious substances.

B) It could increase the cost of many rare elements found on dry land.

C) It could spur a modernization of the methods used in mining today.

D) It could revolutionize scientific research of deep-sea marine life.

16

Which choice provides the best evidence for the answer to the previous question?

A) Lines 19–22 ("Within ... copper")

B) Lines 22–25 ("Like ... economy")

C) Line 35 ("Poverty ... all")

D) Lines 42–44 ("Developing ... economies")

Strategy

The following questions refer to the passages on page 98. Work on your own using the Cut and Paste strategy to answer questions 17 and 18.

17

The author of Passage 1 claims which of the following is a motivating factor for companies interested in deep-sea mining?

A) Learning about the ecosystem of the seafloor

B) Attaining global recognition from the International Seabed Authority

C) Utilizing precious minerals in tandem with electricity production

D) Extracting a large supply of precious materials

18

Which choice provides the best evidence for the answer to the previous question?

A) Lines 2–3 ("That's ... seafloor")

B) Lines 19–22 ("Within ... copper")

C) Lines 38–41 ("Redistributing ... locals")

D) Lines 44–46 ("Others ... professionals")

Strategy

Working Backward

If you are struggling to select the answers for the citing textual evidence question pair, you can simplify the process by working backward. Here's how ...

1. Identify the topic of the first question in the pair.

2. Eliminate answer choices from the second question if they do not provide information that is helpful to answer the previous question.

3. Use the remaining choices in the second question to pick an answer for the first question.

4. Pick the answer in the second question that was most helpful for answering the first question.

Review questions 19 and 20 with your teacher. Use the Working Backward strategy to answer the questions as a class.

19

Which of the following best portrays the attitude of the authors of Passage 2 toward "deep-sea exploration" (line 47)?

A) They are worried about developing countries relying on it for economic growth.

B) They are unconcerned about its potential impact on underwater ecosystems.

C) They are worried about potential negative outcomes above and below the earth's surface.

D) They are confident that their concerns are being heard.

20

Which choice provides the best evidence for the answer to the previous question?

A) Lines 56–59 ("Initially ... disrupting")

B) Lines 59–61 ("But ... consideration")

C) Lines 62–64 ("Some ... disturbing it")

D) Lines 80–83 ("One ... regulations")

The following questions refer to the passages on page 98. Work on your own using the Working Backward strategy to answer questions 21 and 22.

21

In Passage 2, the authors most strongly imply that some people are unmoved by environmental concerns because they

A) believe that underwater mining will not have any impacts on ocean life.

B) understand very well the enormous benefits of mineral extraction to humanity.

C) are more interested in immediate, personal desires and how to meet them.

D) know that soon there will be precise regulations protecting the environment.

22

Which choice provides the best evidence for the answer to the previous question?

A) Lines 47–48 ("The interest ... business")

B) Lines 62–64 ("Some ... disturbing it")

C) Lines 70–72 ("Ultimately ... wants")

D) Lines 74–75 ("The resources ... globe")

This page intentionally left blank

Practice Set 3 | Complete the practice set. When you have finished, double-check your work.

Questions 15–26 are based on the following passages.

Passage 1 is adapted from Thomas Roy, "Ocean Mining: The Next Gold Rush?" ©2019 by MasteryPrep. Passage 2 is from the editors of MasteryPrep, "Regulating Seafloor Expedition." ©2019 by MasteryPrep.

Passage 1

Chase down profits and you will end up on the ocean floor. That's the word from an exclusive conference on mining the seafloor.

Line
5 Hosted in Jamaica by the International Seabed Authority (ISA), the gathering assembled international scholars, experts from the legal and scientific communities, and government and industry representatives who are all driven to explore the ocean floor.

10 The conference took place right after the 2018 issuance of 29 exploration licenses to government-sponsored companies. Nautilus Minerals of Australia says that it will debut its first underwater exploration probes within five years, while Japan Oil, Gas, and
15 Metals National Corporation has already begun prospecting. Another international company, UK Seabed Resources, hopes to be harvesting deep-sea minerals in the near future, including rare, precious metals.

Within a few years, these companies might be able
20 to exploit the abundance of marine resources in order to satisfy the growing demand for rare earth elements and minerals, such as copper. Like the scientists who transformed the world through their discovery of electricity, unearthed resources could transform
25 the global economy. The revenue from rare earth minerals and precious metals could potentially lead to unprecedented economic growth and improved quality of life.

With this in mind, the ISA and the various
30 governments involved would ensure the participation of developing states. "In this world, what is better: a country whose citizens struggle or a country where people are given the chance to prosper?" asks Diedre McDorman of the International Seabed Authority.
35 "Poverty helps no one. Prosperity helps us all."

Revenue generated from mineral extraction would be evenly distributed to developing countries directly from the ISA or from the mining companies. Redistributing the profits in this way allows for greater investment in
40 infrastructure, so that investments in mining operations benefit locals.

Developing countries are open to ocean mining if it boosts job growth, negotiating power, and exports, which could easily improve local economies. Others
45 hope to use the investment to improve training for engineers and other mining professionals.

Passage 2

The interest in deep-sea exploration is moving from scientific investigation to big business. We have recently seen an expansion in the number of licenses offered to
50 government-sponsored companies to mine the seafloor. This will certainly enrich a few investors, but all of humanity may benefit: a sustainable supply of critical minerals could help us all.

However, prior to government-backed companies
55 embarking on ocean mining, we ought to consider several issues. Initially, seabed mining does not appear to impact some environmental factors; there is (probably) very little life at such depths, and therefore few ecosystems to worry about disrupting. But other
60 potential consequences—both on the ocean floor and on the ground above—are worthy of consideration.

This is partially about ethics. Some have argued that the ocean's riches should not be exploited, that we know too little about life on the seafloor to risk disturbing it.
65 Others have declared that we should stop degrading the earth in order to sustain our consumer lifestyles.

History shows that such concerns are often overridden, and the public may not be interested in protecting a deep-sea ecosystem that they see as devoid
70 of life. Ultimately, the world on the ocean floor is hidden, and few people are likely to value what they can't see over their everyday needs and wants.

We must also consider international economic competition. The resources that are found in the ocean
75 are coveted by nations around the globe. Issues regarding their governance have scarcely been addressed—and the applicable laws and regulations are incomplete and piecemeal, to say the least.

Ocean prospectors, like their Old West predecessors,
80 are frequently averse to addressing these issues. One businessman at the recent ISA conference in Jamaica entreated his peers to lobby against additional regulations. Yet companies stand to profit from clear and fair oversight of the extraction of sea minerals. In the
85 absence of any clear framework, claims will be contested, funding insecure, and profits made uncertain. It is in the best interest of all of humanity to settle these issues before diving in.

23

The authors of Passage 2 would most likely react to the analysis of the future of ocean mining in lines 36–38, Passage 1, by asserting that such a future

A) is not in line with policies of environmental sustainability.

B) will be difficult to achieve without unambiguous regulations.

C) is still out of reach because necessary technology isn't ready.

D) will certainly have a negative impact on the world's economy.

24

Which choice provides the best evidence for the answer to the previous question?

A) Lines 62–64 ("Some … disturbing it")

B) Lines 74–75 ("The resources … globe")

C) Lines 80–83 ("One … regulations")

D) Lines 84–86 ("In the absence … uncertain")

25

According to Passage 1, which choice best describes the future impacts of deep-sea mining?

A) Anticipated shortfalls due to uncertain technological advancements

B) An overabundance of extracted resources devaluing their market price

C) Greater ability to meet the ever-growing need for precious minerals

D) Humanitarian efforts organized by many philanthropic organizations

26

Which choice provides the best evidence for the answer to the previous question?

A) Lines 4–9 ("Hosted … floor")

B) Lines 16–18 ("Another … metals")

C) Lines 29–31 ("With this … states")

D) Lines 42–44 ("Developing … economies")

Mini-Test | Complete the mini-test. When you have finished, double-check your work.

Questions 42–51 are based on the following passage.

This passage is adapted from Jacob Fiorella, *More than Beauty Sleep: The Science of Brain Health.* ©2019 by MasteryPrep.

In 2013, a professor of neurosurgery at the University
of Rochester named Maiken Nedergaard wanted to
know what function, if any, neural activity during sleep
Line serves in the restoration of the brain. When Nedergaard
5 examined the brains of 20 sleeping mice using
fluorescent imaging, he discovered a surprising and
significant phenomenon. The volume of cerebrospinal
fluid (CSF), a fluid that cushions the brain and spinal
cord, was about 95% higher in sleeping mice than in
10 those that were awake—a striking difference. Nedergaard
eventually determined that the mice's brains actually
shrank during sleep to allow for the increased flow of
CSF into the brain. Wakefulness in the mice led to a
sharp decline in CSF levels.

15 The brain is a self-regulating structure, able to—with
some limitations—perform its own maintenance and
cleaning via the regulatory functions of the lymphatic
system. While the brain rests and CSF levels increase,
the lymphatic drainage system acts as a housekeeper,
20 washing away waste products, such as beta-amyloid, that
are harmful to brain cells. Nedergaard's study revealed
that disrupted sleep could be related to a decline in brain
health.

Following Nedergaard's study, neuroscientists began
25 to focus on sleep in people suffering from Alzheimer's
disease. Dr. Laura Lewis of Boston University worked
with a team of researchers from Harvard Medical School
to study 11 healthy people who self-identified as good
sleepers. Dr. Lewis and her team wanted to know if
30 the healthy sleepers' brains—like the brains of mice—
experienced an increase of CSF while simultaneously
experiencing a decrease of beta-amyloid, or if there were
other mechanisms at work helping to rid the human
brain of harmful waste.

35 The scientists used accelerated neuroimaging to
observe physical and neural shifts in the brains of the
participants while they slept inside an MRI machine.
Scientists also measured the movement of CSF
during periods of non-rapid eye movement (NREM)
40 sleep. Lewis and her team surmised that they might
find physiological similarities between the human
participants' brains and the brains of mice, proving
that mammalian brains have similar methods of self-
regulation. When the team analyzed the MRI data, they
45 indeed found that the brains of the study participants
functioned very similarly to those of the mice in the

previous study. In addition, in every human participant,
the pattern of CSF flow in the brain followed the same
pattern as that in the mice. The study showed that the
50 human brain experiences the same "cleaning process"
during sleep, and that healthy sleepers reap the same
neural benefits.

But the scientists found one important difference
between the brains of the mice and those of the humans;
55 when the team analyzed the levels of CSF in the human
brain during NREM sleep, they found that an entirely
different mechanism was allowing for increased levels of
fluid to reach the brain. According to the neuroimaging
data, the brains of the human participants did not shrink
60 like those of the mice, but experienced decreased blood
flow in order to make room for more CSF.

Interestingly, when the humans were in a state of
deep sleep, they experienced two processes in the brain
that appeared to be involved in clearing beta-amyloid
65 (an abundance of which could otherwise contribute
to Alzheimer's disease): neural electrical activity
followed seconds later by large, slow waves of CSF.
This observation raised other questions. Why do these
processes happen during deep sleep, rather than while
70 people are in other states of sleep? Why would the brain
of someone with Alzheimer's not force itself into more
deep sleep in order to help get rid of waste?

Lewis and her team researched other possible
factors to understand exactly what happens in the
75 sleep-deprived brain. The results of their studies
point to numerous factors that may initiate a decrease
in the brain's ability to self-clean, which launches a
vicious cycle whereby beta-amyloid buildup prevents
sleep. Consequently, disrupted sleep results in more
80 amyloid, and more amyloid leads to a decline in brain
functioning. Thus, these scientific investigations into the
connections between sleep, CSF, and the brain lymphatic
system have revealed a possible clue that could lead to a
cure for Alzheimer's.

1 | | | **1**

42

According to the author, Nedergaard's results regarding mice are noteworthy because they

A) show that fluorescent imaging has a variety of applications.

B) support previously established findings about mental decline.

C) establish a potential link between sleep patterns and brain health.

D) shed light on a long-held but erroneous theory of the brain.

43

Which choice provides the best evidence for the answer to the previous question?

A) Lines 7–10 ("The volume ... difference")

B) Lines 10–13 ("Nedergaard ... brain")

C) Lines 15–18 ("The brain ... system")

D) Lines 21–23 ("Nedergaard's ... health")

44

As used in line 62, "state" most nearly means

A) territory.

B) glory.

C) mood.

D) condition.

45

Which question was Lewis' study of healthy sleepers chiefly designed to answer?

A) Does the act of sleeping cause the brain to shrink in response to the introduction of increased levels of CSF?

B) Do patients suffering from Alzheimer's disease exhibit genetic traits that make them more susceptible to mental decline?

C) Does healthy sleep lead to increased levels of CSF that help the brain cleanse itself from dangerous waste?

D) What are the various factors that may contribute to the mental decline of people suffering from brain disease?

46

Which choice provides the best evidence for the answer to the previous question?

A) Lines 24–26 ("Following ... disease")

B) Lines 29–34 ("Dr. Lewis ... waste")

C) Lines 35–37 ("The scientists ... machine")

D) Lines 47–49 ("In addition ... mice")

1   1

47

As used in line 40, "surmised" most nearly means

A) deduced.

B) discovered.

C) investigated.

D) pretended.

48

The main purpose of the fifth paragraph (lines 53–61) is to

A) explain the link between the study of mice and the study of Alzheimer's disease.

B) provide a hypothesis for the surprising results in the human study.

C) point out a significant finding of Lewis' study of the human brain.

D) shift the focus from the results of Lewis' study to her methodology.

49

According to the author, when compared to the brains of mice, the brains of humans

A) had less CSF fluid overall during deep sleep.

B) were more likely to experience mental decline.

C) made room for CSF fluid by different means.

D) had a greater amount of neural activity at rest.

50

The author most strongly implies that healthy sleepers are less likely to develop Alzheimer's because they

A) benefit from the brain's natural lymphatic system during deep sleep.

B) activate regions of the brain at rest that most people are unable to use.

C) have lymphatic brain systems that are exceptionally efficient.

D) report sleep deprivation to doctors as soon as they become aware of it.

51

Which choice provides the best evidence for the answer to the previous question?

A) Lines 62–67 ("Interestingly ... CSF")

B) Line 68 ("This ... questions")

C) Lines 73–75 ("Lewis ... brain")

D) Lines 79–81 ("Consequently ... functioning")

STOP

**If you finish before time is called, you may check your work on this section only.
Do not turn to any other section.**

This page intentionally left blank

Wrap-Up

Complete the wrap-up. When you have finished, double-check your work.

Questions 5–8 are based on the following passage.

This passage is adapted from Zamir Saxena, *The Gut and Gene Therapy.* ©2019 by MasteryPrep.

When scientists first discovered how to alter the genetics of microbes, they began to take stock of the discovery's potentially far-reaching applications
Line for both science and medicine. While the ability to
5 engineer genetics for applied use in medicine was a mere theoretical notion just decades ago, some of today's scientists are aspiring to engineer synthetic microbes that can treat disease. One business is currently achieving this goal. We have entered a world where the
10 human microbiome and synthetic biology meet, through which genetic engineering creates living medicine.

Many of the microbes that naturally live in our gut keep us healthy. Our guts' own bacteria, fungi, and other microorganisms are used to manage metabolism,
15 inflammation, autoimmune conditions, and the production of vitamins within our bodies. The problem is that it's difficult to identify and study these microbes outside of their hosts, and, as a consequence, patients have not been able to benefit from lab-created microbes.
20 The Human Microbiome Project, however, is working to fully identify the microflora of the human gut; if scientists could match a specific microbe to a health problem, they could engineer microbes in the gut to treat dozens of health disorders.

25 Genetic studies conducted in the 1980s and 1990s revealed evidence of the potential for synthetic microbes, as scientists began altering genetic traits in microbes using a technique called microinjection. Initially, this work was limited to academic, lab-
30 based experiments that only interested scientists. Everything changed when SynB, a drug created by the Massachusetts biotech company Synlogic, came onto the scene. SynB is a strain of *Escherichia coli Nissle (E. coli),* a probiotic that can be used to treat life-threatening levels
35 of protein in the bloodstream. The bacteria housed in our gut play an important role in moving excess proteins out of the body. But about 1 in 10,000 babies are born with a genetic disorder that prevents their bodies from expelling these proteins, resulting in a buildup of toxic
40 protein levels that could lead to fatality. Synthetic *E. coli* may reduce these risks, and Synlogic resolved to create the probiotic using genetically engineered microbes.

To manufacture the microbes, Synlogic used microinjection, the same method previously studied for
45 its potential use in the creation of treatments for celiac disease and type 1 diabetes. Scientists isolated a gene from a different microbe that could act as a transporter for protein and inserted it into the probiotic. Next, they partnered the *E. coli* with a promoter (a sequence of
50 DNA that manages gene activity) that is present during protein digestion. Finally, mice were injected with the modified probiotic; when they were fed protein, the promoter activated, and their guts reproduced the probiotic. Scientists were encouraged by the results.
55 SynB went on to undergo clinical trials in 2018, becoming the world's first gene therapy used to treat the rare genetic disorder in children. Eventually, scientists hope to use microinjection techniques to treat other rare diseases.

5

What does the author suggest about the genetic studies done in the 1980s and 1990s?

A) They were hindered by the controversial nature of genetic engineering.

B) They were not driven by a search for practical purposes outside of academia.

C) They were completed when a strain of *E. coli* was identified.

D) They concentrated on the genetic components of protein-inhibiting enzymes.

6

Which choice provides the best evidence for the answer to the previous question?

A) Lines 16–19 ("The problem … microbes")

B) Lines 29–30 ("Initially … scientists")

C) Lines 33–35 ("SnyB … bloodstream")

D) Lines 35–37 ("The bacteria … body")

7

According to the passage, which of the following is true of *E. coli*?

A) It regulates levels of protein in the blood.

B) It is caused by an inherited genetic disorder that is rare in humans.

C) It is a bacterium that does not occur naturally in the human gut.

D) It is a DNA molecule that was first identified in an academic lab.

8

Which choice provides the best evidence for the answer to the previous question?

A) Lines 33–35 ("SynB … bloodstream")

B) Lines 35–37 ("The bacteria … body")

C) Lines 40–42 ("Synthetic … microbes")

D) Lines 48–51 ("Next … digestion")

Review

Entrance

Citing textual evidence questions can be identified by these features:

- All answer choices are line numbers followed by a set of parentheses.
- The question includes the words *best evidence* and *previous question*.

Evidence and Elimination

To answer a citing textual evidence question, follow these steps:

1. Bracket the referenced lines.
2. Use the bracketed lines to answer the previous question.
3. Eliminate choices not used to answer the previous question.

Exit

If you've found the answer ...

Make sure that the bracketed lines in your answer choice directly support the answer to the previous question. If so, mark your answer and continue to the next question.

If you're stuck between two choices ...

Mix and match your bracketed lines and the remaining choices to the previous question. Select the choices that best connect an answer to its support.

If you have no idea what the answer is ...

Go with your gut. Select the choice that contains the most synonyms of words found in the previous question's answer.

4

Chapter

Word Interpretation

LEARNING TARGETS

1. Interpret words and phrases using context.

2. Implement the basic approach for word interpretation questions.

3. Apply the *Predict the Future* and *Plug In* strategies to word interpretation questions.

Warm-Up | Complete the warm-up. When you have finished, double-check your work.

Questions 1–3 are based on the following passage.

This passage is adapted from Jonathan Quimby, "Technology-Enhanced Eyewear: The Next Big Thing?" ©2019 by MasteryPrep.

Peer into the future of next-generation eyewear. That's the takeaway from TechCon, a conference for investors and entrepreneurs looking for the most promising
Line innovations in technology.
5   Inside the Mayo Convention Center in Rochester, Minnesota, industry partners—including optometrists, designers, engineers, and medical professionals—came together to explore the future of "smart wearables": devices that bring the touchscreen of a smartphone right
10 up to eye level.
       The conference follows the launch of two major eyewear technology startups. iSight Technologies Inc. will partner with medical device manufacturers to create specialized goggles that allow surgeons to consult vital
15 data in real time. 4Eye, an optical technology company, intends to bring futuristic technology to conventional eyeglasses, embedding the frame with motion-capture sensors and augmented reality.
       Within a few years, these companies may be meeting
20 consumers' calls for advanced capabilities in eyewear, such as camera-enabled lenses that provide location feedback and a visual search. These startups also hope to perfect specialized applications through which professionals can use enhanced lenses to collaborate
25 with colleagues in remote locations where resources are limited. However, significant obstacles remain, including bandwidth issues and the right industry-specific and cultural fit; all of these considerations could delay a strong rollout of the technology by several more years.
30   Additionally, there are marketing and privacy concerns. Companies are hopeful they can remove the stigma surrounding earlier models of "smart" eyewear, which came across to some as spyware. "People said the same thing about having recorders and cameras in our
35 phones," says Chris Staple, COO of iSight. "Getting used to these things takes time. Eventually people will come around." Staple's confidence that consumers' memories will be short is echoed by other industry executives.
       Efforts to minimize the public's misgivings may
40 include installing hardware components such as blinking LEDs or other visible indicators that can make an interaction more transparent to others, therefore implying consent. Similarly, a sleeker design, along with an aggressive marketing campaign, might elevate
45 advanced eyewear to a fashion statement, thus branding it as a must-have item.

Investors were bullish about similar innovations in the past, but the technology didn't pan out. Perhaps the consumer market wasn't ready. However, as more
50 people go wireless with everyday technology such as headphones, it appears we are becoming more comfortable with our inner cyborgs. Technological advancements in eyewear may accelerate this, repurposing the lens as an all-in-one screen that
55 augments our world with the features of a smartphone, fostering collaboration and connecting people with data for a more integrated world.

1

As used in line 11, "launch" most nearly means

A) blastoff.

B) spectacle.

C) explosion.

D) founding.

2

As used in line 26, "limited" most nearly means

A) insufficient.

B) protected.

C) defined.

D) controlled.

3

Quimby characterizes Staple's point of view in lines 33–37 ("People said . . . around") as both

A) dismissive and unenthusiastic.

B) alarmist and judgmental.

C) resolute and optimistic.

D) jovial and compelling.

Foundation

Read sentences 1–3 with your teacher and interpret the meaning of the word "racket."

1.   The girls got together and made a *racket*.

2.   We knew it would be a sleepless night, as the girls were known to make a *racket*.

3.   The girls gathered craft materials and made a *racket* for the badminton tournament.

Foundation

Work with a partner to match the underlined word in the left column with its correct definition in the right column for questions 4–12. Draw a line to connect each pair. Underline the context clues you used to interpret the word's meaning.

4. Mark's mom knew to <u>refrain</u> from asking how his test went when she saw a sorrowful face come through the door.

comment or statement often repeated

5. Many of the Billboard Top 100 songs each year attribute their success to catchy <u>refrains</u> that people can easily remember.

to keep oneself from doing, feeling, or indulging in something

6. The students have made their opinions clear: a common <u>refrain</u> among them is that they prefer recess before lunch.

a regular, recurring phrase or verse, especially at the end of each stanza or division of a poem or song

7. Removing the legs from the chair was the easiest <u>solution</u> I could find when it did not fit through the doorway.

a mixture of substances

8. When Dad makes soup, he uses a <u>solution</u> of cornstarch and water to thicken the broth.

an action or process of solving a problem

9. Vick worked through the equation but got a different <u>solution</u> when he checked his work with a calculator.

an answer to a question

10. As the emcee began to <u>present</u> her to the audience, Abby took a graceful bow.

an item given to someone as a gift

11. He stepped back to admire the thoughtful <u>present</u> he had been given by his neighbor.

to be in a particular place

12. Jenn pushed herself, knowing how important it was for her to be <u>present</u> at the parade.

to show, introduce, or make known

This page intentionally left blank

Practice Set 1

Complete the practice set. When you have finished, double-check your work.

Questions 1–11 are based on the following passage.

This passage is adapted from Emily Collins, "Taking the Temperature on Health: Climate's Impact on Pharmaceuticals." ©2019 by MasteryPrep.

In 2015, a cardiologist at the Calhoun Center for Cardiovascular Research named Dr. Sarah McCormick began to explore the possible impact of climate change
Line on medications and their side effects. As she reviewed
5 the files of twenty of her patients with similar yet varying conditions, she took note of a striking and significant trend. As the temperatures in northern Arizona began to demonstrate drastic fluctuations throughout each season, patients taking medications for heart conditions
10 began to report increased side effects. McCormick suspected that the sudden rise and fall of temperatures had intensified the side effects of some prescribed drugs. Reports of reactions to medication had increased by thirty percent over five years, which seemed to parallel
15 profound changes in the region's climate.

Medication is an ever-changing issue in health care, frequently studied by those who seek current information about the role of pharmaceuticals in human health. The prevailing notion, understood by most in
20 the medical field, is that certain medications can reduce a person's symptoms—while sometimes also resulting in adverse reactions. However, scientists often overlook another factor: how outside influences such as climate and medication storage could impact certain drugs—and
25 in turn, patients.

Following the observation of increased side effects in her own patients, McCormick became determined to learn more. She already knew that medications intended to treat specific ailments could lose potency,
30 and therefore effectiveness, if exposed to certain external elements. However, she wanted to discover if there was a connection between climate, medication storage, and the side effects that her patients were experiencing. McCormick sought the counsel of Dr. Samuel Giddings
35 and Dr. Victoria Mallard, respiratory physicians at Linden University Hospital of Tallahassee. Together, they initiated an investigation of twelve patients taking the same medication for similar health conditions. The goal of the study was to examine the possible impact of
40 medication storage on side effects among the patients— all of whom resided in the same climate.

The doctors administered a questionnaire to all twelve participants, asking them to report how they stored their medications in their homes. McCormick and
45 the other doctors thought it was possible that, because all of the patients lived in the same climate, the way the medication was stored could influence the incidence of side effects. However, when the doctors began to collect the patients' data, they discovered that all of the patients,
50 regardless of who experienced side effects, stored the medication in corresponding ways: in a pillbox inside a kitchen cabinet.

However, there was one notable contrast between patients who had reported medication side effects and
55 those who had not. Markedly, patients who reported no side effects lived in homes equipped with air conditioning. McCormick's team asked these patients what temperature they typically set their air conditioning to during the day. Most of them reported that they set
60 their thermostats to between 68 and 70 degrees, which is consistent with the medication storage guidelines of most pharmaceutical companies.

On the other hand, those patients who did report increased medication side effects did not utilize air
65 conditioning in their homes. At first, a simple conclusion could have been made: without air conditioning, the medication in these homes was stored at varying temperatures, which impacted the drug's formula. However, the same patients went on to clarify that they
70 were unable to regulate their homes' inside temperature against constant spikes and falls in the outside temperature, which had become customary in recent years.

The results of McCormick's study indeed suggest a
75 correlation between climate change and medication side effects. Recently, drastic changes in weather conditions have resulted in wildly fluctuating temperatures across seasons. The study participants who reported an increase in medication-related symptoms appeared to do so
80 because they lacked a way to regulate their homes' internal temperature against such highs and lows. As a result of these conclusions, McCormick and her research team proposed further study of the connection between medication and climate change, as reports of medication side effects rise with each passing year.

Practice Set 1

1

As used in line 5, "varying" most nearly means

A) differing.

B) threatening.

C) changing.

D) altering.

2

As used in line 12, "intensified" most nearly means

A) deepened.

B) heightened.

C) excited.

D) emphasized.

3

As used in line 14, "parallel" most nearly means

A) go in the same direction.

B) occur simultaneously.

C) happen at different times.

D) be seriously affected by.

Approach

Entrance
Word interpretation questions can be identified by these terms:
 • as used in line(s)
 • most nearly means
 • is characterized as

The following questions refer to the passage on page 118. Review question 4 with your teacher. Do not answer the question.

Entrance Evidence and Elimination Exit

4

As used in line 19, "prevailing" most nearly means

A) victorious.

B) widespread.

C) striking.

D) controversial.

Approach

Review questions 5 and 6 on your own. Circle the parts of the questions that identify them as word interpretation questions. Do not answer the questions.

5

As used in line 39, "examine" most nearly means

A) question.

B) check.

C) quiz.

D) explore.

6

As used in line 34, "sought the counsel of" most nearly means

A) gave research to.

B) deliberated findings with.

C) looked for comfort from.

D) solicited assistance from.

Questions 1–11 are based on the following passage.

This passage is adapted from Emily Collins, "Taking the Temperature on Health: Climate's Impact on Pharmaceuticals." ©2019 by MasteryPrep.

In 2015, a cardiologist at the Calhoun Center for Cardiovascular Research named Dr. Sarah McCormick
Line began to explore the possible impact of climate change
on medications and their side effects. As she reviewed
5 the files of twenty of her patients with similar yet varying
conditions, she took note of a striking and significant
trend. As the temperatures in northern Arizona began
to demonstrate drastic fluctuations throughout each
season, patients taking medications for heart conditions
10 began to report increased side effects. McCormick
suspected that the sudden rise and fall of temperatures
had intensified the side effects of some prescribed drugs.
Reports of reactions to medication had increased by
thirty percent over five years, which seemed to parallel
15 profound changes in the region's climate.

Medication is an ever-changing issue in health
care, frequently studied by those who seek current
information about the role of pharmaceuticals in human
health. The prevailing notion, understood by most in
20 the medical field, is that certain medications can reduce
a person's symptoms—while sometimes also resulting
in adverse reactions. However, scientists often overlook
another factor: how outside influences such as climate
and medication storage could impact certain drugs—and
25 in turn, patients.

Following the observation of increased side effects
in her own patients, McCormick became determined
to learn more. She already knew that medications
intended to treat specific ailments could lose potency,
30 and therefore effectiveness, if exposed to certain external
elements. However, she wanted to discover if there was
a connection between climate, medication storage, and
the side effects that her patients were experiencing.
McCormick sought the counsel of Dr. Samuel Giddings
35 and Dr. Victoria Mallard, respiratory physicians at
Linden University Hospital of Tallahassee. Together,
they initiated an investigation of twelve patients taking
the same medication for similar health conditions. The
goal of the study was to examine the possible impact of
40 medication storage on side effects among the patients—
all of whom resided in the same climate.

The doctors administered a questionnaire to all
twelve participants, asking them to report how they
stored their medications in their homes. McCormick and
45 the other doctors thought it was possible that, because

all of the patients lived in the same climate, the way the
medication was stored could influence the incidence of
side effects. However, when the doctors began to collect
the patients' data, they discovered that all of the patients,
50 regardless of who experienced side effects, stored the
medication in corresponding ways: in a pillbox inside a
kitchen cabinet.

However, there was one notable contrast between
patients who had reported medication side effects and
55 those who had not. Markedly, patients who reported
no side effects lived in homes equipped with air
conditioning. McCormick's team asked these patients
what temperature they typically set their air conditioning
to during the day. Most of them reported that they set
60 their thermostats to between 68 and 70 degrees, which
is consistent with the medication storage guidelines of
most pharmaceutical companies.

On the other hand, those patients who did report
increased medication side effects did not utilize air
65 conditioning in their homes. At first, a simple conclusion
could have been made: without air conditioning,
the medication in these homes was stored at varying
temperatures, which impacted the drug's formula.
However, the same patients went on to clarify that they
70 were unable to regulate their homes' inside temperature
against constant spikes and falls in the outside
temperature, which had become customary in recent
years.

The results of McCormick's study indeed suggest a
75 correlation between climate change and medication side
effects. Recently, drastic changes in weather conditions
have resulted in wildly fluctuating temperatures across
seasons. The study participants who reported an increase
in medication-related symptoms appeared to do so
80 because they lacked a way to regulate their homes'
internal temperature against such highs and lows. As a
result of these conclusions, McCormick and her research
team proposed further study of the connection between
medication and climate change, as reports of medication
side effects rise with each passing year.

Approach

Evidence and Elimination

To answer a word interpretation question, follow these steps:

1 Reread the sentence that contains the identified word or phrase.

2 Underline any context clues you see within or surrounding the sentence and begin forming your understanding of the word's definition.

3 Eliminate any answers that go against your general understanding of the word or context.

Answer question 4 with your teacher.

Entrance   **Evidence and Elimination**   Exit

4

As used in line 19, "prevailing" most nearly means

A) victorious.

B) widespread.

C) striking.

D) controversial.

The following questions refer to the passage on page 122. Answer questions 5 and 6 on your own. Focus on eliminating incorrect answers.

5

As used in line 39, "examine" most nearly means

A) question.

B) check.

C) quiz.

D) explore.

6

As used in line 34, "sought the counsel of" most nearly means

A) gave research to.

B) deliberated findings with.

C) looked for comfort from.

D) solicited assistance from.

Word Interpretation

Approach

Exit

If you've found the answer ...
Plug it into the sentence and confirm that it sounds fine. Mark your answer and continue on to the next question.

If you're stuck between two choices ...
Choose the answer that has the same connotation, or feeling, as the passage.

If you have no idea what the answer is ...
Go with your gut. Select the choice that you think flows the most naturally when you substitute it into the sentence.

Review questions 7 and 8. Work with your teacher to choose the correct answer from the remaining choices.

Entrance 〉 Evidence and Elimination 〉 **Exit**

7

As used in line 47, "influence" most nearly means

A) develop.

B) corrupt.

C) interrupt.

D) impact.

8

In line 51, "corresponding" most nearly means

A) emerging.

B) matching.

C) communicating.

D) competing.

Key Terms

Connotation: the emotion or feeling that a word evokes in addition to its general definition.

Practice Set 2 | Complete the practice set. When you have finished, double-check your work.

Questions 1–11 are based on the following passage.

This passage is adapted from Emily Collins, "Taking the Temperature on Health: Climate's Impact on Pharmaceuticals." ©2019 by MasteryPrep.

In 2015, a cardiologist at the Calhoun Center for Cardiovascular Research named Dr. Sarah McCormick began to explore the possible impact of climate change
Line on medications and their side effects. As she reviewed
5 the files of twenty of her patients with similar yet varying conditions, she took note of a striking and significant trend. As the temperatures in northern Arizona began to demonstrate drastic fluctuations throughout each season, patients taking medications for heart conditions
10 began to report increased side effects. McCormick suspected that the sudden rise and fall of temperatures had intensified the side effects of some prescribed drugs. Reports of reactions to medication had increased by thirty percent over five years, which seemed to parallel
15 profound changes in the region's climate.

Medication is an ever-changing issue in health care, frequently studied by those who seek current information about the role of pharmaceuticals in human health. The prevailing notion, understood by most in
20 the medical field, is that certain medications can reduce a person's symptoms—while sometimes also resulting in adverse reactions. However, scientists often overlook another factor: how outside influences such as climate and medication storage could impact certain drugs—and
25 in turn, patients.

Following the observation of increased side effects in her own patients, McCormick became determined to learn more. She already knew that medications intended to treat specific ailments could lose potency,
30 and therefore effectiveness, if exposed to certain external elements. However, she wanted to discover if there was a connection between climate, medication storage, and the side effects that her patients were experiencing. McCormick sought the counsel of Dr. Samuel Giddings
35 and Dr. Victoria Mallard, respiratory physicians at Linden University Hospital of Tallahassee. Together, they initiated an investigation of twelve patients taking the same medication for similar health conditions. The goal of the study was to examine the possible impact of
40 medication storage on side effects among the patients— all of whom resided in the same climate.

The doctors administered a questionnaire to all twelve participants, asking them to report how they stored their medications in their homes. McCormick and
45 the other doctors thought it was possible that, because all of the patients lived in the same climate, the way the medication was stored could influence the incidence of side effects. However, when the doctors began to collect the patients' data, they discovered that all of the patients,
50 regardless of who experienced side effects, stored the medication in corresponding ways: in a pillbox inside a kitchen cabinet.

However, there was one notable contrast between patients who had reported medication side effects and
55 those who had not. Markedly, patients who reported no side effects lived in homes equipped with air conditioning. McCormick's team asked these patients what temperature they typically set their air conditioning to during the day. Most of them reported that they set
60 their thermostats to between 68 and 70 degrees, which is consistent with the medication storage guidelines of most pharmaceutical companies.

On the other hand, those patients who did report increased medication side effects did not utilize air
65 conditioning in their homes. At first, a simple conclusion could have been made: without air conditioning, the medication in these homes was stored at varying temperatures, which impacted the drug's formula. However, the same patients went on to clarify that they
70 were unable to regulate their homes' inside temperature against constant spikes and falls in the outside temperature, which had become customary in recent years.

The results of McCormick's study indeed suggest a
75 correlation between climate change and medication side effects. Recently, drastic changes in weather conditions have resulted in wildly fluctuating temperatures across seasons. The study participants who reported an increase in medication-related symptoms appeared to do so
80 because they lacked a way to regulate their homes' internal temperature against such highs and lows. As a result of these conclusions, McCormick and her research team proposed further study of the connection between medication and climate change, as reports of medication side effects rise with each passing year.

9

As used in line 53, "notable" is closest in meaning to

A) striking.

B) accomplished.

C) renowned.

D) celebrated.

10

As used in line 72, "had become customary" most nearly means

A) had become a riveting topic of conversation.

B) had resulted in disastrous consequences.

C) had caused widespread illness.

D) had been accepted as a widespread occurrence.

11

As used in line 8 and line 76, "drastic" most nearly means

A) tragic.

B) compelling.

C) radical.

D) foolish.

Strategy

Questions 12–20 are based on the following passage.

This passage is adapted from Amelia Sikes, *Camping in Wonderland*. ©2019 by MasteryPrep.

Jordalee emerged from the tent under a canopy of white pine in the Georgia woods and took a long look at the scenery around her, soaking up the solitude before
Line her uncles woke up. Then, near her feet, she spied a
5 chipmunk gripping an acorn. For Jordalee, the image first appeared to her as a fine example of the whimsical illustrations in children books. The charm she found in the scene diminished, however, when she registered the larger scene around her. The chipmunk existed
10 peacefully, as it were, in miniature. But only as the composition grew to include Jordalee herself standing over the tiny creature, and the hawks watching from the trees, as well as timber rattlers curled up and disguised in the green understory, did it occur to her the true reality
15 of life in the wild. She realized her precariousness to the whims of weather and woodland predators without any natural defenses of her own. Jordalee hadn't been in the woods very much since she was a child and her mother had left. For weeks, she had dreaded this camping trip,
20 which was supposed to be her opportunity to "rough it" alongside the Halls—her relatives on her father's side. For them, it was an exalted outing, a near-religious holiday to connect with nature and each other. But for Jordalee, it was culture shock. While her friends were
25 enjoying the comfortable leisure of spring break, possibly poolside, Jordalee hadn't taken a shower in two days. Instead, she was holed up in the pine woods of Georgia.

She heard the zipper of a tent. Jordalee blinked her way back to reality just as her uncle crawled out, groggy
30 and damp.

"Where were you *this time*, city slicker?" he asked wryly. "Already lost in Wonderland?"

A smirk danced across his face. It's confirmed, Jordalee thought. The Halls are definitely related because
35 her dad says the same thing.

"Just somewhere different," said Jordalee.

"Well, go get changed. We're leaving soon to hike up the mountain," he said. "And leave your phone behind."

Jordalee pictured herself waist-high in brush. The
40 specter of unseen insects moving about underneath made her audibly gasp and grow lightheaded. She could feel them and hear them now, all around. It was deafening.

She shut her eyes and pretended she was on a
45 photography shoot with lights and cameras. At the very least, a real selfie in the rural landscape would be

worthy of social media praise. She imagined her profile picture as she posed, poised to take flight over a rocky outcropping.
50 "Hear what I told you?" her uncle asked.

"Consider it left," she begrudgingly replied.

"And don't act like it's such a chore in front of your father, OK? Every year he counts the days to get out here. So don't ruin it."
55 Her uncle unlocked the food trunk. Soon the rest of the party awoke. After a measly breakfast, the campers began to pack up their temporary abode. Jordalee meticulously folded the tent and put away her things to avoid chatter. She passed her phone between her hands.
60 It wasn't the idea of camping that disgusted her, she noted. It was that this was too ordinary. She had seen TV shows featuring celebrities' glamorous camping, or "glamping": lantern-shaped treehouses, cocoon-like hammocks between banana trees. But this was just
65 camping, with soiled mess kits and canvas tents that smelled of mildew. Her mind wandered and began scrolling through celebrities' social media posts about their sophisticated "camping" trips.

"Morning, Lee."
70 It was her father. His voice jolted her out of her reverie.

"Trust me, honey, there's nothing like being out here in nature. Am I right?"

She knew he was trying to connect.
75 "Sure, you're probably right," Jordalee responded, scolding herself for once again failing to say what she really thought.

Her father looked at Jordalee with solemn eyes. He knew that when her mother left, Jordalee would soon
80 take after her; this part of her childhood—the tomboy, rough-and-tumble "daddy's girl" part—would be lost. But he couldn't have fathomed the struggle to bond with his daughter as she got older. It was harder than he expected. When his child gazed elsewhere, he was keen
85 enough to realize her mind was somewhere far away, in Wonderland. And still, as distant as she was, his efforts to connect with her drove him forward, and he tried again.

"Bring your phone, Lee," he said. "You won't be able
90 to get service, but you can still take some pictures."

Strategy

Predict the Future

When all of the answer choices sound convincing, it can be difficult to know which ones should be eliminated. Use this strategy on word interpretation questions when you feel stuck.

Here's how ...

1 Cover the answers.

2 Read the previous sentence, the sentence that contains the word, and the next sentence. Come up with your own replacement word.

3 Select the choice that best matches your prediction.

Review question 12 with your teacher. Use the Predict the Future strategy to answer the question as a class.

12 As used in line 8, "diminished" most nearly means

A) overlooked.

B) insulted.

C) rejected.

D) lessened.

Strategy

The following questions refer to the passage on page 128. Work on your own using the **Predict the Future strategy** to answer questions 13 and 14.

13

As used in line 17, "defenses" most nearly means

A) protection.

B) excuses.

C) rebuttal.

D) attacks.

14

In line 22, the word "exalted" most nearly means

A) preferred.

B) sacred.

C) raised.

D) perfect.

Strategy

Plug In

Finding the right answer to a word interpretation question becomes even more challenging when you don't know what a word means. By plugging the answer choices into the sentence in place of this unfamiliar word, you can better eliminate incorrect options and select the best definition using the context.

1. Replace the identified word or phrase in the sentence with each answer choice.

2. Eliminate illogical answer choices.

Review question 15 with your teacher. Use the Plug In strategy to answer the question as a class.

15

As used in line 23 and line 74, "connect" most nearly means

A) open.

B) associate.

C) relate.

D) submit.

The following questions refer to the passage on page 128. Work on your own using the Plug In strategy to answer questions 16 and 17.

16

In line 57, "abode" most nearly means

A) habitat.

B) lodging.

C) structure.

D) address.

17

As used in line 82, "fathomed" is closest in meaning to

A) imagined.

B) forgotten.

C) resented.

D) summoned.

This page intentionally left blank

Practice Set 3 | Complete the practice set. When you have finished, double-check your work.

Questions 12–20 are based on the following passage.

This passage is adapted from Amelia Sikes, *Camping in Wonderland*. ©2019 by MasteryPrep.

Jordalee emerged from the tent under a canopy of white pine in the Georgia woods and took a long look at the scenery around her, soaking up the solitude before
Line her uncles woke up. Then, near her feet, she spied a
5 chipmunk gripping an acorn. For Jordalee, the image first appeared to her as a fine example of the whimsical illustrations in children books. The charm she found in the scene diminished, however, when she registered the larger scene around her. The chipmunk existed
10 peacefully, as it were, in miniature. But only as the composition grew to include Jordalee herself standing over the tiny creature, and the hawks watching from the trees, as well as timber rattlers curled up and disguised in the green understory, did it occur to her the true reality
15 of life in the wild. She realized her precariousness to the whims of weather and woodland predators without any natural defenses of her own. Jordalee hadn't been in the woods very much since she was a child and her mother had left. For weeks, she had dreaded this camping trip,
20 which was supposed to be her opportunity to "rough it" alongside the Halls—her relatives on her father's side. For them, it was an exalted outing, a near-religious holiday to connect with nature and each other. But for Jordalee, it was culture shock. While her friends were
25 enjoying the comfortable leisure of spring break, possibly poolside, Jordalee hadn't taken a shower in two days. Instead, she was holed up in the pine woods of Georgia.

She heard the zipper of a tent. Jordalee blinked her way back to reality just as her uncle crawled out, groggy
30 and damp.

"Where were you *this time*, city slicker?" he asked wryly. "Already lost in Wonderland?"

A smirk danced across his face. It's confirmed, Jordalee thought. The Halls are definitely related because
35 her dad says the same thing.

"Just somewhere different," said Jordalee.

"Well, go get changed. We're leaving soon to hike up the mountain," he said. "And leave your phone behind."

Jordalee pictured herself waist-high in brush. The
40 specter of unseen insects moving about underneath made her audibly gasp and grow lightheaded. She could feel them and hear them now, all around. It was deafening.

She shut her eyes and pretended she was on a
45 photography shoot with lights and cameras. At the very least, a real selfie in the rural landscape would be

worthy of social media praise. She imagined her profile picture as she posed, poised to take flight over a rocky outcropping.
50 "Hear what I told you?" her uncle asked.

"Consider it left," she begrudgingly replied.

"And don't act like it's such a chore in front of your father, OK? Every year he counts the days to get out here. So don't ruin it."
55 Her uncle unlocked the food trunk. Soon the rest of the party awoke. After a measly breakfast, the campers began to pack up their temporary abode. Jordalee meticulously folded the tent and put away her things to avoid chatter. She passed her phone between her hands.
60 It wasn't the idea of camping that disgusted her, she noted. It was that this was too ordinary. She had seen TV shows featuring celebrities' glamorous camping, or "glamping": lantern-shaped treehouses, cocoon-like hammocks between banana trees. But this was just
65 camping, with soiled mess kits and canvas tents that smelled of mildew. Her mind wandered and began scrolling through celebrities' social media posts about their sophisticated "camping" trips.

"Morning, Lee."
70 It was her father. His voice jolted her out of her reverie.

"Trust me, honey, there's nothing like being out here in nature. Am I right?"

She knew he was trying to connect.
75 "Sure, you're probably right," Jordalee responded, scolding herself for once again failing to say what she really thought.

Her father looked at Jordalee with solemn eyes. He knew that when her mother left, Jordalee would soon
80 take after her; this part of her childhood—the tomboy, rough-and-tumble "daddy's girl" part—would be lost. But he couldn't have fathomed the struggle to bond with his daughter as she got older. It was harder than he expected. When his child gazed elsewhere, he was keen
85 enough to realize her mind was somewhere far away, in Wonderland. And still, as distant as she was, his efforts to connect with her drove him forward, and he tried again.

"Bring your phone, Lee," he said. "You won't be able
90 to get service, but you can still take some pictures."

18

As used in line 71, "reverie" most nearly means

A) loneliness.

B) despair.

C) obstacle.

D) daydream.

19

The author characterizes Jordalee's feelings in lines 60–66 ("It wasn't ... mildew") as both

A) humorous and lighthearted.

B) sentimental and lonely.

C) irritable and disappointed.

D) idealistic and hopeful.

20

Which choice most closely captures the meaning of the figurative "Wonderland" referred to in line 32 and line 86?

A) Heaven

B) Relaxation

C) Escape

D) Ignorance

Mini-Test

Complete the mini-test. When you have finished, double-check your work.

Questions 22–32 are based on the following passage.

This passage is adapted from Lydia Busenbarrick, "Canines on Patrol: Geese Police." ©2019 by MasteryPrep.

The honking squawks of Canadian geese fill the early morning air, where all else is relatively quiet in the heart of Central Park in New York City. As the summer air
Line thickens, a loud, disturbing flock of geese waddles from
5 path to pond and everywhere in between. "The geese wreak havoc on people enjoying the treasured, green oasis in the middle of an otherwise concrete jungle," says Judy Borger, a park attendant. "Meet the resident geese of New York City." Unlike migratory geese, resident birds
10 settle in residential and urban areas rather than cycle north and south throughout the year. As a result, they can become a nuisance if not kept in check.

In recent years, the goose population in Central Park has grown as some migratory geese have decided to take
15 up residence there year-round. Conservationist Nancy Theld expressed concern not only for the Central Park landscape, but also for the geese, their habitat, and their young. Reports of geese attacks on humans have rapidly increased over the past year. Additionally, nutrients pass
20 through the birds' digestive systems quickly, producing waste at an alarming rate—marring the lush park.

Experts speculate that the sheer number of these birds, their territorial behavior, and a 30-year lifespan all mean that the problem will only get worse, but
25 addressing the issue is tricky. "Dealing with these birds is precarious because all removal practices must be humane, and all species of these birds are protected under the Migratory Bird Treaty Act—regardless of whether or not they have become resident aliens in
30 practice," says Theld. But some municipal leaders, she adds, have suggested the destruction of nests—and consequently, eggs.

To research the matter, Theld contacted Holly Magwan, a dairy farmer in Wisconsin. Magwan's fields
35 had been terrorized by geese for some time, but after some experimentation, she had arrived at a solution that humanely halted the invasion. The secret? Border collies. Magwan had discovered that the dogs' instinctual abilities to herd kept the geese in check. The addition of
40 the dogs had proven extremely effective for Magwan, as the dogs corralled the birds with minimal harm.

Theld suspected that a similar initiative would be effective in Central Park, but she knew that there would need to be solid data to justify the funding for the
45 project. So she initiated a study that observed the impact of border collies in Central Park over the course of six

months. The study began with the addition of one dog to the park, and more collies were added as time went on. After two months, the dogs were removed to see if their
50 herding had lasting effects. Changes in the levels of geese excrement left in the park, in addition to the numbers of attack reports, would provide key data to support the study.

Immediately, the border collies began to herd the
55 geese, which were shrewd enough to gauge the border collies' body language. Hunched down with their shoulders back, the collies stared at the geese until they moved. To geese, this behavior mimicked that of a threatening predator.

60 "I had never seen anything like it," reported Theld. "The dogs would hunch and stare, and the geese immediately moved away from undesirable areas, finding refuge by the ponds and puddles." Theld and her team established new patterns for the collies as they
65 tracked where the geese retreated.

The experiment revealed promising findings. Once the dogs were added to Central Park, reports of geese hostility decreased. Additionally, maintenance crews reported a 20% reduction in waste. After the dogs were
70 removed, reports of geese hostility increased again, and workers reported a mere 5% overall decrease in waste compared to the previous 20%.

As expected, when the collies returned, reports of geese attacks decreased again, and maintenance crews
75 reported that waste plummeted by a whopping 55%.

Results of Theld's study opened the door for funding and gave canine companions to the resident geese in Central Park. Experts hope that through the dogs' safe herding, within several years, these geese may decide to
80 divide more of their time between the north and south as they used to do. "This is the safest solution," Theld explained. "We have successfully alleviated a lot of the problems these rather impressive creatures can cause."

22

The primary purpose of the passage is to

A) present opposing ideas using data.

B) convey a problem and potential solution.

C) provide a counterclaim to an argument.

D) illustrate a ground-breaking discovery.

23

As used in line 6, "treasured" is closest in meaning to

A) cherished.

B) conserved.

C) collected.

D) desired.

24

Which statement about Canadian geese can be most reasonably inferred from the passage?

A) Canadian geese may carry diseases that are easily spread.

B) Migratory Canadian geese are not threatening to humans.

C) Geese's invasion of urban parks nationwide is a serious issue.

D) Resident geese could cause problems in other areas.

25

As used in line 36, "arrived at" most nearly means

A) greeted by.

B) figured out.

C) stumbled onto.

D) entered into.

26

As used in line 44, "solid" most nearly means

A) sound.

B) dense.

C) thick.

D) complete.

27

What did Theld do as part of her study that most directly allowed her to conclude that the dog herding was responsible for the decrease in geese attacks?

A) She relied on maintenance crews and rangers to report the results.

B) She canvassed the area and asked park-goers for their opinions.

C) She documented the use of border collies in the park for one year.

D) She introduced border collies to the park and later withdrew them to track data.

28

As used in line 58, "mimicked" most nearly means

A) disguised.

B) confused.

C) dramatized.

D) resembled.

29

As it is used in line 63, "finding refuge" most nearly means

A) looking for home.

B) encountering danger.

C) seeking food.

D) reaching safety.

30

In describing the report by maintenance crews that the decrease in waste was "mere" (line 71), the author most likely means that

A) the previous levels of waste returned.

B) the decrease in waste was not significant.

C) the maintenance crews disapproved of the border collie experiment.

D) Theld was unable to measure the effects of the experiment.

31

According to the passage, Theld's study offers an answer to which of the following questions?

A) How can residents dispose of the waste left by Canadian geese in their yards?

B) Is herding an effective and humane way to control Canadian geese in Central Park?

C) Could extreme temperatures be to blame for the settlement of Canadian geese?

D) Are border collies a potential solution to eliminating unwanted pests?

32

Which choice provides the best evidence for the answer to the previous question?

A) Lines 25–30 ("Dealing . . . Theld")

B) Lines 61–63 ("The dogs . . . puddles")

C) Lines 73–75 ("As expected . . . 55%")

D) Lines 78–81 ("Experts . . . do")

STOP

**If you finish before time is called, you may check your work on this section only.
Do not turn to any other section.**

This page intentionally left blank

Wrap-Up | Complete the wrap-up. When you have finished, double-check your work.

Questions 4–6 are based on the following passage.

This passage is adapted from Jonathan Quimby, "Technology-Enhanced Eyewear: The Next Big Thing?" ©2019 by MasteryPrep.

Peer into the future of next-generation eyewear. That's the takeaway from TechCon, a conference for investors and entrepreneurs looking for the most promising
Line innovations in technology.
5   Inside the Mayo Convention Center in Rochester, Minnesota, industry partners—including optometrists, designers, engineers, and medical professionals—came together to explore the future of "smart wearables": devices that bring the touchscreen of a smartphone right
10 up to eye level.
The conference follows the launch of two major eyewear technology startups. iSight Technologies Inc. will partner with medical device manufacturers to create specialized goggles that allow surgeons to consult vital
15 data in real time. 4Eye, an optical technology company, intends to bring futuristic technology to conventional eyeglasses, embedding the frame with motion-capture sensors and augmented reality.
Within a few years, these companies may be meeting
20 consumers' calls for advanced capabilities in eyewear, such as camera-enabled lenses that provide location feedback and a visual search. These startups also hope to perfect specialized applications through which professionals can use enhanced lenses to collaborate
25 with colleagues in remote locations where resources are limited. However, significant obstacles remain, including bandwidth issues and the right industry-specific and cultural fit; all of these considerations could delay a strong rollout of the technology by several more years.
30   Additionally, there are marketing and privacy concerns. Companies are hopeful they can remove the stigma associated with earlier models of "smart" eyewear, which came across to some as spyware. "People said the same thing about having recorders and cameras in our
35 phones," says Chris Staple, COO of iSight. "Getting used to these things takes time. Eventually people will come around." Staple's confidence that consumers' memories will be short is echoed by other industry executives.
Efforts to minimize the public's misgivings may
40 include installing hardware components such as blinking LEDs or other visible indicators that can make an interaction more transparent to others, therefore implying consent. Similarly, a sleeker design, along with an aggressive marketing campaign, might elevate the
45 advanced eyewear to a fashion statement, thus branding it as a must-have item.

Investors were bullish about similar innovations in the past, but the technology didn't pan out. Perhaps the consumer market wasn't ready. However, as more
50 people go wireless with everyday technology such as headphones, it appears we are becoming more comfortable with our inner cyborgs. Technological advancements in eyewear may accelerate this, repurposing the lens as an all-in-one screen that
55 augments our world with the features of a smartphone, fostering collaboration and connecting people with data for a more integrated world.

4

As used in line 42, "transparent" most nearly means

A) obvious.

B) uncolored.

C) fair.

D) see-through.

5

As used in line 44, "aggressive" most nearly means

A) hostile.

B) competitive.

C) vigorous.

D) offensive.

6

As used in line 48, "pan out" most nearly means

A) revolutionize the industry.

B) grow in popularity.

C) remain available.

D) become a reality.

This page intentionally left blank

Review

Entrance

Word interpretation questions can be identified by these terms:

- as used in line(s)
- most nearly means
- is characterized as

Evidence and Elimination

To answer a word interpretation question, follow these steps:

1. Reread the sentence that contains the identified word or phrase.
2. Underline any context clues you see within or surrounding the sentence and begin forming your understanding of the word's definition.
3. Eliminate any answers that go against your general understanding of the word or context.

Exit

If you've found the answer ...

Plug it into the sentence and confirm that it sounds fine. Mark your answer and continue on to the next question.

If you're stuck between two choices ...

Choose the answer that has the same connotation or feeling as the passage.

If you have no idea what the answer is ...

Go with your gut. Select the choice that you think flows the most naturally when you substitute it into the sentence.

Chapter

5

Central Ideas and Themes

LEARNING TARGETS

1. Identify central ideas in paragraphs and passages.

2. Implement the basic approach for central ideas and themes questions.

3. Apply the *Answers to Answers* and *Back to the Front* strategies to central ideas and themes questions.

Warm-Up

Complete the warm-up. When you have finished, double-check your work.

Questions 1–3 are based on the following passage.

This passage is adapted from Margaret McCarthy, "How Many People Will There Be in the Future?" ©2020 by MasteryPrep.

The growth of the world's population is a recurrent newspaper headline, but experts debate whether this trend will continue. New data on global population
Line growth rates suggest that the planet will need to support
5 nearly 10 billion people by 2050, yet not all experts agree with this conclusion—and they have their own evidence.

There are two popular arguments regarding human population growth: it will continue apace, or it will plateau. Over the past century, the global population has
10 rapidly increased, and a recent demographics study and analysis completed by the United Nations supports the claim that this trend will continue. Previous models of population growth assumed that birth rates would fall around the world, but researchers are now reconsidering
15 this assumption. "It's likely that there will be between 9.6 and 12.3 billion people on Earth by 2100," summarized Aoife Boyle, a researcher from the UN study.

The study, published in *Science*, uses a probabilistic analysis to project future population growth.
20 Demographers study population trends through the three dimensions of fertility, mortality, and immigration. The study reports that rapid declines in fertility rates need to occur in sub-Saharan Africa if population growth is to slow. Experts hope to reduce population
25 growth, as it may threaten Earth's resources.

Brazil's rapid population growth rate decline is an interesting example of what is possible; its fertility rate dropped dramatically and rapidly over two generations, from 6.3 children to 1.73 children per woman. By
30 improving educational opportunities and increasing access to contraception, the Brazilian government helped lower the fertility rate to below the global average. "Something *happened*," Brazilian demographer José Alberto Carvalho says, emphasizing the nation's
35 accomplishment in slowing population growth. "What took 120 years in England took 40 years here."

"The UN research evokes the global overconsumption of natural resources," argues population biologist Paul Ehrlich. The past half-century has been labeled the
40 "Great Acceleration" due to an increase in human activity. Since World War II, the world's population has tripled and drastically ramped up resource utilization, from water used in irrigation and croplands to oil for gas and industrial production. Ehrlich's research predicted
45 mass famine in the 1970s and 1980s due to this rapid

population growth and its related resource drain.

"Our collective burden on the planet is not determined by statistics only," Ehrlich stated. He developed a formula showing that impact equals
50 population multiplied by affluence multiplied by technology (IPAT for short) in order to model increased natural resource consumption.

Studies of global consumption patterns reveal that humans are utilizing natural resources beyond their
55 predicted capacity as both the world population and global demand for goods grow at an unprecedented rate. However, one-fifth of Earth's population still has no access to reliable electricity. Lack of such access impacts educational opportunities, a key factor in fertility
60 rate decline. The connection between these concepts illuminates the complexity of the population debate and resource consumption trends, as well as the resulting question of whether natural resources can support such growth.
65 "Population growth is not straightforward," says Raunaq Paul, an ecologist at the University of North Dakota, warning us to always consider all of the dimensions of our collective and individual impact. Choices that societies make regarding educational
70 opportunities, public health, and material consumption all have real consequences for the environment. Whether population growth continues or slows, "the human population has a dynamic and complex role to play when it comes to the quality of our environment."

1

What is a main idea of the second paragraph (lines 7-17)?

A) Debate about population growth trends has been contentious and ardent.

B) Consistent population growth has been seen in the last dozen years.

C) Evidence supports the theory that population growth will continue.

D) Early models of population growth predicted a decrease in global birth rates.

2

The central idea of the fourth paragraph
(lines 26–36) is that

A) governments should work to improve
educational opportunities.

B) dramatic fertility decline is possible through
focused effort.

C) Brazil's decrease in fertility should be attempted
elsewhere.

D) England's decrease in fertility occurred within
one century.

3

One central claim of the passage is that

A) population growth affects resource availability
and consumption.

B) collective environmental impacts are more
significant than individual impacts.

C) demographers will soon shift their focus to
immigration and mortality.

D) fertility is the most consequential dimension of
population study.

Foundation

Work on your own to read the paragraph below and complete the following activity.

(1) Located in southeast Colorado, the town of Picket Wire Canyon is home to one of the largest sets of dinosaur tracks in North America. (2) The 150-million-year-old tracks date back to the Jurassic period, when the canyonlands of the area had a tropical climate enjoyed by herbivorous Apatosaurs and carnivorous Allosaurs. (3) The tracks not only show that the dinosaurs once roamed the area but also imply the social behaviors of these two types of dinosaurs. (4) Now, tourists can hike, bike, or ride horseback to visit the 1,900 individual footprints on 130 trackways or see rock art that could be 4,500 years old.

In each bubble, write a 3–5 word summary of each sentence in the paragraph.

(1)

(2)

(3)

(4)

What is the subject of the paragraph in 1–2 words?

Key Terms

Central idea: the most important or central thought of a paragraph or larger section of text.

Foundation

Read the passage below with a partner. As you read, work together to write a one-sentence summary of each paragraph on the lines provided.

(1) While the Mojave Desert of Arizona may seem like an odd choice of location for duplicating the North Pole, it's the home of a little town named Santa Claus. (2) Over 80 years ago, an entrepreneur named Nina Talbot and her husband moved from their home in California and founded Santa Claus, Arizona. (3) They created a town and erected Christmas-themed buildings and a "Santa's Land" sign, intending to draw residents into their workshop-modeled town. (4) For years, Santa Claus, AZ, was a highlight of the Arizona desert.

_____

_____

_____

(5) Talbot was never successful in attracting buyers and sold the town in the 1940s, but the Christmas motif lived on for some time. (6) The town continued to draw tourists for decades, ironically bringing Christmas's winter wonderland to the desert outside of Kingman, Arizona, all year round. (7) Restaurants and businesses were themed, as well as shops that sold related souvenirs and paraphernalia in every season. (8) A post office was erected, and ads were later placed in magazines so that children

could receive letters postmarked "Santa Claus, AZ." (9) The Santa Claus Inn—which was not an inn at all, but a restaurant—gained acclaim, even after the name was changed to Christmas Tree Inn. (10) Christmas Tree Inn was visited by cake-mix king Duncan Hines, who declared it the best in the region, and 1950s actress Jane Russell hosted a small dinner party there.

_____

_____

(11) However, the town did not outlast the desert sun, and it became a tourist desert itself. (12) Today, Santa Claus is a shell of its former self, having lost its postal service remailing rights and ending with a population of 10. (13) To the dismay of children everywhere, Santa Claus, Arizona, is no longer a real town but instead has become a legend, much like its namesake.

_____

_____

In the vertical space between the columns, write the main idea of the passage using a single sentence. Consider the one-sentence summary and main idea of each paragraph.

Practice Set 1 | Complete the practice set. When you have finished, double-check your work.

Questions 1–8 are based on the following passages.

Passage 1 is adapted from Adam Nowicki, "Farm to Table: Fad or the Future?" ©2019 by MasteryPrep. Passage 2 is from the editors of MasteryPrep, "Does Local Eating Matter?" ©2019 by MasteryPrep.

Passage 1

Dishes made with ingredients that are sourced nearby are healthier for you. That is the idea behind the farm-to-table movement. Although it may seem like a fad, this local-eating initiative has roots in the "hippie era"
5 of the 1960s and 1970s, when young people rejected the status quo, including the consumption of processed and canned foods.

In the 21st century, the idea of "eating local" is spreading through communities and making its way
10 into restaurants and cafeterias. In over 1,000 school districts around the country, administrations work with local farms to provide fresh fruits and vegetables to students. Restaurants—from boutique, luxury dining establishments to fast-casual chains—are adjusting their
15 menus to offer seasonal ingredients and locally sourced fare.

According to the movement's proponents, eating locally is not only healthier, since fresher foods retain more nutrients, but also more sustainable, since a focus
20 on purchasing local products supports smaller farms. As a result, farm-fresh goods are now making their way to nearby cities, where locally sourced foods are not readily available. Moreover, in recent years, community gardens and farmers markets have sprung up in communities
25 that have historically been underserved, providing a source of recently harvested produce where previously only processed and preserved food was readily available.

Through such efforts, the ideals of eating local and building communities intersect. "We have to look at
30 community gardening as more than food production," says Bob Wilson, community garden and urban farm expert. "We have to look at it as building stronger, healthier communities by bringing people together."

Implementing farm-to-table efforts is beneficial
35 for people throughout the community. Restaurants that commit to supporting local purveyors often boost their own sales, while community gardens and farmers markets help build a sense of unity.

Many are meeting demands for locally grown,
40 seasonal food, both in institutional settings, such as schools, and in the marketplace. Others hope to capitalize on the increased interest in creating farmers markets and community gardens. The variety of

approaches to improving food supply and consumption
45 demonstrates the adaptability and creativity of local food movement advocates (such as urban farmers and chefs) in promoting their mission.

Passage 2

The local food movement is gaining traction as a nutritious, sustainable approach to food. In recent years
50 the "locavore" trend has popped up in restaurants and grocery stores around the country. It's possible that the farm-to-table movement could help both small farms and our communities: the nourishing food and related benefits hold a lot of promise.

55 However, despite the growing trend, we shouldn't be too quick to jump on board. At first glance, the farm-to-table movement seems to address environmental, nutritional, economic, and social concerns: it seems logical to bring communities and farms together and
60 have them support each other. But how farm-to-table actually works—both for suppliers and consumers—warrants further examination.

One concern is misrepresentation of the products. Some critics argue that because the term "farm-to-table"
65 is so broad, it is used by restaurants and other companies to falsely imply that their products are locally-sourced. For instance, produce may be labeled as "farm-to-table," despite being imported from traditional factory farms hundreds of miles away.

70 The growing trend of local food suggests people are unconcerned with that argument, and it appears difficult to encourage the public to be more discerning.

In addition, critics argue that the potential impact of eating local on the urban environment and economy
75 needs to be considered. Urban locavores' primary desire is to increase the public's access to fresh, high-quality food, but accessibility to such ingredients may increase their carbon footprint by increasing the number of farm trucks on the road. Consumers might have to choose
80 between access to fresh food and a "green" lifestyle—a difficult choice for consumers who want both, to put it bluntly.

Farmers, along with consumers, are largely unconvinved by such concerns. A coalition of urban
85 farmers led by Bob Wilson argued recently that there should be fewer restrictions on the term "local food." However, farmers stand to benefit from a universal definition of farm-to-table. Without agreement, the label of "locally sourced" stands to be corrupted, misleading
90 customers and damaging the movement's environmental claims. It is in the entire community's interest to carefully consider these critiques.

Practice Set 1

1

The central idea of the fourth paragraph (lines 28–33) of Passage 1 is that

A) community gardening experts support bringing people together.

B) the development of stronger communities is a key aspect of the local food movement.

C) people should buy their food from community gardens or farmers markets whenever possible.

D) urban farmers want healthier communities.

2

What is a main idea of the fifth paragraph (lines 73–82) of Passage 2?

A) Locavores consume more than typical amounts of fresh produce.

B) Misled consumers will be collateral damage in the locavore controversy.

C) The environmental impact of local eating is being scrutinized by critics.

D) Eating local increases the carbon footprint of urban residents.

3

The main idea of the final paragraph (lines 39–47) of Passage 1 is that

A) more seasonal food is being introduced in institutional settings.

B) farmers markets and community gardens are opening in response to increased demand.

C) supporters of the local food movement use a variety of methods to meet its goals.

D) urban farmers and chefs aim to make money from the local food movement.

Approach

Entrance

Central ideas and themes questions can be identified by these terms:

- main idea
- central idea
- central claim
- central problem

The following questions refer to the passages on page 148. Review question 4 with your teacher. Do not answer the question.

Entrance > Evidence and Elimination > Exit

4

The central idea of the first paragraph of Passage 2 (lines 48–54) is that

A) the local food movement has been embraced nationwide.

B) many restaurants and grocery stores have welcomed the "locavore" trend.

C) small farms are supported by the farm-to-table movement.

D) communities receive nourishing food and other benefits from eating local.

Review questions 5 and 6 on your own. Circle the part of the question that identifies it as a central ideas and themes question. Do not answer the questions.

5

What is a main idea of the first paragraph (lines 1–7) of Passage 1?

A) The hippies of the 1960s and 1970s are responsible for many modern trends.

B) Eating locally first began as a counterculture movement before it became mainstream.

C) The local food movement can be found in communities across America.

D) Processed and canned foods are losing appeal in light of local eating movements.

6

The central claim of Passage 2 is that the local food movement appears to benefit its followers but

A) its definition and methods should be carefully examined.

B) its incompatibility with urbanization makes it more damaging than beneficial to the environment.

C) those benefits may not be accessible enough to residents of low-income communities.

D) the resulting increase in the carbon footprint is unappealing to young consumers.

Questions 1–8 are based on the following passages.

Passage 1 is adapted from Adam Nowicki, "Farm to Table: Fad or the Future?" ©2019 by MasteryPrep. Passage 2 is from the editors of MasteryPrep, "Does Local Eating Matter?" ©2019 by MasteryPrep.

Passage 1

Dishes made with ingredients that are sourced nearby are healthier for you. That is the idea behind the farm-to-table movement. Although it may seem like a fad,
Line this local-eating initiative has roots in the "hippie era"
5 of the 1960s and 1970s, when young people rejected the status quo, including the consumption of processed and canned foods.

In the 21st century, the idea of "eating local" is spreading through communities and making its way
10 into restaurants and cafeterias. In over 1,000 school districts around the country, administrations work with local farms to provide fresh fruits and vegetables to students. Restaurants—from boutique, luxury dining establishments to fast-casual chains—are adjusting their
15 menus to offer seasonal ingredients and locally sourced fare.

According to the movement's proponents, eating locally is not only healthier, since fresher foods retain more nutrients, but also more sustainable, since a focus
20 on purchasing local products supports smaller farms. As a result, farm-fresh goods are now making their way to nearby cities, where locally sourced foods are not readily available. Moreover, in recent years, community gardens and farmers markets have sprung up in communities
25 that have historically been underserved, providing a source of recently harvested produce where previously only processed and preserved food was readily available.

Through such efforts, the ideals of eating local and building communities intersect. "We have to look at
30 community gardening as more than food production," says Bob Wilson, community garden and urban farm expert. "We have to look at it as building stronger, healthier communities by bringing people together."

Implementing farm-to-table efforts is beneficial
35 for people throughout the community. Restaurants that commit to supporting local purveyors often boost their own sales, while community gardens and farmers markets help build a sense of unity.

Many are meeting demands for locally grown,
40 seasonal food, both in institutional settings, such as schools, and in the marketplace. Others hope to capitalize on the increased interest in creating farmers markets and community gardens. The variety of approaches to improving food supply and consumption
45 demonstrates the adaptability and creativity of local food movement advocates (such as urban farmers and chefs) in promoting their mission.

Passage 2

The local food movement is gaining traction as a nutritious, sustainable approach to food. In recent years
50 the "locavore" trend has popped up in restaurants and grocery stores around the country. It's possible that the farm-to-table movement could help both small farms and our communities: the nourishing food and related benefits hold a lot of promise.

55 However, despite the growing trend, we shouldn't be too quick to jump on board. At first glance, the farm-to-table movement seems to address environmental, nutritional, economic, and social concerns: it seems logical to bring communities and farms together and
60 have them support each other. But how farm-to-table actually works—both for suppliers and consumers— warrants further examination.

One concern is misrepresentation of the products. Some critics argue that because the term "farm-to-table"
65 is so broad, it is used by restaurants and other companies to falsely imply that their products are locally-sourced. For instance, produce may be labeled as "farm-to-table," despite being imported from traditional factory farms hundreds of miles away.

70 The growing trend of local food suggests people are unconcerned with that argument, and it appears difficult to encourage the public to be more discerning.

In addition, critics argue that the potential impact of eating local on the urban environment and economy
75 needs to be considered. Urban locavores' primary desire is to increase the public's access to fresh, high-quality food, but accessibility to such ingredients may increase their carbon footprint by increasing the number of farm trucks on the road. Consumers might have to choose
80 between access to fresh food and a "green" lifestyle—a difficult choice for consumers who want both, to put it bluntly.

Farmers, along with consumers, are largely unconvinved by such concerns. A coalition of urban
85 farmers led by Bob Wilson argued recently that there should be fewer restrictions on the term "local food." However, farmers stand to benefit from a universal definition of farm-to-table. Without agreement, the label of "locally sourced" stands to be corrupted, misleading
90 customers and damaging the movement's environmental claims. It is in the entire community's interest to carefully consider these critiques.

Evidence and Elimination

To answer a central ideas and themes question, follow these steps:

1. Reread the introduction and conclusion.
2. Come up with a loose interpretation of the central idea.
3. Eliminate answer choices that don't agree with the central idea.
4. Eliminate answer choices that give details instead of central ideas.

Answer question 4 with your teacher.

Entrance **Evidence and Elimination** Exit

4

The central idea of the first paragraph of Passage 2 (lines 48–54) is that

A) the local food movement has been embraced nationwide.

B) many restaurants and grocery stores have welcomed the "locavore" trend.

C) small farms are supported by the farm-to-table movement.

D) communities receive nourishing food and other benefits from eating local.

Approach

The following questions refer to the passages on page 152. Answer questions 5 and 6 on your own. Focus on eliminating incorrect answers.

5

What is a main idea of the first paragraph (lines 1–7) of Passage 1?

A) The hippies of the 1960s and 1970s are responsible for many modern trends.

B) Eating locally first began as a counterculture movement before it became mainstream.

C) The local food movement can be found in communities across America.

D) Processed and canned foods are losing appeal in light of local eating movements.

6

The central claim of Passage 2 is that the local food movement appears to benefit its followers but

A) its definition and methods should be carefully examined.

B) its incompatibility with urbanization makes it more damaging than beneficial to the environment.

C) those benefits may not be accessible enough to residents of low-income communities.

D) the resulting increase in the carbon footprint is unappealing to young consumers.

Approach

Exit

If you've found the answer ...
Compare your answer to the details of the paragraph or passage to ensure they all support the central idea. Mark your answer and keep moving.

If you're stuck between two choices ...
Select the choice that is most closely related to the conclusion.

If you have no idea what the answer is ...
Select the choice that reflects the claim or topic suggested by the title.

Review questions 7 and 8. Work with your teacher to choose the correct answer from the remaining choices.

Entrance > Evidence and Elimination > Exit

7

The central claim of Passage 1 is that

A) ~~the spread of local food movements throughout the country will make farming more interesting to city dwellers.~~

B) eating food from farther than 100 miles from its origin has detrimental effects on the human population.

C) eating local offers nutritional and community benefits.

D) ~~small farms benefit when the surrounding neighborhoods support them financially by purchasing fresh produce and goods.~~

8

What is a main idea of the third paragraph (lines 63–69) of Passage 2?

A) Restaurateurs have been known to make false claims about their services.

B) ~~Chefs create seasonal menus based on partnerships with local farms.~~

C) ~~Farm to table is a concept that attracts customers who value nutrition.~~

D) Restaurants and other companies are being criticized for taking advantage of the "farm-to-table" trend.

Practice Set 2 | Complete the practice set. When you have finished, double-check your work.

Questions 9–13 are based on the following passage.

This passage is adapted from Ann Schuster, "Greenfrastructure: Saving Our Homes and Ourselves Through Urban Green Spaces." ©2019 by MasteryPrep.

Although many people migrate to cities for the benefits of urban life, this lifestyle has its drawbacks, such as chronic stress, insufficient physical activity, and
Line regular exposure to environmental pollution. To offset
5 the downsides of city life, residents living in urban centers should have access to "greenfrastructure": urban green space that may contribute to a more balanced lifestyle by supporting residents' mental and physical well-being.
10 Urban greenfrastructure includes forests, parks, playgrounds, and gardens. Green spaces in cities in Europe, the continent with the most urban greenfrastructure, are an essential part of daily life. Every day, millions of people gather in parks, an essential
15 common space, and use these areas to exercise, relax, and interact with the community and nature. In the era of mass urbanization, greenfrastructure is fundamental.

Despite this growth, there is a lack of availability of green spaces in economically marginalized
20 neighborhoods—in these places, greenfrastructure is seen as a potential hotspot for crime or too costly to develop. In some cases, this is understandable: badly maintained parks are a dangerous eyesore. If you've spent time in American cities, you know that there are
25 many poorly planned green spaces that have become dangerous; they are inaccessible environments strewn with debris. Given this experience, why would we want more greenfrastructure?

Urban residents in the United States deserve better.
30 By committing to equitable access to green space, city officials can make life cleaner, healthier, and more enjoyable. One way local governments have met this challenge is by utilizing obsolete or underutilized transportation infrastructure, such as train tracks or
35 remnant urban land, transforming it into attractive greenfrastructure. For example, the Heights community of Memphis, Tennessee, created a pilot project to demonstrate how a former trolley line could become a multi-use "linear park" with solar lights, plants,
40 and benches for the public's enjoyment. In Paris, city officials turned traditional roadways (that contributed to congestion) into parks with bike paths. Around the world, communities are unifying around a common goal and investing resources to increase residents' exposure
45 to nature and green life—improving the health, comfort, and well-being of urban citizens.

While conventional wisdom celebrates the benefits of being in nature, scientific studies firmly support the advantages of access to the outdoors. Time spent outside,
50 whether in a human-made space or a rural countryside, has been proven to support both mental and physical health. Studies have shown that spending time in nature can reduce symptoms of depression, anxiety, and even post-traumatic stress disorder (PTSD). Schoolchildren
55 have consistently been shown to demonstrate higher levels of concentration following playtime at recess. Access to nature can spark creativity and inspiration, invigorate the mind and body, and reduce technological distraction. Spending time outside has also been widely
60 proven to support physical well-being, including cardiovascular health, immunity, and recovery from illness. As such, increasing the availability, accessibility, and attractiveness of urban green spaces has become an issue of environmental justice and societal health. City
65 planners and municipal leaders around the world should ensure that access to greenfrastructure is equitable in all urban areas.

Practice Set 2

9

The central idea of the third paragraph (lines 18–28) is that

A) greenfrastructure attracts crime in economically marginalized neighborhoods.

B) American cities have poorly planned green spaces.

C) there are barriers to developing parks in disadvantaged American communities.

D) parks that are not maintained are an eyesore.

10

One central idea of the passage is that

A) exposure to green space has many benefits.

B) parks, gardens, and grassy areas are considered urban green space.

C) researchers are studying the effects of exposure to natural light.

D) green spaces are not easily incorporated into urban areas.

11

What is a main idea of the first paragraph (lines 1–9)?

A) Stress and pollution are two negative effects of urban life.

B) Exposure to nature may help balance the detriments of urban life.

C) Those migrating to cities often overlook the downsides of urban living.

D) Urban residents need positive experiences to outweigh the limitations of city life.

Strategy

Answers to Answers

It can be difficult to determine whether an answer choice describes the central idea of a paragraph, rather than just a detail. However, by comparing the answers to one another, you'll be able to more effectively eliminate the details and zero in on the central idea.

1 Eliminate any choice that could be used as support for another choice.

The following questions refer to the passage on page 156. Review question 12 with your teacher. Use the Answers to Answers strategy to answer the question as a class.

12

The central idea of the fourth paragraph (lines 29–46) is that

A) communities in Tennessee excel at greenfrastructure.

B) some international greenfrastructure initiatives focus on repurposing congested roadways into bike paths.

C) urban centers in the United States should adopt French greenfrastructure policies when possible.

D) some cities around the world have prioritized urban green space creation and access.

Work on your own using the Answers to Answers strategy to answer question 13.

13

What is a main idea of the second paragraph (lines 10–17)?

A) Urban green space includes forests, parks, playgrounds, and gardens.

B) The majority of urban residents live in cities dominated by infrastructure.

C) Greenfrastructure is an important part of everyday life for city dwellers.

D) European cities have more parks than American cities.

Questions 14–18 are based on the following passage.

This passage is adapted from Joaquim Cerqueira, "Is Gentrification Ever Ethical?" ©2019 by MasteryPrep.

Recent debates on gentrification (defined as the transformation of neighborhoods from low market value to high market value) have posed the question, "Who does this process help?"

Property owners argue that a community's financial and aesthetic value rises when there is investment in the built environment. Others contend that gentrification too often results in the displacement of longtime residents who can no longer afford to live in their neighborhoods. Both arguments have merit, so before we decry or embrace the concept, varying points of view must be evaluated.

The first point of contention is over the definition of gentrification. *Merriam-Webster's Collegiate Dictionary* defines gentrification as a process that rebuilds homes and businesses in deteriorating neighborhoods (usually in urban areas). *Merriam-Webster* further describes the rebuilding process as accompanied by the subsequent influx of affluent people—an occurrence that often displaces previous, typically poorer, residents. Is displacement of residents part of what defines gentrification? Another definition of gentrification from anthropologist Sabiyha Prince does not refer to its consequences, but simply defines the term as an influx of capital goods and services in "locales where those resources were previously non-existent": a definition that foregrounds financial investment. Though Prince's definition does not address the issue of resident displacement, this aspect of gentrification is often assumed.

While it does not define gentrification, a recent article in *The Economist* claims that the term itself has been tarred, and that the words "reinvestment" or "renaissance" would more appropriately describe the process. Such a shift in perspective may alter the stigma associated with gentrification. These various sources agree on simple facts: gentrification brings a different set of residents into a neighborhood, as well as new options for goods and services that were not previously available. But does life improve for *everyone* involved when a neighborhood changes, or is there too much collateral damage for longtime residents? *The Economist* dismisses reports of widespread resident displacement as largely exaggerated. However, even if the consequences of gentrification are overstated, they are a harsh reality for many people.

Methods of displacement vary; in most cases of gentrification, rental prices increase beyond what longtime residents can afford. These increases could result from higher real estate prices—the more landlords have to pay for their buildings, the more they have to charge their tenants. Sometimes, building owners sell to developers, who raise tenants' rents. Depending on the city's layout and housing options, residents displaced through gentrification may have to not only leave their homes but vacate the local area altogether.

While the displacement of longtime neighborhood residents is at the heart of the debate over gentrification, setting that aside, there are potential benefits. Studies show that, in gentrified areas, crime rates often decrease, businesses grow and prosper because safe neighborhoods attract more patrons, and employment rates often rise. Growth in these areas benefits both new and longtime business owners and residents, suggesting a neighborhood renaissance offers numerous advantages.

Understandably, it is challenging to definitively say whether gentrification is advantageous or harmful for residents, or whether it is beneficial to neighborhoods overall. The idea that the greatest objection—displacement of vulnerable residents—may be exaggerated only underscores the complexity of the subject. But studies in some areas of New York City, San Francisco, and Philadelphia show that gentrification without widespread displacement is indeed possible. Depending on the area's economy, longtime residents and businesses may be able to stay and thrive in a community as it changes.

That many metropolitan neighborhoods are transforming aesthetically and culturally is inarguable. As city living becomes more desirable and affordable, the flow of people from all socioeconomic statuses into urban communities will continue to alter both housing and commercial markets. But with careful planning and consideration, community input, and equitable processes, neighborhoods undergoing gentrification can flourish and retain longtime residents. If so, the word "gentrification" could come to be defined as a change in the right direction for all involved.

Strategy

Back to the Front

The main idea is often identified in the introduction of a paragraph or passage and then summarized in the conclusion. By finding the thread that connects the two, you can more effectively identify the central claim.

Use this strategy on central ideas and themes questions when the answer choices are difficult to eliminate.

1. Read the conclusion.

2. Read the introduction.

3. Select the answer choice that connects them.

Review question 14 with your teacher. Use the Back to the Front strategy to answer the question as a class.

14

One central idea of the passage is that

A) housing prices that are affordable to some are unattainably expensive to others.

B) it is impossible to predict how the influx of new residents will affect a neighborhood.

C) gentrification is occurring in cities across the country.

D) conclusions about gentrification are dependent on one's perspective.

The following question refers to the passage on page 160. Work on your own using the Back to the Front strategy to answer question 15.

15

The central idea of the fifth paragraph (lines 47–56) is that

A) gentrification can displace residents from their cities.

B) resident displacement can result from different factors.

C) developers often raise rental prices.

D) tenants can be displaced due to commercial renovations.

This page intentionally left blank

Practice Set 3 | Complete the practice set. When you have finished, double-check your work.

Questions 16–18 are based on the following passage.

This passage is adapted from Joaquim Cerqueira, "Is Gentrification Ever Ethical?" ©2019 by MasteryPrep.

Recent debates on gentrification (defined as the transformation of neighborhoods from low market value to high market value) have posed the question, "Who
Line does this process help?"

5   Property owners argue that a community's financial and aesthetic value rises when there is investment in the built environment. Others contend that gentrification too often results in the displacement of longtime residents who can no longer afford to live in their
10   neighborhoods. Both arguments have merit, so before we decry or embrace the concept, varying points of view must be evaluated.

The first point of contention is over the definition of gentrification. *Merriam-Webster's Collegiate Dictionary*
15   defines gentrification as a process that rebuilds homes and businesses in deteriorating neighborhoods (usually in urban areas). *Merriam-Webster* further describes the rebuilding process as accompanied by the subsequent influx of affluent people—an occurrence
20   that often displaces previous, typically poorer, residents. Is displacement of residents part of what defines gentrification? Another definition of gentrification from anthropologist Sabiyha Prince does not refer to its consequences, but simply defines the term as an influx
25   of capital goods and services in "locales where those resources were previously non-existent": a definition that foregrounds financial investment. Though Prince's definition does not address the issue of resident displacement, this aspect of gentrification is often
30   assumed.

While it does not define gentrification, a recent article in *The Economist* claims that the term itself has been tarred, and that the words "reinvestment" or "renaissance" would more appropriately describe the
35   process. Such a shift in perspective may alter the stigma associated with gentrification. These various sources agree on simple facts: gentrification brings a different set of residents into a neighborhood, as well as new options for goods and services that were not previously
40   available. But does life improve for *everyone* involved when a neighborhood changes, or is there too much collateral damage for longtime residents? *The Economist* dismisses reports of widespread resident displacement as largely exaggerated. However, even if the consequences
45   of gentrification are overstated, they are a harsh reality for many people.

Methods of displacement vary; in most cases of gentrification, rental prices increase beyond what longtime residents can afford. These increases could
50   result from higher real estate prices—the more landlords have to pay for their buildings, the more they have to charge their tenants. Sometimes, building owners sell to developers, who raise tenants' rents. Depending on the city's layout and housing options, residents displaced
55   through gentrification may have to not only leave their homes but vacate the local area altogether.

While the displacement of longtime neighborhood residents is at the heart of the debate over gentrification, setting that aside, there are potential benefits. Studies
60   show that, in gentrified areas, crime rates often decrease, businesses grow and prosper because safe neighborhoods attract more patrons, and employment rates often rise. Growth in these areas benefits both new and longtime business owners and residents, suggesting
65   a neighborhood renaissance offers numerous advantages.

Understandably, it is challenging to definitively say whether gentrification is advantageous or harmful for residents, or whether it is beneficial to neighborhoods overall. The idea that the greatest
70   objection—displacement of vulnerable residents—may be exaggerated only underscores the complexity of the subject. But studies in some areas of New York City, San Francisco, and Philadelphia show that gentrification without widespread displacement is indeed possible.
75   Depending on the area's economy, longtime residents and businesses may be able to stay and thrive in a community as it changes.

That many metropolitan neighborhoods are transforming aesthetically and culturally is inarguable.
80   As city living becomes more desirable and affordable, the flow of people from all socioeconomic statuses into urban communities will continue to alter both housing and commercial markets. But with careful planning and consideration, community input, and equitable
85   processes, neighborhoods undergoing gentrification can flourish and retain longtime residents. If so, the word "gentrification" could come to be defined as a change in the right direction for all involved.

16

The central idea of the third paragraph (lines 13–30) is that

A) the definition of gentrification is debatable.

B) gentrification is not an appropriate word for trends in neighborhood change.

C) damage and displacement are unavoidable as communities change.

D) change in urban communities results in advancement and improvement.

17

What is the main idea of the sixth paragraph (lines 57–65)?

A) Crime rates often decrease in areas that have undergone gentrification.

B) Gentrification is often accompanied by many beneficial side effects.

C) Despite perceived advantages, gentrification causes controversial displacement.

D) New and longtime business owners can work together to offer new services.

18

The main idea of the final paragraph (lines 78–88) is that

A) urban areas will increasingly benefit from an influx of new residents.

B) urban neighborhoods around the country will definitely be altered.

C) measures can be taken so that gentrification benefits all involved.

D) affordable city living will frequently create conflict in communities.

Mini-Test

Complete the mini-test. When you have finished, double-check your work.

Questions 1–10 are based on the following passage.

This passage is adapted from Elizabeth Cady Stanton's speech "Our Girls," originally delivered in 1880.

Every girl should be something in and of herself, have an individual aim and purpose in life. As the boy approaches manhood, he gathers up his forces
Line and concentrates them on some definite work, trade,
5 or profession, has a wish, a will, a way of his own that everybody respects, hence he begins life with enthusiasm, early learns the pleasure of self-dependence, growing stronger, nobler, braver, every day he lives. But, alas for the girl, she leaves school with her ambition at
10 white heat; perchance she has outstripped the foremost in the sciences and languages, she has her tools ready to carve her way to distinction. She, too, has a will of her own and desires the dignity and independence of self-support.

15 But any career for a woman is tabooed by the world, and nothing that she proposes to do is acceptable to family and friends. If, in spite of opposition, a woman does step outside all conventional trammels to do something that her grandmother did not do, she meets a
20 dozen obstacles where a man does one. Surely the battle of life without any artificial trammels is hard enough, for multitudes of young men even perish in the struggle, but the girl who earns her bread, or makes for herself a name, has all the boy has to surmount, and these
25 artificial barriers of law and custom in addition.

Do you wonder that so few are ready to take their rights? Multitudes of our noblest girls are perishing for something to do. The hope of marriage, all we offer girls, is not enough to feed an immortal mind, and if
30 that goal is never reached, what then? The more fire and genius a girl has with no outlets for her powers, the more complete is her misery when all these forces are turned back upon herself. The pent-up fires that might have glowed with living words of eloquence in
35 courts of justice, in the pulpit, or on the stage, are today consuming their victims in lunatic asylums, in domestic discontent and disgust, in peevish wailings about trifles, or in the vain pursuit of pleasure and fashion, longing for that peace that is found only in action. Thus, multitudes
40 of girls live and die unloving and unloved, who might have stood high in the shining walks of life a blessing to others and themselves ...

I know a beautiful girl just eighteen ... She has a passion for tragedy; all her desires, her longings, her
45 hopes and aspirations center there; she thinks of the stage by day, dreams of it by night, and fruitlessly friends try to change the current of her thoughts, her heart's desire, the purpose of her life. They have the power to say to her nay, to control her action, thwart her will,
50 pervert her nature, darken all life, but how can they fill the mighty void that one strong passion unsatisfied makes in the human soul? The weary hours of such a blasted life cannot be cheated with the dull round of ordinary duties, with the puerile pleasures said to
55 be legitimate to woman's sphere. Fathers, brothers, husbands die, banks fail, houses are consumed with fire, friends prove treacherous, creditors grasping, and debtors dishonest; the skill and cunning of a girl's own brains and hands are the only friends that are ever with
60 her, the only sure means of self-protection and support.

To train your daughter to a good trade or profession is far better than to leave her an unhappy dependent or a fortune without the necessary knowledge to take care of it. Every thinking man must see how entirely a
65 woman's virtue and dignity are involved in her pecuniary independence.

The universe of matter and mind is [the masculine] domain; no constitutions, customs, creeds, or codes block his onward way, but all combine to urge him on.
70 His triumphs in science, literature and art are hailed with loud huzzas. He accepts the homage of the multitude as his sole right and looks with jealous eye on any girl that dares to tread upon his heels. In these artificial distinctions, boys learn their first lessons of contempt
75 for all womankind.

Your creeds, codes, and conventionalisms have indeed fallen with crushing weight on the head of woman in all ages, but nature is mightier than law and custom, and in spite of the stone on her head, behold her
80 today close upon the heels of man in the whole world of thought, in art, science, literature, and government.

1 | | **1**

1

The central problem that Stanton describes in the passage is that women have been

A) denied the right to vote, which has resulted in unjust laws.

B) discouraged from pursuing a career, which has kept them from reaching their potential.

C) blocked from getting an education, which has led them to make poor decisions.

D) prevented from being happy, which has caused societal problems.

2

What is the main idea of the first paragraph (lines 1–14)?

A) Boys are able to pursue careers and be self-dependent.

B) Girls are not as ambitious as boys.

C) Just like boys, girls have the capacity to be self-reliant.

D) Knowledge of the sciences and languages are tools at girls' disposal.

3

Stanton claims that which of the following is a barrier to women's progress in her time?

A) The lack of formal education

B) The inheritance of a fortune

C) The tedium of life

D) The norms and rules of society

4

The central idea of the second paragraph (lines 15–25) is that

A) life is a difficult battle.

B) society puts up barriers to women who want to work.

C) women should act like men whenever possible.

D) many young men struggle to earn a living.

5

As used in line 72, "jealous" most nearly means

A) mean.

B) anxious.

C) aware.

D) possessive.

6

What is a main idea of the third paragraph (lines 26–42)?

A) The options available to women do not allow them to reach their full potential.

B) Problems arise when people are unhappy in their marriages.

C) Women are generally very intelligent.

D) It isn't clear what is causing women to be miserable.

7

The main idea of the fourth paragraph (lines 43–60) is that

A) women do not enjoy doing domestic duties.

B) men universally are not to be relied upon.

C) women need to pursue their passions in order to attain fulfillment and self-reliance.

D) female society is largely concerned with pleasure.

8

Stanton contends that the situation she describes in the passage is so dismal in part because men have

A) not allowed women the same privileges they enjoy.

B) refused to acknowledge the problem.

C) been disgusted with women who want an education.

D) enforced unjust laws and customs.

9

Which choice provides the best evidence for the answer to the previous question?

A) Lines 20–25 ("Surely . . . addition")

B) Lines 48–52 ("They have . . . soul")

C) Lines 71–73 ("He accepts . . . heels")

D) Lines 73–75 ("In these . . . womankind")

10

What is a main idea of the fifth paragraph (lines 61–66)?

A) Most women do not know how to manage a fortune.

B) Living as a dependent makes women unhappy.

C) Earning a living is a way for women to maintain their dignity.

D) Men should train women in a trade or profession.

STOP

**If you finish before time is called, you may check your work on this section only.
Do not turn to any other section.**

This page intentionally left blank

Wrap-Up | Complete the wrap-up. When you have finished, double-check your work.

Questions 4–6 are based on the following passage.

This passage is adapted from Margaret McCarthy, "How Many People Will There Be in the Future?" ©2020 by MasteryPrep.

The growth of the world's population is a recurrent newspaper headline, but experts debate whether this trend will continue. New data on global population
Line growth rates suggest that the planet will need to support
5 nearly 10 billion people by 2050, yet not all experts agree with this conclusion—and they have their own evidence.

There are two popular arguments regarding human population growth: it will continue apace, or it will plateau. Over the past century, the global population has
10 rapidly increased, and a recent demographics study and analysis completed by the United Nations supports the claim that this trend will continue. Previous models of population growth assumed that birth rates would fall around the world, but researchers are now reconsidering
15 this assumption. "It's likely that there will be between 9.6 and 12.3 billion people on Earth by 2100," summarized Aoife Boyle, a researcher from the UN study.

The study, published in *Science*, uses a probabilistic analysis to project future population growth.
20 Demographers study population trends through the three dimensions of fertility, mortality, and immigration. The study reports that rapid declines in fertility rates need to occur in sub-Saharan Africa if population growth is to slow. Experts hope to reduce population
25 growth, as it may threaten Earth's resources.

Brazil's rapid population growth rate decline is an interesting example of what is possible; its fertility rate dropped dramatically and rapidly over two generations, from 6.3 children to 1.73 children per woman. By
30 improving educational opportunities and increasing access to contraception, the Brazilian government helped lower the fertility rate to below the global average. "Something *happened*," Brazilian demographer José Alberto Carvalho says, emphasizing the nation's
35 accomplishment in slowing population growth. "What took 120 years in England took 40 years here."

"The UN research evokes the global overconsumption of natural resources," argues population biologist Paul Ehrlich. The past half-century has been labeled the
40 "Great Acceleration" due to an increase in human activity. Since World War II, the world's population has tripled and drastically ramped up resource utilization, from water used in irrigation and croplands to oil for gas and industrial production. Ehrlich's research predicted
45 mass famine in the 1970s and 1980s due to this rapid population growth and its related resource drain.

"Our collective burden on the planet is not determined by statistics only," Ehrlich stated. He developed a formula showing that impact equals
50 population multiplied by affluence multiplied by technology (IPAT for short) in order to model increased natural resource consumption.

Studies of global consumption patterns reveal that humans are utilizing natural resources beyond their
55 predicted capacity as both the world population and global demand for goods grow at an unprecedented rate. However, one-fifth of Earth's population still has no access to reliable electricity. Lack of such access impacts educational opportunities, a key factor in fertility
60 rate decline. The connection between these concepts illuminates the complexity of the population debate and resource consumption trends, as well as the resulting question of whether natural resources can support such growth.
65 "Population growth is not straightforward," says Raunaq Paul, an ecologist at the University of North Dakota, warning us to always consider all of the dimensions of our collective and individual impact. Choices that societies make regarding educational
70 opportunities, public health, and material consumption all have real consequences for the environment. Whether population growth continues or slows, "the human population should consider all the dimensions of our collective and individual impact on the environment."

4

The main idea of the final paragraph (lines 65–74) is that

A) people need to be mindful of their impact on society.

B) it is difficult to predict whether population growth rates will continue to rise.

C) the environment is affected by the choices of societies in multiple ways.

D) predictions of population growth developed by ecologists are complex.

5

What is a main idea of the seventh paragraph (lines 53–64)?

A) Some people in the world do not have access to electricity.

B) As the population grows, there is a greater strain on natural resources.

C) Access to educational opportunities is important for reducing the fertility rate.

D) The relationship between natural resource consumption and population growth is complex.

6

One central idea of the passage is that

A) human decisions play a role in both population growth and resource use.

B) sometimes population growth rises unexpectedly.

C) environmentalists are justified in their concerns.

D) natural resources will replenish with enough time.

Review

Entrance

Central ideas and themes questions can be identified by these terms:

- main idea
- central idea
- central claim
- central problem

Evidence and Elimination

To answer a central ideas and themes question, follow these steps:

1. Reread the introduction and conclusion.
2. Come up with a loose interpretation of the central idea.
3. Eliminate answer choices that don't agree with the central idea.
4. Eliminate answer choices that give details instead of central ideas.

Exit

If you've found the answer ...

Compare your answer to the details of the paragraph or passage to ensure they all support this central idea. Mark your answer and keep moving.

If you're stuck between two choices ...

Select the choice that is most closely related to the conclusion.

If you have no idea what the answer is ...

Select the choice that reflects the claim or topic suggested by the title.

6

Chapter

Understanding Relationships

LEARNING TARGETS

1. Identify connections made between individuals, events, or ideas in SAT Reading passages.

2. Implement the basic approach for understanding relationships questions.

3. Apply the *Predict the Future* strategy to understanding relationships questions.

Warm-Up

Complete the warm-up. When you have finished, double-check your work.

Questions 1–3 are based on the following passage.

This passage is adapted from Henry Frank, *George Digory*. George had been an infamous miser when his wealth was suddenly stolen away. He later adopted a poor woman's daughter, Becca, who had lost everything herself.

But unlike money—which was locked away from
the sunlight, was oblivious to the sounds of nature, and
didn't react to people's voices—Becca was a living being
Line of boundless desires and increasing interests, searching
5 for and enjoying the sunlight and world around her. The
money had trapped his mind in a never-ending cycle,
going nowhere beyond itself; but Becca was a thing
filled with novelty and optimism that pushed his mind
forward, propelling it beyond its old, endless, fervent
10 striving. She called him away from his work and re-
awakened him to life's simple joys.
   And in the summer, when the daisies were dense
in the fields, George might be found in the bright
afternoon, or at dusk when the shadows grew longer
15 under the shrubbery, ambling out with bare feet to
bring Becca to where the flowers blossomed, so he
could relax as Becca waddled to pick them; she spoke
to the flying things that buzzed happily around them,
constantly calling "Daddy's" attention and giving him
20 flowers. Then she would turn her head to the song of a
bird, and George discovered he could make her happy
by motioning to remain quiet, so that when the next call
sounded, she would jump up and her laughter would
bubble in triumph. Sitting like this, George would
25 sometimes start remembering his past, but he would
shyly push the encroaching memories aside, taking
shelter in Becca's simple life, which weighed nothing on
his fatigued soul.
   As Becca's mind developed, George's own
30 consciousness grew: his spirit, long-dazed and trapped
in a dark tunnel, was quivering slowly into complete
awareness.
   Her influence on George became greater with each
passing year. As Becca grew, her words became more
35 sophisticated and required articulate responses; objects
and noises became more distinct to Becca's eyes and ears,
and there was more that "Daddy" had to acknowledge
and respond to as well. By the time Becca turned four
years old, she had established an acute ability for trouble
40 and mischief, which put to practice not only George's
endurance, but his attentiveness and scrutiny. It was at
times such as these, especially, that George struggled to
understand how discipline and love could coexist.

1

The narrator indicates that George's desire for wealth has lessened because

A) Becca has opened his eyes to the simple joys of life.

B) someone has stolen his life savings.

C) he must devote all of his time and energy to Becca.

D) he feels as though he had earned enough money.

2

In describing the relationship between Becca and George, the narrator draws a connection between Becca's

A) physical dependence and George's emotional instability.

B) zeal for her surroundings and George's newfound appreciation for life.

C) limitless vigor and George's voracious ambition for fortune.

D) physical growth and George's negative perception of life.

3

Which statement best describes the relationship between George and Becca that is presented in the passage?

A) Both are sorrowful, but they vary significantly in how they deal with the sadness in their lives.

B) Both depend on each other, but George is too busy to care for Becca's needs.

C) Both enjoy life, but George's enjoyment of life began only when he encountered Becca's carefree spirit.

D) Both lost everything, but only George was able to recover what had been stolen from him.

Foundation

Work with your teacher to read the passage and answer 1–3.

Passage 1

"Here you go," my mom says with delight as she slides her latest concoction in front of me. I try to keep the horror off my face as the scent of sulfur and boiled ground beef wafts to my nostrils.

"Looks great, mom," I reply, promptly grabbing my fork as if it were a tool for delicious consumption rather than a device of a torturous culinary test of will power.

She turns back to the counter and begins to serve herself; a hint of worry tingles at the back of my mind. I may be able to fake the *mmms* and *this is greats*, but as soon as she takes that first bite, she'll know the last three hours of her life were wasted. But it's too late for that. I grip my fork and focus on the business at hand.

When she has her back turned, I try to slip a little bite to Dodger, our golden retriever, who's been sitting patiently under the table waiting for a scrap. It's a no go. Once it touches his tongue, he rears back and gives me a look that I can only describe as an insinuation that I've offended even his ancestors. Okay. Looks like this is up to me.

"What do you think, honey?" She looks over her shoulder as she pulls some ketchup out of the fridge. Maybe I can coat my own plate in that lifesaving condiment to help me get this down? But, no. I don't want to give her any indication that I'm not enjoying this mess of a meal.

"It's great, Mom!" I reply, quickly shoving a bite into my mouth before I get cold feet. My resulting smile contorts my face, my gag reflex threatens to give me away, and I turn my face to my plate. Bad idea. The smell hits me again, and my eyes begin to water. *I can do this. I can do this … I can't do this.*

1. In describing this moment between a mother and son, the narrator depicts a cause and effect relationship between two events. What *causes* the son to lie to his mother?

   _____

   _____

   _____

   _____

2. Which sentence best explains *why* the son didn't want to complain about the meal? Underline that sentence.

3. What elements of the passage contain lies? When is the narrator being honest?

   _____

   _____

   _____

   _____

Work on your own to read the passage and answer questions 4–6.

Passage 2

It's 2 p.m. on a Tuesday, and the mall is dead. And yet, here I sit, working the slowest afternoon of the week at the smoothie stand in the center of the food court. I always feel ridiculous with my uniform's paper pirate hat on, offering anyone who might pass ample opportunity to smirk or offer a sympathetic smile. Neither one makes me feel better. I look around at what must be a hundred empty tables. Just four are filled.

Need-a-Job Ned is clearly waiting on an interview. He's wearing dress slacks and a tie, but it looks too new and too uncomfortable. No way he wears this regularly. His leg is jiggling like crazy, and he's unsuccessfully trying to smooth the wrinkles in the few pages of text he's brought with him. Definitely a resume.

James is here today, too. He's a big dude, like linebacker big. He's covered in tattoos. He even has a tribal thorn branch that runs from ear to ear over the path of his forehead. His leather jacket and motorcycle boots don't make him any less intimidating, which is clear from the way the few in the food court avoid him. They literally walk several feet out of their way to avoid passing his table. What they don't know is that he's a sweet guy; he always leaves good tips for us and smiles when he says "thanks" for his drink. You don't realize how few people have good manners until you work in a service job like this.

There's a mom in the corner with a stroller, and she has that exhausted look on her face. She'll probably head to the coffee shop rather than in my direction. And there's the group of older women sitting close together at a far table. They come here every week to walk and complain about everything they see, including me. They'll *definitely* be heading my way soon. Maybe I should stop daydreaming and get that orange juice working.

4. The other people in the food court regard James as

_____.

5. The character most likely to offer a sympathetic smile to the narrator is

_____.

6. Underline the sentence in the passage that *best* supports your answer to the previous question.

Foundation

Each passage contains a *cause and effect* or a *compare and contrast* relationship. Work with your teacher to answer question 7.

7. Buying a car is an investment in a variety of opportunities, such as being able to maintain a job or attend college while living off-campus. Buying a new car will involve a bigger investment, while older cars offer a less expensive way to get around. However, a vehicle's purchase price is only one aspect to consider, since investing in any car, new or used, will involve ongoing expenses such as gasoline, insurance, and maintenance.

   What kind of relationship is expressed in this paragraph? _____

   According to the passage, what do new and used cars have in common? Underline the sentence that provides this information.

Work on your own to answer questions 8 and 9.

8. Streaming apps are popular because they give people the power to select what they hear. Music streaming means the lyrics and melody fill your ears, while streaming music *videos* gives you the opportunity to enjoy a visual along with the music. Radio tells you what to listen to, but streaming gives you all the power.

   What kind of relationship is expressed in this paragraph? _____

   What contrast exists between listening to the radio and listening to streamed music? Underline the sentence that provides this information.

9. People find reasons to quit their jobs every day. The negative impact of an uncaring, overly critical boss forces even the best of workers to abandon careers they love in search of something new. Other times, people leave in search of better pay or flexibility.

   What kind of relationship is expressed in this paragraph? _____

   The passage tells us that most people quit their jobs because of what? Underline the sentence that provides this information.

Practice Set 1 | Complete the practice set. When you have finished, double-check your work.

Questions 1–11 are based on the following passages.

Passage 1 is adapted from Michael Bates, "Social Media Prevents Bonding, Restructures Brains." © 2019 by MasteryPrep Passage 2 is from Arnold Franzinger, "Social Bonds Through Social Media." © 2019 by MasteryPrep.

Passage 1

The consequences of relying on social media to connect with others are not entirely negative. Many relationships are strengthened by the use of social
Line media. This tends to apply most to relationships between
5 people who do not live nearby, such as distant relatives or old friends. One study found that those who use social media are ten times more likely to be aware of the happenings of their relatives than those who don't use social media. Furthermore, social media users were five
10 times more likely to have had some form of contact with remote friends within the past month.

It's also likely that social media usage can strengthen communication skills, particularly those that are commonly used in modern business environments.
15 A study of recent college graduates in Germany found that those who were adept at navigating online networking platforms were far more likely to be hired for communications positions than those candidates who did not engage in social media. The more we interact
20 online, the more effective we become at communicating through today's technology.

But it would be a misstep to focus solely on the positive effects of social media usage and conclude that technology alone can strengthen interpersonal
25 relationships and make us better communicators. In a *Technology* article published last year, leading social psychologist Pricilla Brown reviewed over 30 studies on the effects of social media on our social interactions and communication. She concluded that "social media
30 develops online social skills at the expense of face-to-face social skills." Our growing use of social media, she concedes, has led to "extensive and sophisticated development of worldwide human connections." But those go hand in hand with a weakening of the "depth"
35 of those interpersonal connections that result in long-lasting feelings of "belonging, comradeship, and trust."

Researchers have concluded that the human brain is adaptable; the connections in our brains adjust to changing circumstances. When we immerse ourselves
40 in a cultural phenomenon such as social media, for example, our brains adapt to follow suit. That means our use of social media impacts how we interact with others even when we are not online, explains John McMiller,

an expert in neuroscience. We exercise the parts of our
45 brains used for communicating and processing mass social information while neglecting the parts used for understanding body language and deep emotions.

Passage 2

Critics of social media usually support their claims with sociological studies that demonstrate how "face-
50 to-face communication is the only way to develop deep relationships." But other experts aren't so convinced. Yes, in-person interaction can deepen emotional bonds, but that doesn't mean it is the only way to build and maintain meaningful relationships.

55 Lack of face-to-face contact does not prevent us from creating lasting bonds and friendships. In fact, some of the most resilient and lasting friendships have come about in unconventional ways. For example, the famous rivalry between John Adams and Thomas Jefferson
60 eventually evolved into friendship when, starting in 1812, they exchanged 158 letters long-distance over the next 14 years. Legend claims their friendship was so deep that it explains why they quite literally died the same day and hour, though they were separated by miles.
65 Likewise, a reliance on social media does not hinder us from forming deep personal bonds, as made evident by the familiar story of married couples who found each other online.

Furthermore, the benefit of face-to-face interaction
70 is specific to each encounter. If strangers routinely ride an elevator together to and from their workplaces, they are unlikely to become more than acquaintances exchanging polite conversation—unless more effort is made. That is, deep relationships don't always result
75 from face time, even when it is frequent. Instead, meaningful connections form through communication and trust. Communication is a building block of human relationships that is unhindered by technology.

The negative effects of relying on social media
80 are likely more overblown than some claim. Critics talk as if using technology to communicate results in "simulated" relationships. However, people who connect through social media develop enduring friendships all the time. As ancient philosophers feared that the
85 development of written language would degrade our capacity for true intellect and wisdom, social media critics fear that status updates and emojis will deprive our relationships of any true value or depth.

Practice Set 1

1

The author of Passage 1 indicates that people who are adept at social media are more likely to be hired for communications positions because

A) they are practiced in communicating through technology.

B) they are more likely to be aware of what is happening in other people's lives.

C) their brains have adapted to a new social phenomenon.

D) they have studied neuroscience and psychology.

2

In Passage 1, the author implies that the widespread use of social media can have which consequence?

A) Communication skills may decline across the board.

B) People can improve certain communication skills at the expense of other skills.

C) Individuals are unable to repair broken emotional bonds.

D) Most people gain more social connections than they need.

3

In Passage 1, the author describes the relationship between social media and our brains by drawing a connection between social media's

A) expanding network and the brain's growing intelligence.

B) subtle impact on interpersonal behavior and the brain's adaptation to new forms of communication.

C) positive effect on employability and the brain's resistance to change.

D) growing popularity and the brain's enhanced resilience.

Approach

Entrance
Understanding relationships questions can be identified by this feature: • a question asking you to relate two things to each other

The following questions refer to the passage on page 178. Review question 4 with your teacher. Circle the part of the question that identifies it as an understanding relationships question. Do not answer the question.

> Entrance Evidence and Elimination > Exit
>
> **4**
>
> The author of Passage 1 indicates that social media usage can be beneficial because
>
> A) it results in increased communication with distant family and friends.
>
> B) people are able to exercise different parts of the brain.
>
> C) it leads to a lucrative and successful career.
>
> D) those with an active online presence are perceived as intelligent.

Approach

Review questions 5 and 6 on your own. Circle the part of the question that identifies it as an understanding relationships question. Do not answer the questions.

5

According to the author of Passage 2, one benefit of using social media is that people

A) can express their deep emotions with ease.

B) can more easily find a spouse.

C) seem to be more accepting of others.

D) can make connections that result in long-term relationships.

6

In Passage 2, the author implies that long-distance, unconventional forms of communication could have which result?

A) The ability to truly connect would be limited.

B) People could establish deeply meaningful relationships.

C) Face-to-face communication would be rendered unnecessary.

D) People would struggle to have in-person relationships.

Questions 1–11 are based on the following passages.

Passage 1 is adapted from Michael Bates, "Social Media Prevents Bonding, Restructures Brains." © 2019 by MasteryPrep
Passage 2 is from Arnold Franzinger, "Social Bonds Through Social Media." © 2019 by MasteryPrep

Passage 1

The consequences of relying on social media to connect with others are not entirely negative. Many relationships are strengthened by the use of social media. This tends to apply most to relationships between people who do not live nearby, such as distant relatives or old friends. One study found that those who use social media are ten times more likely to be aware of the happenings of their relatives than those who don't use social media. Furthermore, social media users were five times more likely to have had some form of contact with remote friends within the past month.

It's also likely that social media usage can strengthen communication skills, particularly those that are commonly used in modern business environments. A study of recent college graduates in Germany found that those who were adept at navigating online networking platforms were far more likely to be hired for communications positions than those candidates who did not engage in social media. The more we interact online, the more effective we become at communicating through today's technology.

But it would be a misstep to focus solely on the positive effects of social media usage and conclude that technology alone can strengthen interpersonal relationships and make us better communicators. In a *Technology* article published last year, leading social psychologist Pricilla Brown reviewed over 30 studies on the effects of social media on our social interactions and communication. She concluded that "social media develops online social skills at the expense of face-to-face social skills." Our growing use of social media, she concedes, has led to "extensive and sophisticated development of worldwide human connections." But those go hand in hand with a weakening of the "depth" of those interpersonal connections that result in long-lasting feelings of "belonging, comradeship, and trust."

Researchers have concluded that the human brain is adaptable; the connections in our brains adjust to changing circumstances. When we immerse ourselves in a cultural phenomenon such as social media, for example, our brains adapt to follow suit. That means our use of social media impacts how we interact with others even when we are not online, explains John McMiller,

an expert in neuroscience. We exercise the parts of our brains used for communicating and processing mass social information while neglecting the parts used for understanding body language and deep emotions.

Passage 2

Critics of social media usually support their claims with sociological studies that demonstrate how "face-to-face communication is the only way to develop deep relationships." But other experts aren't so convinced. Yes, in-person interaction can deepen emotional bonds, but that doesn't mean it is the only way to build and maintain meaningful relationships.

Lack of face-to-face contact does not prevent us from creating lasting bonds and friendships. In fact, some of the most resilient and lasting friendships have come about in unconventional ways. For example, the famous rivalry between John Adams and Thomas Jefferson eventually evolved into friendship when, starting in 1812, they exchanged 158 letters long-distance over the next 14 years. Legend claims their friendship was so deep that it explains why they quite literally died the same day and hour, though they were separated by miles. Likewise, a reliance on social media does not hinder us from forming deep personal bonds, as made evident by the familiar story of married couples who found each other online.

Furthermore, the benefit of face-to-face interaction is specific to each encounter. If strangers routinely ride an elevator together to and from their workplaces, they are unlikely to become more than acquaintances exchanging polite conversation—unless more effort is made. That is, deep relationships don't always result from face time, even when it is frequent. Instead, meaningful connections form through communication and trust. Communication is a building block of human relationships that is unhindered by technology.

The negative effects of relying on social media are likely more overblown than some claim. Critics talk as if using technology to communicate results in "simulated" relationships. However, people who connect through social media develop enduring friendships all the time. As ancient philosophers feared that the development of written language would degrade our capacity for true intellect and wisdom, social media critics fear that status updates and emojis will deprive our relationships of any true value or depth.

Approach

Evidence and Elimination

To answer an understanding relationships question, follow these steps:

1. Identify the relationship in the question.
2. Use the type of relationship to help find evidence in the passage.
3. Eliminate choices that don't accurately describe the relationship.

Answer question 4 with your teacher.

Entrance | **Evidence and Elimination** | Exit

4

The author of Passage 1 indicates that social media usage can be beneficial because

A) it results in increased communication with distant family and friends.

B) people are able to exercise different parts of the brain.

C) it leads to a lucrative and successful career.

D) those with an active online presence are perceived as intelligent.

Approach

The following questions refer to the passage on page 182. Answer questions 5 and 6 on your own. Focus on eliminating incorrect answers.

5

According to the author of Passage 2, one benefit of using social media is that people

A) can express their deep emotions with ease.

B) can more easily find a spouse.

C) seem to be more accepting of others.

D) can make connections that result in long-term relationships.

6

In Passage 2, the author implies that long-distance, unconventional forms of communication could have which result?

A) The ability to truly connect would be limited.

B) People could establish deeply meaningful relationships.

C) Face-to-face communication would be rendered unnecessary.

D) People would struggle to have in-person relationships.

Approach

Exit

If you've found the answer ...
Verify that it is supported with textual evidence. If so, mark your answer and continue to the next question.

If you're stuck between two choices ...
Talk yourself through why each answer choice might be right. Select the answer that needs the least explanation.

If you have no idea what the answer is ...
Go with your gut. Select the answer choice that best matches the main idea of the passage.

Review questions 7 and 8. Work with your teacher to choose the correct answer from the remaining choices.

Entrance > Evidence and Elimination > **Exit**

7

In describing critics' concerns about social media, the author of Passage 2 draws a connection between social media's

A) proven shortcomings and previous limitations of language.

B) perceived harm and past sociological developments.

C) negative influence and slow historical progress.

D) potential fallout and the new developments in communication.

8

According to the author of Passage 2, what do all meaningful relationships have in common?

A) They develop over long periods of time.

B) They result from face-to-face interaction.

C) They are based on honest and open dialogue.

D) They are built through communication and trust.

Practice Set 2 | Complete the practice set. When you have finished, double-check your work.

Questions 1–11 are based on the following passages.

Passage 1 is adapted from Michael Bates, "Social Media Prevents Bonding, Restructures Brains." © 2019 by MasteryPrep Passage 2 is from Arnold Franzinger, "Social Bonds Through Social Media." © 2019 by MasteryPrep

Passage 1

The consequences of relying on social media to connect with others are not entirely negative. Many relationships are strengthened by the use of social
Line media. This tends to apply most to relationships between
5 people who do not live nearby, such as distant relatives or old friends. One study found that those who use social media are ten times more likely to be aware of the happenings of their relatives than those who don't use social media. Furthermore, social media users were five
10 times more likely to have had some form of contact with remote friends within the past month.

It's also likely that social media usage can strengthen communication skills, particularly those that are commonly used in modern business environments.
15 A study of recent college graduates in Germany found that those who were adept at navigating online networking platforms were far more likely to be hired for communications positions than those candidates who did not engage in social media. The more we interact
20 online, the more effective we become at communicating through today's technology.

But it would be a misstep to focus solely on the positive effects of social media usage and conclude that technology alone can strengthen interpersonal
25 relationships and make us better communicators. In a *Technology* article published last year, leading social psychologist Pricilla Brown reviewed over 30 studies on the effects of social media on our social interactions and communication. She concluded that "social media
30 develops online social skills at the expense of face-to-face social skills." Our growing use of social media, she concedes, has led to "extensive and sophisticated development of worldwide human connections." But those go hand in hand with a weakening of the "depth"
35 of those interpersonal connections that result in long-lasting feelings of "belonging, comradeship, and trust."

Researchers have concluded that the human brain is adaptable; the connections in our brains adjust to changing circumstances. When we immerse ourselves
40 in a cultural phenomenon such as social media, for example, our brains adapt to follow suit. That means our use of social media impacts how we interact with others even when we are not online, explains John McMiller,

an expert in neuroscience. We exercise the parts of our
45 brains used for communicating and processing mass social information while neglecting the parts used for understanding body language and deep emotions.

Passage 2

Critics of social media usually support their claims with sociological studies that demonstrate how "face-
50 to-face communication is the only way to develop deep relationships." But other experts aren't so convinced. Yes, in-person interaction can deepen emotional bonds, but that doesn't mean it is the only way to build and maintain meaningful relationships.

55 Lack of face-to-face contact does not prevent us from creating lasting bonds and friendships. In fact, some of the most resilient and lasting friendships have come about in unconventional ways. For example, the famous rivalry between John Adams and Thomas Jefferson
60 eventually evolved into friendship when, starting in 1812, they exchanged 158 letters long-distance over the next 14 years. Legend claims their friendship was so deep that it explains why they quite literally died the same day and hour, though they were separated by miles.
65 Likewise, a reliance on social media does not hinder us from forming deep personal bonds, as made evident by the familiar story of married couples who found each other online.

Furthermore, the benefit of face-to-face interaction
70 is specific to each encounter. If strangers routinely ride an elevator together to and from their workplaces, they are unlikely to become more than acquaintances exchanging polite conversation—unless more effort is made. That is, deep relationships don't always result
75 from face time, even when it is frequent. Instead, meaningful connections form through communication and trust. Communication is a building block of human relationships that is unhindered by technology.

The negative effects of relying on social media
80 are likely more overblown than some claim. Critics talk as if using technology to communicate results in "simulated" relationships. However, people who connect through social media develop enduring friendships all the time. As ancient philosophers feared that the
85 development of written language would degrade our capacity for true intellect and wisdom, social media critics fear that status updates and emojis will deprive our relationships of any true value or depth.

9

Which choice best describes the relationship between the two passages?

A) Passage 2 presents personal anecdotes that contrast with the neurological data presented in Passage 1.

B) Passage 2 argues against some of the conclusions drawn from the research discussed in Passage 1.

C) Passage 2 cites specific research regarding an effect that Passage 1 examines more broadly.

D) Passage 2 predicts the negative repercussions that the findings discussed in Passage 1 might produce.

10

Which choice best describes the ways in which the two authors perceive the impact of social media on society?

A) Bates believes social media has both benefits and drawbacks, while Franzinger believes that concerns about social media are unjustified.

B) Bates believes that social media should not be used to assess employability, while Franzinger does not address social media's role in the workplace.

C) Bates believes that social media can play a key role in relationship building, while Franzinger thinks social media has no bearing on personal relationships.

D) Bates believes that social media should be used with caution, while Franzinger believes social media should take the place of other forms of communication.

11

Which statement best expresses the relationship between social media and human connections as presented in both of the passages?

A) Both passages convey equal concern about the effects of social media on our relationships, but they differ dramatically in how these concerns should be addressed.

B) Both passages convey that using social media helps our brains become better at connecting to other people, but Passage 1 conveys that social media should be used only in conjunction with traditional methods of communication.

C) Both passages convey that using social media can change how we connect to others, but only Passage 1 conveys that this can be detrimental to our relationships.

D) Both passages convey that using social media can have negative effects on our relationships, but only Passage 2 conveys that there are also some positive effects.

Strategy

Questions 12–20 are based on the following passage.

This passage is adapted from Walter Bryant, "Shade on Solar Power: Why Renewable Energy May Not Be So Powerful." © 2019 by MasteryPrep.

When it comes to electricity, everyone wants reliability. Providing a stable supply of electricity is a common objective that most political leaders can agree
Line on, though they occasionally disagree on the best way
5 to do it. Efficient electricity generation results in more power using fewer resources, which is beneficial for the energy industry and (in some cases) beneficial to the environment, too. In an increasingly technologically-advanced world, the only sustainable way to continue
10 our quest for reliable energy is to get more with less. Everyone can agree on that.

But turn the discussion to using renewable energy, and the most powerful methods of generating electricity start to look questionable. Nuclear power plants have
15 become incredibly robust and reliable when considering pure electricity generation. Thanks to technological advancements and chemical engineering, a typical nuclear power plant can supply electricity to one million homes a year. Nuclear power plants produce
20 more electricity with fewer resources—about 7.9 billion kilowatt hours per year when running at 90% capacity, for example—which means less oil or coal is burned. And since the demand for electricity is expected to rise 30% by 2030—increasing air and water pollution as
25 well—any method that could reduce the burning of oil or coal while producing more electricity would be in everyone's best interest.

Of course, that's not what environmentalists consider the best option, especially in the long run. They believe
30 renewable energy sources are better for the world—more efficient and safer, too—considering the radioactive waste produced by nuclear power plants. On the other hand, renewable sources—which do not consume material and generate less waste—are thought to be far
35 better long-term. Solar energy, for example, is expected to produce 35% of the United States' electricity by 2050, up from 7% in 2015—and homeowners are investing in solar panels as much for the environment as their budgets.
40 However, a recent study in *Power* did the math and came to a difficult conclusion: renewable energy produces 27% less power on average than nuclear power. Renewable energy requires clear skies or windy days—and that means renewable energy may not be as
45 dependable as we might hope.

Researchers from the University of Michigan conducted a meta-analysis of 55 articles comparing renewable energy and nuclear power across 32 countries, from North America to Asia. They discovered that
50 nuclear power was the primary method of producing electricity in every country, though the results varied. In countries with governmental incentives for solar power, such as the United States or Germany, nuclear power surpassed renewable energy by only 6%. Yet in most
55 other countries, especially Eastern countries—which collectively are the largest consumers of electricity—nuclear power outproduced renewable energy by more than 23%.

The primary difference is what resources are utilized.
60 A basic nuclear power plant uses 27 tons of uranium per year, which produces as much electricity as a solar power plant using 45 to 75 square miles of land. When we talk about energy efficiency, we are actually discussing what resources are consumed—and different resources come
65 with different consequences.

The uranium used in nuclear power burns clean, but it has waste. This radioactive waste isn't disposable, dangerously radiating the environment for tens of thousands of years. We already have quarantined zones
70 all over the planet that store the waste indefinitely, which is not sustainable long-term. Renewable energy uses a lot of land, on the other hand, which can harm the environment in other ways.

What that means is that while nuclear sites generate
75 more power—in most cases, much more power—than renewable energy, there are pros and cons with each. Thus, an ideal worldwide energy system, according to the study's researchers, will draw the best strategies from both methods, as Andrew Felix of the University of
80 Michigan suggested:

The final conclusion? Today's renewable energy systems are best utilized in countries with large areas of unusable land, or where land (in comparison to population) is readily available. But in terms of
85 generating pure electricity, especially in countries that are overcrowded or where available land is sparse, nuclear power has an advantage.

In the future, however, I believe we will need to develop both methods (especially in ways
90 that make nuclear power more sustainable and renewable energy more productive) so that they are both effective—technologically, environmentally, economically, etc.

Strategy

Predict the Future

Understanding relationships questions can be challenging because you're asked to look at how two elements of a passage relate to each other, and each answer choice gives you more and more to think about. The extra reading and time spent considering your options can leave you feeling bogged down. Take some of that weight off and reduce the time it takes to answer these kinds of questions by using the Predict the Future strategy.

❶ Cover the answers.

❷ Read the question and come up with your own answer.

❸ Select the answer that best matches your prediction.

Review question 12 with your teacher. Use the Predict the Future strategy to answer the question as a class.

12

The passage suggests that the comparative use of nuclear power varies among countries because it is

A) more efficient in some regions than in others.

B) predominantly used in Western countries as opposed Eastern countries.

C) cost-prohibitive for some developing countries.

D) less relied upon in countries that offer incentives for renewable energy use.

Strategy

The following questions refer to the passage on page 188. Work on your own using the Predict the Future strategy to answer questions 13 and 14.

13

According to the author of the passage, what do nuclear power and renewable energy have in common?

A) They are too hazardous to be effective ways of generating electricity.

B) They are the most inexpensive methods of generating electricity.

C) They are exciting technologies for scientists to study.

D) They can each be useful and efficient in the right environment.

14

Which statement best expresses a relationship between nuclear power and renewable energy that is presented in the passage?

A) Both are equally sustainable, but they differ significantly in the amount of land they require to produce electricity.

B) Both rely on resources to generate electricity, but nuclear power uses chemicals in addition to large areas of land.

C) Both use resources to generate electricity, but only nuclear power uses a resource that is unsustainable long-term.

D) Both generate a significant amount of waste, but only the radioactive waste produced by nuclear power is dangerous to the planet.

Strategy

Avoiding Trap Answers

Understanding relationships questions ask you to find how two topics, people, groups, or authors relate to one another. On top of that, these kinds of questions look at many different types of relationships, so there are lots of opportunities for you to make mistakes. The SAT will put attractive trap answers into every question in order to cross you up. You can avoid selecting trap answers if you actively watch out for them. Look for the following traps ...

1. Recycled Words

2. Half-Truths

3. Outside Knowledge

Review question 15 with your teacher. Use these tips for avoiding traps to answer the question as a class.

15

Which statement best characterizes the relationship between renewable energy and nuclear power?

A) Renewable energy is safer than nuclear energy, but it generates more waste.

B) Renewable energy is less productive than nuclear power but better for the environment.

C) Renewable energy doesn't require resources to generate electricity, but nuclear power does.

D) Renewable energy came about because of nuclear power's technological advancements.

The following questions refer to the passage on page 188. Work on your own to answer questions 16 and 17.

16

In the passage, the author implies that the burning of coal and oil has what consequence?

A) There will not be enough of these resources to provide electricity long-term.

B) The air and water are more polluted.

C) Less electricity is generated compared to what could be generated using nuclear power.

D) Woodlands are damaged by emissions.

17

Based on the passage, which choice best describes the relationship between the environmental impacts of nuclear power and those of renewable energy systems?

A) Both nuclear power and renewable energy systems negatively impact the environment because of the resources they require.

B) Nuclear power's environmental impact is manageable, but renewable energy's impact is unknown.

C) Nuclear power generates better-quality electricity than renewable energy techniques.

D) With nuclear power, there are risks to the environment if a facility is compromised, whereas renewable energy facilities are relatively risk-free.

This page intentionally left blank

Practice Set 3 | Complete the practice set. When you have finished, double-check your work.

Questions 12–20 are based on the following passage.

This passage is adapted from Walter Bryant, "Shade on Solar Power: Why Renewable Energy May Not Be So Powerful." © 2019 by MasteryPrep.

When it comes to electricity, everyone wants reliability. Providing a stable supply of electricity is a common objective that most political leaders can agree
Line on, though they occasionally disagree on the best way
5 to do it. Efficient electricity generation results in more power using fewer resources, which is beneficial for the energy industry and (in some cases) beneficial to the environment, too. In an increasingly technologically-advanced world, the only sustainable way to continue
10 our quest for reliable energy is to get more with less. Everyone can agree on that.

But turn the discussion to using renewable energy, and the most powerful methods of generating electricity start to look questionable. Nuclear power plants have
15 become incredibly robust and reliable when considering pure electricity generation. Thanks to technological advancements and chemical engineering, a typical nuclear power plant can supply electricity to one million homes a year. Nuclear power plants produce
20 more electricity with fewer resources—about 7.9 billion kilowatt hours per year when running at 90% capacity, for example—which means less oil or coal is burned. And since the demand for electricity is expected to rise 30% by 2030—increasing air and water pollution as
25 well—any method that could reduce the burning of oil or coal while producing more electricity would be in everyone's best interest.

Of course, that's not what environmentalists consider the best option, especially in the long run. They believe
30 renewable energy sources are better for the world—more efficient and safer, too—considering the radioactive waste produced by nuclear power plants. On the other hand, renewable sources—which do not consume material and generate less waste—are thought to be far
35 better long-term. Solar energy, for example, is expected to produce 35% of the United States' electricity by 2050, up from 7% in 2015—and homeowners are investing in solar panels as much for the environment as their budgets.
40 However, a recent study in *Power* did the math and came to a difficult conclusion: renewable energy produces 27% less power on average than nuclear power. Renewable energy requires clear skies or windy days—and that means renewable energy may not be as
45 dependable as we might hope.

Researchers from the University of Michigan conducted a meta-analysis of 55 articles comparing renewable energy and nuclear power across 32 countries, from North America to Asia. They discovered that
50 nuclear power was the primary method of producing electricity in every country, though the results varied. In countries with governmental incentives for solar power, such as the United States or Germany, nuclear power surpassed renewable energy by only 6%. Yet in most
55 other countries, especially Eastern countries—which collectively are the largest consumers of electricity—nuclear power outproduced renewable energy by more than 23%.

The primary difference is what resources are utilized.
60 A basic nuclear power plant uses 27 tons of uranium per year, which produces as much electricity as a solar power plant using 45 to 75 square miles of land. When we talk about energy efficiency, we are actually discussing what resources are consumed—and different resources come
65 with different consequences.

The uranium used in nuclear power burns clean, but it has waste. This radioactive waste isn't disposable, dangerously radiating the environment for tens of thousands of years. We already have quarantined zones
70 all over the planet that store the waste indefinitely, which is not sustainable long-term. Renewable energy uses a lot of land, on the other hand, which can harm the environment in other ways.

What that means is that while nuclear sites generate
75 more power—in most cases, much more power—than renewable energy, there are pros and cons with each. Thus, an ideal worldwide energy system, according to the study's researchers, will draw the best strategies from both methods, as Andrew Felix of the University of
80 Michigan suggested:

The final conclusion? Today's renewable energy systems are best utilized in countries with large areas of unusable land, or where land (in comparison to population) is readily available. But in terms of
85 generating pure electricity, especially in countries that are overcrowded or where available land is sparse, nuclear power has an advantage.

In the future, however, I believe we will need to develop both methods (especially in ways
90 that make nuclear power more sustainable and renewable energy more productive) so that they are both effective—technologically, environmentally, economically, etc.

Practice Set 3

18

According to the narrator, one consequence of using renewable energy to generate electricity is that it

A) is never able to produce enough power.

B) has no impact on the environment.

C) seems unsustainable in the long run.

D) can require a significant amount of land.

19

In describing the relationship between nuclear power and renewable energy, the narrator draws a connection between nuclear power's

A) political consequences and renewable energy's greater production.

B) powerful energy generation and renewable energy's long-term sustainability.

C) impact on technology and renewable energy's popularity around the world.

D) environmental benefits and renewable energy's inaccessibility to consumers.

20

The author indicates that environmentalists prefer renewable energy to nuclear power primarily because

A) they believe renewable energy is better and safer long-term.

B) renewable energy systems outperform nuclear power.

C) nuclear power is polluting the air.

D) renewable energy does not utilize large areas of land.

Mini-Test

Complete the mini-test. When you have finished, double-check your work.

Questions 1–10 are based on the following passage.

This passage is adapted from Caroline Lotte, *The Landlord*, originally published in 1897.

No one likes admitting they may have selected the wrong educational path, and anyone with initial confidence will struggle long against the obstacles in
Line the road before humbling themselves to say "I am lost!"
5 and return to whom they left behind. From my first day at the red house, everything was bothersome. The place itself—a square room with a small closet—was tasteless and cramped enough, but had that been the only thing, I could have long endured it; I am not the inflexible type,
10 and certainly determined to not only prove to myself, but to others, that I had what it takes to graduate from a university, I should have persevered despite the creaking floorboards and the musty stench of my facility; I should not have complained, even internally, that I deserved
15 better living conditions; I should have held in every sigh by which my soul might express its desperation to escape from the lack of privacy, the thin walls, the gaudy decor, and the neglected maintenance of the red house; I should have instead set before myself the discipline
20 of Patience, the practice of Self-Control, and I should have worshipped them like gods on my doorframe, from which my prized, secretly beloved, Hope, for better or for worse, should never, by great or by small, have parted me from them. But this wasn't everything; the abhorrence
25 which shot up between myself and my landlord became deeper and darker by the day, preventing me from enjoying a single minute of the opportunity I had; and I started to feel like a budding tree that got planted in the slick gloom at the bottom of a well.
30 Abhorrence is the only word that accurately describes the way Mr. Mickle felt toward me—a feeling that, in unnatural speed, was propagated by every innocent, regular thing I did or said. My classical music irritated him; my sophisticated vocabulary annoyed him; my
35 cleanliness, cologne, and decency secured his hatred, and provided it an ample supply of loathing seated in jealousy; he hated that I was smarter than him. Had I been in any way lesser than him, he may have not disliked me so completely, but I knew more than he did,
40 and worse yet, he knew that I was too perfectly polite to ever gloat at my acceptance to the revered college. If he could have in some way ridiculed me or proven me arrogant, he might have vented some of his anger away, but I was protected by three things—Dedication,
45 Preparation, and Awareness; and knocking and chatting as was Mr. Mickle's custom; he could never stump the

fox-mind of mine, as craftiness and intelligence were my natural abilities. Day after day his scornful eyes watched for me, hoping to perhaps catch me on my way
50 out, prepared to rip wolf-like into me; but intellect, if disciplined with preparation, is never caught unaware.
I had just received my letter of commendation from the college president, and was returning to my apartment, filled with the satisfaction that the prideful
55 landlord had yet to prove any reason why I didn't belong at the university. (I no longer felt indebted to Mr. Mickle for renting me a room just days before the term began.) He was even worse than my parents; he strove to rise above me almost as much as they did. Doubts, not timid
60 but certain, filled my mind, two voices sounding inside me, repeating the same words. The first: "Jason, you can't live like this for four more years." The other: "Who are you proving yourself to?" I scurried along, because it was freezing on that night in December; as I came to my
65 apartment, my attention shifted from my ponderings to whether the tape I had used to cover the hole in my window had held fast against the weather; and gazing upon it, I saw it flapping in the breeze like a flag hanging by a thread.
70

1

The narrator indicates that Jason is living at the red house because

A) he needed a place to stay while attending college.

B) he wanted a better place to stay.

C) he wanted the freedom of living on his own.

D) his parents were worse than his landlord.

2

Which choice provides the best evidence for the answer to the previous question?

A) Lines 24–29 ("But this ... well")

B) Lines 33–37 ("My classical ... him")

C) Lines 48–51 ("Day after day ... unaware")

D) Lines 56–57 ("I no ... began")

1   1

3

The passage indicates that Mr. Mickle's behavior was mainly caused by his

A) annoyance with the narrator's joyful personality.

B) contempt for the narrator's lowly beginnings.

C) outrage at the narrator's reckless lifestyle.

D) jealousy of the narrator's superior intellect.

4

According to the narrator, one consequence of Jason living at Mr. Mickle's house is that he

A) can't listen to the music he likes.

B) does not take on adult responsibilities.

C) seems less willing to accept help from others.

D) questions his decision to attend the university.

5

According to the narrator, what do Mr. Mickle and Jason's parents have in common?

A) They have unrealistic expectations for Jason.

B) They disagree on suitable living conditions.

C) They don't respect Jason's privacy.

D) They want to appear superior to Jason.

6

Which choice best summarizes the passage?

A) A student struggles with a new living arrangement and questions his decisions.

B) Two people who live in the same house take increasing measures to avoid each other.

C) A young man regrets a choice he made privately but defends it publicly.

D) A new student experiences hope, then annoyance, and finally, depression.

1 ▸ ◂ **1**

7

The references to "budding" and "gloom" at the end of the first paragraph mainly have what effect?

A) They describe the narrator's hopes that were quickly spoiled.

B) They evoke the narrator's growing malicious intent.

C) They reflect the narrator's increasing fear of isolation.

D) They reveal the narrator's love for growing things.

8

In describing the relationship between Mr. Mickle and Jason, the narrator draws a connection between Mr. Mickle's

A) boring conversations and Jason's dull music.

B) constant watching and Jason's vigilant preparedness.

C) unpleasant home and Jason's impossible standards of living.

D) unwelcome attention and Jason's negative outlook on his future.

9

The narrator indicates that Jason has put tape on his apartment window because

A) the window has a hole in it.

B) he used it as a reminder to persevere.

C) he was trying to annoy his landlord.

D) the landlord had refused to fix it.

10

At the end of the second paragraph, the comparisons of abstract qualities between a fox and a wolf mainly have the effect of

A) contrasting two theoretical choices to make.

B) depicting the precariousness of a decision.

C) predicting the chances of a confrontation.

D) illustrating the nature of a rival relationship.

STOP

**If you finish before time is called, you may check your work on this section only.
Do not turn to any other section.**

This page intentionally left blank

Wrap-Up

Complete the wrap-up. When you have finished, double-check your work.

Questions 4–6 are based on the following passage.

This passage is adapted from Henry Frank, *George Digory*. George had been an infamous miser when his wealth was suddenly stolen away. He later adopted a poor woman's daughter, Becca, who had lost everything herself.

But unlike money—which was locked away from the sunlight, was oblivious to the sounds of nature, and didn't react to people's voices—Becca was a living being
Line of boundless desires and increasing interests, searching
5 for and enjoying the sunlight and world around her. The money had trapped his mind in a never-ending cycle, going nowhere beyond itself; but Becca was a thing filled with novelty and optimism that pushed his mind forward, propelling it beyond its old endless, fervent
10 striving. She called him away from his work and re-awakened him to life's simple joys.

And in the summer, when the daisies were dense in the fields, George might be found in the bright afternoon, or at dusk when the shadows grew longer
15 under the shrubbery, ambling out with bare feet to bring Becca to where the flowers blossomed, so he could relax as Becca waddled to pick them; she spoke to the flying things that buzzed happily around them, constantly calling "Daddy's" attention and giving him
20 flowers. Then she would turn her head to the song of a bird, and George discovered he could make her happy by motioning to remain quiet, so that when the next call sounded, she would jump up and her laughter would bubble in triumph. Sitting like this, George would
25 sometimes start remembering his past, but he would shyly push the encroaching memories aside, taking shelter in Becca's simple life, which weighed nothing on his fatigued soul.

As Becca's mind developed, George's own
30 consciousness grew: his spirit, long-dazed and trapped in a dark tunnel, was quivering slowly into complete awareness.

Her influence on George became greater with each passing year. As Becca grew, her words became more
35 sophisticated and required articulate responses; objects and noises became more distinct to Becca's eyes and ears, and there was more that "Daddy" had to acknowledge and respond to as well. By the time Becca turned four years old, she had established an acute ability for trouble
40 and mischief, which put to practice not only George's endurance, but his attentiveness and scrutiny. It was at times such as these, especially, that George struggled to understand how discipline and love could coexist.

4

The passage indicates that Becca's change in behavior is mainly caused by her

A) frustration with George's lack of attention.

B) sorrow over the loss of her mother.

C) desire to spend more time with George outside.

D) growth in language, awareness, and needs.

5

According to the narrator, one result of George adopting Becca is that he

A) struggles to forget the past.

B) better understands his own mortality.

C) seems more willing to help others around him.

D) wrestles with combining love and discipline.

6

Based on the passage, which choice best describes the relationship between George's interactions with Becca when he first adopts her and his interactions with Becca as she grows older?

A) In both cases, George is fully engaged and attentive to Becca's growing needs.

B) George could not properly care for Becca when he first adopted her, and he struggles to handle her now that she is older.

C) George cared for Becca when he first adopted her, but as she grows older, he relies on her for help.

D) George was surprised by Becca's behavior when he first adopted her, but he accepts her behavior now that she is older.

This page intentionally left blank

Review

Entrance

Understanding relationships questions can be identified by these features:

- a question asking you to relate two things to each other

Evidence and Elimination

To answer an understanding relationships question, follow these steps:

1. Identify the relationship in the question.
2. Use the type of relationship to help find evidence in the passage.
3. Eliminate choices that don't accurately describe the relationship.

Exit

If you've found the answer ...

Verify that it is supported with textual evidence. If so, mark your answer and continue to the next question.

If you're stuck between two choices ...

Talk yourself through why each answer choice might be right. Select the answer that needs the least explanation.

If you have no idea what the answer is ...

Go with your gut. Select the answer choice that best matches the main idea of the passage.

7
Chapter

Word Choice

LEARNING TARGETS

1. Determine which meaning of a word is most appropriate based on context clues.

2. Implement the basic approach for word choice questions.

3. Apply the *Half and Half* and *Match the Emotion* strategies to word choice questions.

Warm-Up

Complete the warm-up. When you have finished, double-check your work.

Questions 1–3 are based on the following passage.

This passage is adapted from Frederick Douglass, "On the Occasion of the Unveiling of the Freedman's Monument." Originally delivered in 1876.

Fellow citizens, shall we say that in what we have said and done today, and in what we may say and do hereafter, we do disclaim everything like arrogance
Line and assumption, and shall we say we have superior
5 devotion to history? Men generally, at such a time of firsts as this, think that they fully comprehend the relation of Abraham Lincoln both to ourselves and to the white people of the United States. They think that, when speaking of a great public man, the truth is proper
10 and beautiful. But it must be admitted that Abraham Lincoln was not either our man or our model. It must be admitted. Why not acknowledge that in his associations, and in his prejudices, he was a white man? Why not state he was preeminently the white man's President? Why not
15 reckon that he was entirely devoted to the welfare of the white man? …
Though he loved Caesar less than Rome, though the Union was more to him than our freedom, be thankful, be thankful; gradually we saw ourselves lifted from the
20 depths of slavery—under his wise and beneficent rule. When he tarried long in the mountain, or told us we were the cause of war, our faith in him was taxed and strained to the uttermost; we are at best only his step-children, children by adoption, children by force of
25 circumstances (for we were brought to this Golden Land against our will). Yet I say, let us multiply his statues. For while Abraham Lincoln saved for you a country, he delivered us from a bondage that was such an unsavory remnant of the past.
30 Whatever else in this world may be partial, unjust, and uncertain, time is impartial, just, and certain. The honest statesman endeavors to do his duty. He had many affairs to attend to. He was assailed by Abolitionists, slaveholders, and men who were for peace at any price.
35 A man cannot do everything, but must do something; and the judgement of the present hour—this anniversary of the end of the Civil War—is that there was hardly any man better fitted for his mission than Abraham Lincoln.
We have done a good work for our race today. In
40 doing honor to the memory of our friend and liberator, we have been doing highest honors to ourselves and those who come after us. When now it shall be said that the colored man is soulless, that he has no appreciation of benefits or benefactors, we may calmly point to the
45 monument we have erected to the memory of Abraham Lincoln.

1

In the first paragraph (lines 1–16), the description of Abraham Lincoln mainly serves to

A) reveal Frederick Douglass's adoration of his subject.

B) show how Lincoln served as a role model to the American people.

C) underscore that Lincoln was part of the white race.

D) introduce the evolution of presidential history.

2

The author uses the phrase "tarried long in the mountain" in line 21 most likely to

A) describe how long it took for Lincoln to travel across the country.

B) show that mountain climbing can be difficult.

C) describe how Caesar acted to cause the fall of Rome.

D) suggest that Lincoln didn't act as quickly as he could have to free the slaves.

3

The most likely purpose of the parenthetical information in lines 25–26 is to

A) explain a biological concept.

B) define a technical term.

C) describe a new hypothesis.

D) support a claim.

Foundation

Work with a partner to complete the table by listing the words from the word bank under the correct category.

Support	Demonstrate	Imply	Emphasize	Explain	Critique
advance	show		highlight		

Word Bank				
acknowledge	counter	~~highlight~~	popularize	~~show~~
~~advance~~	criticize	hint	provide	stress
clarify	depict	indicate	raise doubts	substantiate
condemn	describe	introduce	recount	suggest
confirm	evoke	illustrate	refute	underline
contrast	establish	identify	reinforce	underscore
convey	express	list	reveal	

Foundation

Work with your teacher to evaluate the topic sentence of a paragraph and determine the purpose of sentence 1. Use the answer choice bank to fill in the blank.

I've decided that I want to be a Japanese train pusher when I grow up.

Emphasize	Define	Clarify	Anticipate and Correct

1. *The official name of the Japanese train pusher is "oshiya," and their job is to smush people onto subway trains so that as many people as possible fit in each train car.*

   Purpose:_____

Work on your own to determine the purpose of sentences 2–4 that make up the rest of the paragraph below. Use the answer choice bank to fill in the blanks.

2. *They stand on the train platform and push from the outside, making sure that the doors are still able to close once everyone is on.*

   Purpose:_____

3. *It might sound like a weird job, but think about how great it would be to get revenge on all those rude commuters who are already shoving everyone else.*

   Purpose:_____

4. *I just can't imagine anything more fun!*

   Purpose:_____

Foundation

With your teacher, read the following sentences, and write the letter of the matching reason in the space provided.

5. _____ A. The morning was full of brightness and possibility.

    _____ B. It was morning.

    _____ C. It was a gloomy morning, and dark clouds began forming in the sky.

D. to create a neutral setting

E. to create an ominous setting

F. to increase a sense of excitement

Read the following sentences. Write the letter of the matching reason in the space provided.

6. _____ A. The boy lazily and half-heartedly completed his SAT homework.

    _____ B. The boy finished his SAT homework.

    _____ C. The boy completed his SAT homework with eagerness and enthusiasm.

D. to describe a character behaving in a neutral manner

E. to describe someone who is diligent

F. to describe someone who is inactive

7. _____ A. The abandoned building reeked of death and despair.

    _____ B. The building was located in a residential neighborhood.

    _____ C. The building, recently upgraded with the latest renovations, was a spectacular sight to see.

D. to create a sense of admiration

E. to create a sense of fear

F. to describe a neutral setting

Key Terms

Connotation: an idea or feeling associated with a word in addition to its literal or primary meaning.

Practice Set 1 | Complete the practice set. When you have finished, double-check your work.

Questions 1–11 are based on the following passage.

This passage is from Jessie Hill, *The Science of Questions*. © 2020 by MasteryPrep. The narrator, a scientist, recalls her most vivid childhood memories.

From an early age, I was fascinated with observing the world around me. As I child, I had learned to carry a small notebook with me everywhere. Although
Line others thought it was strange that I carefully recorded
5 innocuous details like the temperature, humidity, and cloud cover, the natural world and its countless possibilities drew me in; I found in every detail a microcosm, a miniature world whose meaning resonated throughout the universe, sparking a million questions
10 that distracted me even when my home life made asking such questions difficult. My parents were very skeptical of science. There was something about my experiments—and the relentless note-taking—that annoyed them. They used to tell me that when I grew
15 up, I was going to have to give up this bizarre habit and get a real job. I felt I had to hide my experiments in the basement and check on them when my parents were out. One day, they came back early and found me doing water quality tests in the backyard and became very
20 upset. They took away my test tubes and locked up my notebooks.

"You need to find yourself a normal hobby, like a sport, kid."

My parents were somewhat stiff-necked but,
25 regardless of their skepticism, provided me with whatever educational opportunities I asked for. They were convinced I was going to become a doctor, or a lawyer, or take on some other kind of illustrious, well-paid profession, but I had no intention of following
30 along that path; I knew what I wanted to do.

I spent every spare moment I could at the teeny Strotham Natural History Museum on Broad Street. Every corner of the old building was stacked with strange specimens, their dusty, handwritten labels
35 peeling off, browned on the edges like wilting flower petals. The docent often let me in by the side door and allowed me to wander the corridors unsupervised. When it was slow, she would guide me around the place and explain to me why various specimens were important.
40 Everything had meaning—even the microscopic specimens (those that were too small to be seen with the naked eye). When the closing bell rang, I reluctantly packed up my observation notebooks and headed home, my head buzzing with questions. Each day, I fervently
45 wished the closing bell would break and the museum

would stay open all night.

One afternoon, Ms. Strotham greeted me at the door with a small grey rock, about the size of an egg, in her hand. It was worn smooth on three sides, but the rough
50 side glinted promisingly.

"There's no label on it," I said, turning the rock over in my palm.

Upon closer inspection, the rock wasn't only grey but also had specks of pink and black. Ms. Strotham raised
55 her eyebrows, watching me observe the specimen closely. Why did it appear to be hard on one side and easily scratched on the other? Why did it seem to be made up of layers of rocks of different colors and consistencies?

"Is it a rare gem?"
60 "A rare gem? Yes, very. You will have to find out just how rare it is yourself."

When the closing bell rang, I slipped the rock Ms. Strotham gave me into my coat pocket so my parents wouldn't see me coming home with it, and my mind
65 began racing with questions. Over spring break, I turned the rock over and over in my hands, imagining every possible experiment I could do with the presumably magical stone. After a few weeks, I still wasn't sure what the rock was made of, but I knew just what kind of scientist I was going to be.

1

The main purpose of the opening sentence of the passage is to

A) clarify the narrator's perspective on an argument.

B) provide background information useful in understanding the narrator's character.

C) describe the central conflict of the narrator.

D) contrast the narrator's childhood interests with her adult interests.

2

The sentence in lines 3–11 ("Although ... difficult") mainly serves to

A) disclose a secret about the narrator's past.

B) emphasize that the narrator is a logical and rational scientist.

C) show that the narrator finds herself drawn to natural science.

D) underscore the narrator's technical knowledge of science.

3

The main purpose of lines 11–21 ("My parents ... notebooks") is to

A) describe the narrator's passions before she met Ms. Strotham.

B) characterize the important people in the narrator's story.

C) include more information about the challenges in the narrator's childhood.

D) introduce the narrator's science experiments.

SAT Mastery

Approach

Entrance

Word choice questions can be identified by these features:

- answer choices starting with verbs
- a question asking you about a word or short phrase in the passage

... and by these terms:

- purpose
- effect
- function
- serves to
- uses the word/phrase

The following questions refer to the passage on page 208. Review question 4 with your teacher. Circle the part of the question that identifies it as a word choice question. Do not answer the question.

Entrance Evidence and Elimination Exit

4

The main purpose of the analogy of the flower petals (lines 35–36) is to

A) clarify a scientific theory.

B) analyze a specific finding.

C) critique the museum collection.

D) describe the appearance of the specimens.

Approach

Review questions 5 and 6 on your own. Circle the parts of the questions that identify them as word choice questions. Do not answer the questions.

5

Hill repeatedly uses the word "they" in the first paragraph mainly to

A) underscore the consistent helpfulness of her parents.

B) reflect the sense of anger from her parents.

C) create a distance between herself and her parents.

D) emphasize the need for respect from her parents.

6

The author uses the phrase "stiff-necked" (line 24) most likely to

A) describe the physical ailments of the narrator's parents.

B) highlight the narrator's parents' advanced ages.

C) clarify the ideas that the narrator's parents have about hobbies.

D) emphasize the rigid point of view of the narrator's parents towards the narrator.

Approach

Questions 1–11 are based on the following passage.

This passage is from Jessie Hill, *The Science of Questions*. © 2020 by MasteryPrep. The narrator, a scientist, recalls her most vivid childhood memories.

From an early age, I was fascinated with observing the world around me. As I child, I had learned to carry a small notebook with me everywhere. Although
Line others thought it was strange that I carefully recorded
5 innocuous details like the temperature, humidity, and cloud cover, the natural world and its countless possibilities drew me in; I found in every detail a microcosm, a miniature world whose meaning resonated throughout the universe, sparking a million questions
10 that distracted me even when my home life made asking such questions difficult. My parents were very skeptical of science. There was something about my experiments—and the relentless note-taking—that annoyed them. They used to tell me that when I grew
15 up, I was going to have to give up this bizarre habit and get a real job. I felt I had to hide my experiments in the basement and check on them when my parents were out. One day, they came back early and found me doing water quality tests in the backyard and became very
20 upset. They took away my test tubes and locked up my notebooks.

"You need to find yourself a normal hobby, like a sport, kid."

My parents were somewhat stiff-necked but,
25 regardless of their skepticism, provided me with whatever educational opportunities I asked for. They were convinced I was going to become a doctor, or a lawyer, or take on some other kind of illustrious, well-paid profession, but I had no intention of following
30 along that path; I knew what I wanted to do.

I spent every spare moment I could at the teeny Strotham Natural History Museum on Broad Street. Every corner of the old building was stacked with strange specimens, their dusty, handwritten labels
35 peeling off, browned on the edges like wilting flower petals. The docent often let me in by the side door and allowed me to wander the corridors unsupervised. When it was slow, she would guide me around the place and explain to me why various specimens were important.
40 Everything had meaning—even the microscopic specimens (those that were too small to be seen with the naked eye). When the closing bell rang, I reluctantly packed up my observation notebooks and headed home, my head buzzing with questions. Each day, I fervently
45 wished the closing bell would break and the museum would stay open all night.

One afternoon, Ms. Strotham greeted me at the door with a small grey rock, about the size of an egg, in her hand. It was worn smooth on three sides, but the rough
50 side glinted promisingly.

"There's no label on it," I said, turning the rock over in my palm.

Upon closer inspection, the rock wasn't only grey but also had specks of pink and black. Ms. Strotham raised
55 her eyebrows, watching me observe the specimen closely. Why did it appear to be hard on one side and easily scratched on the other? Why did it seem to be made up of layers of rocks of different colors and consistencies?

"Is it a rare gem?"
60 "A rare gem? Yes, very. You will have to find out just how rare it is yourself."

When the closing bell rang, I slipped the rock Ms. Strotham gave me into my coat pocket so my parents wouldn't see me coming home with it, and my mind
65 began racing with questions. Over spring break, I turned the rock over and over in my hands, imagining every possible experiment I could do with the presumably magical stone. After a few weeks, I still wasn't sure what the rock was made of, but I knew just what kind of scientist I was going to be.

Word Choice

Approach

Evidence and Elimination

To answer a word choice question, follow these steps:

❶ Identify the verbs in the answer choices.

❷ Re-read the identified portion of the text.

❸ Use the selected text to eliminate irrelevant answers.

❹ Use the context to eliminate answers that don't capture the author's why.

Answer question 4 with your teacher.

Entrance ▸ Evidence and Elimination ▸ Exit

4

The main purpose of the analogy of the flower petals (lines 35–36) is to

A) clarify a scientific theory.

B) analyze a specific finding.

C) critique the museum collection.

D) describe the appearance of the specimens.

The following questions refer to the passage on page 212. Answer questions 5 and 6 on your own. Focus on eliminating incorrect answers.

5

Hill repeatedly uses the word "they" in the first paragraph mainly to

A) underscore the consistent helpfulness of her parents.

B) reflect the sense of anger between her parents.

C) create a distance between herself and her parents.

D) emphasize the need for respect from her parents.

6

The author uses the phrase "stiff-necked" (line 24) most likely to

A) describe the physical ailments of the narrator's parents.

B) highlight the narrator's parents' advanced ages.

C) clarify the ideas that the narrator's parents have about hobbies.

D) emphasize the rigid point of view of the narrator's parents towards the narrator.

Approach

Exit

If you've found the answer ...

Check the passage for evidence and confirm that it supports your answer. Mark your answer and continue to the next question.

If you're stuck between two choices ...

Channel your inner lawyer and use logic to eliminate an incorrect answer.

If you have no idea what the answer is ...

Go with your gut. Select the choice that makes the most sense and that best aligns with what the entire passage is about.

Review questions 7 and 8. Work with your teacher to choose the correct answer from the remaining choices.

Entrance ⟩ Evidence and Elimination ⟩ **Exit**

7

It can reasonably be inferred that the phrase "a normal hobby" (line 22) was generally intended to

A) ~~identify the narrator as a skilled person.~~

B) ~~support the narrator's interest in science.~~

C) criticize the narrator's lack of participation in sports.

D) scrutinize the narrator's desire to do something unusual.

8

The most likely purpose of the parenthetical information in lines 41–42 is to

A) ~~analyze a claim.~~

B) describe a scientific discovery.

C) ~~illustrate a procedure.~~

D) clarify a term.

Practice Set 2

Complete the practice set. When you have finished, double-check your work.

Questions 1–11 are based on the following passage.

This passage is from Jessie Hill, *The Science of Questions*. © 2020 by MasteryPrep. The narrator, a scientist, recalls her most vivid childhood memories.

From an early age, I was fascinated with observing the world around me. As I child, I had learned to carry a small notebook with me everywhere. Although
Line others thought it was strange that I carefully recorded
5 innocuous details like the temperature, humidity, and cloud cover, the natural world and its countless possibilities drew me in; I found in every detail a microcosm, a miniature world whose meaning resonated throughout the universe, sparking a million questions
10 that distracted me even when my home life made asking such questions difficult. My parents were very skeptical of science. There was something about my experiments—and the relentless note-taking—that annoyed them. They used to tell me that when I grew
15 up, I was going to have to give up this bizarre habit and get a real job. I felt I had to hide my experiments in the basement and check on them when my parents were out. One day, they came back early and found me doing water quality tests in the backyard and became very
20 upset. They took away my test tubes and locked up my notebooks.

"You need to find yourself a normal hobby, like a sport, kid."

My parents were somewhat stiff-necked but,
25 regardless of their skepticism, provided me with whatever educational opportunities I asked for. They were convinced I was going to become a doctor, or a lawyer, or take on some other kind of illustrious, well-paid profession, but I had no intention of following
30 along that path; I knew what I wanted to do.

I spent every spare moment I could at the teeny Strotham Natural History Museum on Broad Street. Every corner of the old building was stacked with strange specimens, their dusty, handwritten labels
35 peeling off, browned on the edges like wilting flower petals. The docent often let me in by the side door and allowed me to wander the corridors unsupervised. When it was slow, she would guide me around the place and explain to me why various specimens were important.
40 Everything had meaning—even the microscopic specimens (those that were too small to be seen with the naked eye). When the closing bell rang, I reluctantly packed up my observation notebooks and headed home, my head buzzing with questions. Each day, I fervently
45 wished the closing bell would break and the museum would stay open all night.

One afternoon, Ms. Strotham greeted me at the door with a small grey rock, about the size of an egg, in her hand. It was worn smooth on three sides, but the rough
50 side glinted promisingly.

"There's no label on it," I said, turning the rock over in my palm.

Upon closer inspection, the rock wasn't only grey but also had specks of pink and black. Ms. Strotham raised
55 her eyebrows, watching me observe the specimen closely. Why did it appear to be hard on one side and easily scratched on the other? Why did it seem to be made up of layers of rocks of different colors and consistencies?

"Is it a rare gem?"
60 "A rare gem? Yes, very. You will have to find out just how rare it is yourself."

When the closing bell rang, I slipped the rock Ms. Strotham gave me into my coat pocket so my parents wouldn't see me coming home with it, and my mind
65 began racing with questions. Over spring break, I turned the rock over and over in my hands, imagining every possible experiment I could do with the presumably magical stone. After a few weeks, I still wasn't sure what the rock was made of, but I knew just what kind of scientist I was going to be.

9

The questions in lines 56–58 primarily serve to

A) create doubt about the narrator's knowledge of natural science.

B) identify and highlight the curiosities and queries of the narrator when observing the rock.

C) suggest that the narrator's questions about the rock differ from Ms. Strotham's.

D) elaborate on and underscore the relationship between the narrator's interest in natural science and Ms. Strotham.

10

The sentence in lines 26–30 ("They were … do") primarily serves which function in the passage?

A) It raises and refutes objections to the parents' perspective.

B) It identifies and concedes the parents' shortcomings.

C) It acknowledges and substantiates the parents' point of view.

D) It anticipates and counters the parents' expectations.

11

The word "rare" is used three times in lines 59–61 to

A) reinforce the value of the collections in the museum.

B) highlight the characters' combative relationship.

C) emphasize the potential significance of the gem.

D) suggest that the narrator was being greedy.

Strategy

Questions 12–20 are based on the following passage.

This passage is adapted from Victoria Williams, *Coming to My Senses: A Botanist's Love Affair with Plants.* ©2016 by MasteryPrep.

Arguably, the most infamous carnivore in horticulture is the Venus flytrap [*Dionaea muscipula*], which snaps its leaves shut to trap insects for food. There
Line are, however, over 470 plant species, generally referred
5 to as carnivorous plants, that use ingenious techniques such as this to obtain food. To compensate for poor soil quality and limited nutrients, these plants have had to devise elaborate mechanisms to attract, capture, kill, and digest other forms of food.

10 Some carnivorous plants, like sundews, produce a gluey substance that sticks to the legs of visiting insects until they can no longer move. Others have leaves with bladders that swallow animals whole through trap doors. Still others, so-called "pitcher plants," seduce
15 insects to the rim of their "pitcher," which leads to a pit with slippery walls and downward-pointing hairs that make it impossible for the insect to escape. One of the most sophisticated of these plants is the cobra lily, whose upside-down pitcher and forked leaves resemble
20 a rearing cobra about to attack. Its leaves' translucent patches confuse the prey trapped inside with the false hope of an escape. Only after repeated attempts to break free will the insect typically tire out and fall down into the cobra lily's digestive pit. But how do these plants
25 digest and convert the energy from the captured insects? And why did carnivorous plants evolve this way?

These unusual plant adaptations have fascinated scientists since carnivory was notably described in botanical literature by Charles Darwin in 1875. By 2014,
30 Victoria Albert at the University of Buffalo in New York determined that these mechanisms are the result of a natural process whereby some plants develop the ability to adapt to otherwise stressful environments. "We're really looking at a classic case of convergent evolution,"
35 affirms the plant genome scientist. "This is a process whereby unrelated species independently develop similar traits." Convergent evolution results in plants with structures that were not present in their ancestors. The cobra lily is a key example of a plant that has evolved
40 a set of adaptations—including carnivory—in order to survive.

Scientists have found that the cobra lily relies mostly on symbiotic bacteria to break down (digest) animal proteins into simpler compounds. This process
45 supports an entire ecology that helps the plant survive, store energy, and adapt to extreme events such as

flooding. We see these symbiotic relationships across all biological systems. Ecologists use their findings about the mutualism between predatory plants and bacteria
50 to further investigate how these processes may work in other organisms. In humans, for example, veritable colonies of bacteria and protozoa exist in our gut to aid in digestion and metabolism.

Past research confirms this theory. In 1997,
55 researchers discovered a quick-and-dirty method for investigating digestive enzymes. It is possible to test for proteases (enzymes that catalyze the breakdown of proteins into smaller components) by using photographic film. When the film is placed in the pitcher
60 or base of the plant, the proteases dissolve the gelatin on the film. When the film is developed, the images reveal clear spots where the protease "digested" the gelatin. Other evidence of these proteases can be found in subtle chemical tests of potentially carnivorous plants; however,
65 these methods are limited as the levels of conventional mammalian proteases are low and difficult to measure. It is possible that each carnivorous plant develops its own digestive protease—as unique as a fingerprint— depending on the pH level and temperature in their
70 native environments. There are likely other mechanisms by which carnivorous plants absorb nutrients from their prey. Preliminary studies suggest that these plants may use their root systems and cell structures to absorb nutrients such as phosphatase through water intake.

Strategy

Half and Half
The Half and Half strategy is a great option to use when you can't figure out what the function of a word, phrase, or sentence is within the passage. ❶ Separate the verb from the rest of the sentence. ❷ Eliminate choices that are half-wrong.

Review question 12 with your teacher. Use the Half and Half strategy to answer the question as a class.

12

The author uses the phrase "devise elaborate mechanisms" in line 8 most likely to

A) explain how the construction of technical inventions help Venus flytraps.

B) show that Venus flytraps have similarities to humans.

C) describe the cultivation of Venus flytraps in colonies.

D) suggest that carnivorous plants develop unique adaptations in order to survive.

The following questions refer to the passage on page 218. Work on your own using the Half and Half strategy to answer questions 13 and 14.

The following questions refer to the passage on page 218.

13

The questions in lines 24–26 primarily serve to

A) describe the physical modifications that increase the savagery of carnivorous plants.

B) introduce the biology behind the adaptive features of plant carnivory.

C) imply that trap mechanisms may lack a physiological purpose.

D) emphasize the environmental factors that make the plants interesting.

14

The sentence in lines 48–51 ("Ecologists ... organisms") mainly serves to

A) emphasize that scientists are not interested in the sensational descriptions of plant carnivory.

B) demonstrate the importance of the ecological concept of mutualism.

C) show that the symbiosis between plant species and bacteria has relevance to other life forms.

D) convey that plants are an important part of human digestion and metabolism.

Strategy

Match the Emotion
When you feel yourself struggling to choose an answer for word choice questions that include comparison, analogy, or figurative language, aim to match the emotion of the answer to the passage.   ❶ Underline words that indicate a positive, negative, or neutral emotion in the passage and answer choices.   ❷ Select the answer choice that best matches the emotion in the passage.

Review question 15 with your teacher. Use the Match the Emotion strategy to answer the question as a class.

15

At the end of the fourth paragraph, the discussion of human digestion mainly has the effect of

A) supporting the idea that symbiosis between organisms occurs in other life forms.

B) conveying the complicated nature of ecosystems.

C) suggesting that humans are related to mere plants.

D) calling into question the concept of mutualism.

The following questions refer to the passage on page 218. Work on your own using the Match the Emotion strategy to answer questions 16 and 17.

16

The author uses the phrase "quick-and-dirty" (line 55) most likely to

A) emphasize that the test is likely to be messy to complete.

B) highlight the fact that researchers often work quickly to test chemicals.

C) underscore the scientific importance of new methods of testing.

D) reinforce the idea that the test is imperfect but simple.

17

The author uses the comparison to a fingerprint (line 68) most likely to

A) suggest that carnivorous plants are similar to humans.

B) illuminate a side of carnivorous plants that scientists were unaware of.

C) reinforce the idea that the carnivorous plants' effectiveness stems from its deceptive design.

D) emphasize the distinct characteristics of carnivorous plants' digestive enzymes.

222   Warm-Up >   Foundation >   Approach >   **Strategy** >   Mini-Test >   Wrap-Up >   Review

This page intentionally left blank

Questions 12–20 are based on the following passage.

This passage is adapted from Victoria Williams, *Coming to My Senses: A Botanist's Love Affair with Plants.* ©2016 by MasteryPrep.

Arguably, the most infamous carnivore in horticulture is the Venus flytrap [*Dionaea muscipula*], which snaps its leaves shut to trap insects for food. There
Line are, however, over 470 plant species, generally referred
5 to as carnivorous plants, that use ingenious techniques such as this to obtain food. To compensate for poor soil quality and limited nutrients, these plants have had to devise elaborate mechanisms to attract, capture, kill, and digest other forms of food.
10 Some carnivorous plants, like sundews, produce a gluey substance that sticks to the legs of visiting insects until they can no longer move. Others have leaves with bladders that swallow animals whole through trap doors. Still others, so-called "pitcher plants," seduce
15 insects to the rim of their "pitcher," which leads to a pit with slippery walls and downward-pointing hairs that make it impossible for the insect to escape. One of the most sophisticated of these plants is the cobra lily, whose upside-down pitcher and forked leaves resemble
20 a rearing cobra about to attack. Its leaves' translucent patches confuse the prey trapped inside with the false hope of an escape. Only after repeated attempts to break free will the insect typically tire out and fall down into the cobra lily's digestive pit. But how do these plants
25 digest and convert the energy from the captured insects? And why did carnivorous plants evolve this way?
These unusual plant adaptations have fascinated scientists since carnivory was notably described in botanical literature by Charles Darwin in 1875. By 2014,
30 Victoria Albert at the University of Buffalo in New York determined that these mechanisms are the result of a natural process whereby some plants develop the ability to adapt to otherwise stressful environments. "We're really looking at a classic case of convergent evolution,"
35 affirms the plant genome scientist. "This is a process whereby unrelated species independently develop similar traits." Convergent evolution results in plants with structures that were not present in their ancestors. The cobra lily is a key example of a plant that has evolved
40 a set of adaptations—including carnivory—in order to survive.
Scientists have found that the cobra lily relies mostly on symbiotic bacteria to break down (digest) animal proteins into simpler compounds. This process
45 supports an entire ecology that helps the plant survive, store energy, and adapt to extreme events such as

flooding. We see these symbiotic relationships across all biological systems. Ecologists use their findings about the mutualism between predatory plants and bacteria
50 to further investigate how these processes may work in other organisms. In humans, for example, veritable colonies of bacteria and protozoa exist in our gut to aid in digestion and metabolism.
Past research confirms this theory. In 1997,
55 researchers discovered a quick-and-dirty method for investigating digestive enzymes. It is possible to test for proteases (enzymes that catalyze the breakdown of proteins into smaller components) by using photographic film. When the film is placed in the pitcher
60 or base of the plant, the proteases dissolve the gelatin on the film. When the film is developed, the images reveal clear spots where the protease "digested" the gelatin. Other evidence of these proteases can be found in subtle chemical tests of potentially carnivorous plants; however,
65 these methods are limited as the levels of conventional mammalian proteases are low and difficult to measure. It is possible that each carnivorous plant develops its own digestive protease—as unique as a fingerprint— depending on the pH level and temperature in their
70 native environments. There are likely other mechanisms by which carnivorous plants absorb nutrients from their prey. Preliminary studies suggest that these plants may use their root systems and cell structures to absorb nutrients such as phosphatase through water intake.
75

18

The sentence in lines 39–41 ("The cobra ... survive"), mainly serves to

A) highlight the pitcher's lack of dependence on water.

B) illustrate the ecological principle of convergent evolution.

C) give an example of innovative methods of plant survival.

D) illustrate how the cobra lily's roots absorb nutrients.

19

The author uses the phrase "false hope" in lines 21–22 most likely to

A) demonstrate the emotion necessary to grow carnivorous plants.

B) highlight the fact that insects are like humans.

C) emphasize that prey cannot easily escape carnivorous plants once captured.

D) contrast the apparent violence of carnivorous plants with their biological function.

20

The author uses the image of a cobra (lines 17–20) most likely to

A) reveal the sophisticated nature of the pitcher plant.

B) illustrate the symbiotic relationship between plants and animals.

C) explain the origin of the plant's alternate name.

D) examine the sophistication of the trap mechanism.

Mini-Test | Complete the mini-test. When you have finished, double-check your work.

Questions 11–21 are based on the following passage.

This passage is adapted from Aruna Mumble and Sadie Mueller, "Dropping the Ball: College Preparedness and Athletic Spending" from *International Journal of Education*. ©2019 MasteryPrep.

Even for children, participation in extracurricular sports—from little league to competitive travel teams—can be overwhelming and hectic. While some children
Line spend their free time on other pursuits, over three
5 million students spend most of their weekends on a court or field. Many of these students are involved in a variety of competitive athletic endeavors, including playing on school teams, in community leagues, and with the YMCA. Many children thrive in these high-
10 pressure circles because their shared goals and rivalries help to strengthen bonds among classmates and teammates. Conversely, some shudder at the thought of joining a team sport; they worry that they will be mocked instead of celebrated and that their efforts
15 will result in failure rather than victory. This dizzying array of extracurriculars can benefit young people and bolster local communities. However, it can also exclude large numbers of students and siphon valuable financial resources away from schools.
20 Coaches describe sports participation as a positive experience that serves various social, educational, and psychological functions. Some educators, on the other hand, are less impressed with the impact of team sports on academics. According to Downey (2016), many
25 schools seem to care more about their superior athletic teams than about well-educated students. In fact, some schools are so motivated to compete with neighboring schools that they spend more money on building sports complexes than they do on curriculum or teacher
30 salaries (a phenomenon known as "the stadium arms race"). For example, a high school in Missouri spent over 30 million dollars to build a new stadium but invests only five million dollars a year on teacher salaries. Do school districts care more about winning athletic
35 trophies than supporting their faculty? Some high school teachers seem to think so.

What many classroom educators do not understand is that though administrators recognize the costs associated with organized sports, they continue to
40 spend huge amounts of money on athletics, especially when their rivals do so. Sociologists propose a potential explanation for this behavior: many school administrators believe that the more they spend on school athletics, the more successful their students will

45 be. Although this perceived correlation might seem reasonable to administrators, research has shown that it is unfounded. In fact, the opposite appears to be true. Summative testing—assessments performed at the completion of four years of high school—show that
50 students are less prepared to succeed in college when their high school spends a disproportionate amount of money on athletics compared to academics.

Why do some school administrators continue to insist that organized sports are integral to the high
55 school experience? According to Ripley (2013), the prevailing view is that high school sports give students a sense of belonging, as well as a connection to their school. This may help explain why many school administrators feel obligated to prioritize student
60 athletics; they believe that the resulting "school spirit" retains and motivates adolescents. As for the students—especially those who do not participate in these vaunted programs—the fiscal investment in high school sports is like spending precious resources on fool's gold. In the
65 end, is it worth it?

This cognitive disconnect between administrators and students is confusing because both parties exist in the same environment; further, school officials were once students themselves. In sociological terms, some
70 adults working in schools fail to take into account their own experiences with high school sports, both positive and negative, and instead make decisions based on the prevailing culture of school athletics. It's time for school districts to take a step back and examine the key
75 factors, both educational and extracurricular, that lead to student engagement and success beyond high school.

1   1

Administrators' Perceived and Students' Actual College Preparedness

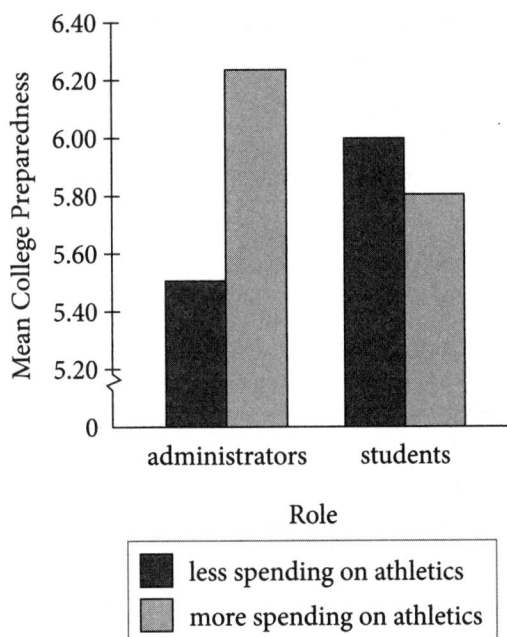

11

The main purpose of the first paragraph ("Even for … schools") is to

A) introduce a hypothesis that is later examined.

B) depict the worst-case scenario when athletics are over-emphasized.

C) summarize the central conflict in the passage.

D) list the pitfalls of an emphasis on extracurricular sports.

12

The primary purpose of lines 48–49 ("assessments … school") is to

A) explain a term.

B) support a claim.

C) describe a process.

D) suggest a solution.

13

The authors indicate that administrators value team sports because they feel they

A) are an important way to showcase athletic talent.

B) function as a way to build physical strength.

C) require students to develop strong character.

D) can strengthen the bonds students have with their school.

14

Which of the following provides the best evidence for the answer to the previous question?

A) Lines 45–47 ("Although … unfounded")

B) Lines 55–58 ("According … school")

C) Lines 58–61 ("This may … adolescents")

D) Lines 69–73 ("In sociological … athletics")

15

The authors use the phrase "the stadium arms race" in lines 30–31 in order to

A) compare the competitive nature among schools to intense political rivalry.

B) show that participating in team sports can be a rewarding experience.

C) suggest that students experience negative consequences because of school sports.

D) describe how administrators finance expensive stadiums by cutting teacher pay.

16

The sentence in lines 35–36 ("Some … think so") mainly serves to

A) stress that teachers are more apt to understand students than administrators.

B) underscore the idea that teachers are underpaid.

C) imply that high school teachers are threatening to take action.

D) emphasize the previous point about prioritizing athletics over instructors.

17

The phrase "fool's gold" in line 64 most directly implies that

A) administrators have done a great deal of research on the best methods to boost student achievement.

B) administrator expenditures have greatly increased over time.

C) the idea that spending more money on athletics to boost student achievement is misguided.

D) sports teams have proven to be financially beneficial to school districts.

18

As it is used in line 17, "bolster" most nearly means

A) threaten.

B) strengthen.

C) force.

D) motivate.

19

The question in lines 53–55 serves mostly to

A) raise doubts about the decision-making ability of some school administrators.

B) imply that administrators undermine research in order to ensure their school has winning sports teams.

C) introduce the information that follows, which explains why administrators support certain programs in schools.

D) explain the connection between administrators' actions and cultural pressure from parents.

20

The graph following the passage suggests that administrators' perception of their students' college preparedness is based on

A) the measure of college preparedness of their students.

B) the extent of financial investment in athletics.

C) their own level of academic success.

D) their relationships with the student body.

21

The authors would likely attribute the differences in administrators' perceived and students' actual college preparedness as represented in the graph to

A) a failure to interpret what leads to success.

B) a growing distaste for extracurricular activities.

C) an increasingly sports-focused society.

D) a misunderstanding of priorities.

STOP

**If you finish before time is called, you may check your work on this section only.
Do not turn to any other section.**

This page intentionally left blank

Wrap-Up

Complete the wrap-up. When you have finished, double-check your work.

Questions 4–6 are based on the following passage.

This passage is adapted from Frederick Douglass, "On the Occasion of the Unveiling of the Freedman's Monument." Originally delivered in 1876.

Fellow citizens, shall we say that in what we have said and done today, and in what we may say and do hereafter, we do disclaim everything like arrogance
Line and assumption, and shall we say we have superior
5 devotion to history? Men generally, at such a time of firsts as this, think that they fully comprehend the relation of Abraham Lincoln both to ourselves and to the white people of the United States. They think that, when speaking of a great public man, the truth is proper
10 and beautiful. But it must be admitted that Abraham Lincoln was not either our man or our model. It must be admitted. Why not acknowledge that in his associations, and in his prejudices, he was a white man? Why not state he was preeminently the white man's President? Why not
15 reckon that he was entirely devoted to the welfare of the white man? …
Though he loved Caesar less than Rome, though the Union was more to him than our freedom, be thankful, be thankful; gradually we saw ourselves lifted from the
20 depths of slavery—under his wise and beneficent rule. When he tarried long in the mountain, or told us we were the cause of war, our faith in him was taxed and strained to the uttermost; we are at best only his step-children, children by adoption, children by force of
25 circumstances (for we were brought to this Golden Land against our will). Yet I say, let us multiply his statues. For while Abraham Lincoln saved for you a country, he delivered us from a bondage that was such an unsavory remnant of the past.
30 Whatever else in this world may be partial, unjust, and uncertain, time is impartial, just, and certain. The honest statesman endeavors to do his duty. He had many affairs to attend to. He was assailed by Abolitionists, slaveholders, and men who were for peace at any price.
35 A man cannot do everything, but must do something; and the judgement of the present hour—this anniversary of the end of the Civil War—is that there was hardly any man better fitted for his mission than Abraham Lincoln.
We have done a good work for our race today. In
40 doing honor to the memory of our friend and liberator, we have been doing highest honors to ourselves and those who come after us. When now it shall be said that the colored man is soulless, that he has no appreciation of benefits or benefactors, we may calmly point to the
45 monument we have erected to the memory of Abraham Lincoln.

4

The author uses the phrase "unsavory remnant of the past" in line 28–29 most likely to

A) emphasize that Americans should look toward the future.

B) show that the U.S. government does not acknowledge the past.

C) describe how slavery was a moral stain on the country's past.

D) suggest that only scraps of America's past are known.

5

The most likely purpose of the parenthetical information in lines 36–37 is to

A) describe an argument.

B) illustrate a complicated concept.

C) emphasize a theory.

D) clarify a phrase.

6

In the final paragraph, the reference to "a good work for our race today" (line 39) mainly serves to

A) reveal the author's motivation for writing the speech.

B) show how Lincoln's work to end slavery influenced the author.

C) acknowledge the historical significance of the monument's unveiling.

D) describe how much Lincoln appreciated the speech.

This page intentionally left blank

Review

Word choice questions can be identified by these features:

- answer choices starting with verbs
- a question asking you about a word or short phrase in the passage

... and by these terms:

- purpose
- effect
- function
- serves to
- uses the word/phrase

Evidence and Elimination

To answer a word choice question, follow these steps:

1. Identify the verbs in the answer choices.
2. Re-read the identified portion of the text.
3. Use the selected text to eliminate irrelevant answers.
4. Use the context to eliminate answers that don't capture the author's why.

Exit

If you've found the answer ...

Check the passage for evidence and confirm that it supports your answer. Mark your answer and continue to the next question.

If you're stuck between two choices ...

Channel your inner lawyer and use logic to eliminate an incorrect answer.

If you have no idea what the answer is ...

Go with your gut. Select the choice that makes the most sense and that best aligns with what the entire passage is about.

8

Chapter

Purpose

LEARNING TARGETS

1. Identify the author's purpose for writing a passage, paragraph, or aspect of a paragraph.

2. Implement the basic approach for purpose questions.

3. Apply the *Convince Yourself* strategy and avoid trap answers on purpose questions.

Warm-Up | Complete the warm-up. When you have finished, double-check your work.

Questions 1–3 are based on the following passage.

This passage is adapted from Daniel Kroeper, "School Bells and Sleep Debt." ©2019 by MasteryPrep.

A combination of school start times and heavy academic loads is causing chronic sleep debt for adolescents across America. Those with extracurricular
Line activities and/or part-time jobs are at an even bigger
5 disadvantage. Combining the necessity to "burn the midnight oil" to complete homework and the need to wake early for school the following day, many adolescents are simply not getting the sleep they need. Numerous reports have shown that delaying school start
10 times can improve sleep patterns and help adolescents live healthier, more balanced lives. However, many school districts are reticent to adjust their operations. Therefore, parent advocacy is a must. Parents must understand the effect of sleep deprivation on their
15 children; further, if they understand that later school start times can alleviate the problem, they may be willing to help convince school administrators.

Sleep debt is accrued like financial debt. When a teen does not get the recommended nine-plus hours of sleep
20 per night (maintain a positive bank balance), a sleep deficit (insufficient funds) is created. As consecutive days of insufficient sleep are accrued, the greater the sleep debt grows. Unlike financial debt, however, sleep debt is not recovered; deficits in sleep throughout the
25 week cannot be made up by sleeping in on weekends. Rather, the body needs adequate and consistent sleep throughout the week. Chronic sleep deprivation in adolescents leads to mental and physical fatigue, which can drastically affect academic performance.

30 In 2017, experts created a study based on the hypothesis that many parents either misperceived their teen's sleep needs or misunderstood the correlation between early school start times and health and academic performance. The resulting National Poll
35 on Children's Health revealed that some parents indeed supported shifting school hours to allow their adolescents adequate sleep. In fact, parents whose child had a school start time at or before 7:30 a.m. were three times more likely to support delaying the
40 start bell. Other parents did not support delaying school start times, perceiving negative outcomes such as interference with family schedules, after-school activities, and transportation to and from school. Many of these parents also misunderstood the sleep needs
45 of adolescents, reporting the belief that approximately seven hours of sleep per night is sufficient.

Parent education on the importance of sleep (particularly in adolescence) along with the effect of sleep deprivation on student performance may
50 encourage advocacy for delayed school hours. Research has shown that shifting school start times to after 8:30 a.m. can have positive effects on students' mental and physical health, academic performance, and even attitude. Increased parental pressure on schools to
55 accommodate the sleep needs of teens is a simple and effective solution to chronic adolescent sleep debt in America.

1

The last paragraph serves mainly to

A) propose future research on solving disagreements between parents and administrators about high school policy.

B) recommend solutions to the problems discussed in the passage related to early school start times and adolescent sleep debt.

C) summarize the findings of a study regarding parental awareness about adolescent sleep requirements.

D) reinforce the importance of re-examining the results of sleep deprivation in high school students.

2

The author's main purpose of including the information about students' workloads and schedules is to

A) establish that high school students deal with higher levels of stress than those in younger grades.

B) present an alternative hypothesis about the amount of sleep teens are actually getting.

C) provide support for the author's claim that adolescents suffer from sleep debt.

D) argue that the extracurricular involvement among high school students should be limited.

3

In the second paragraph (lines 18–29), the discussion of financial debt primarily functions to

A) use a practical example to illustrate how sleep debt can grow.

B) advance a hypothesis about the role that sleep plays in student health and academic performance.

C) stress the distinction between the cause of financial debt and the cause of sleep debt.

D) emphasize adolescents' capacity to incur significant financial debt if left unchecked.

Foundation

With your teacher, read the passage and identify the main idea and purpose.

1. *Okay. There she is. Act cool.* I sat at my usual table in the cafeteria, with my usual ham sandwich and bag of chips, with my usual book and headphones. Jules, the most gorgeous girl I've ever laid eyes on, never seems to notice me. As usual.

    I tried to casually, not-so-obviously do something obvious to catch her attention. *I know! I'll toss up my apple, snag it from the air, and take a bite.* I plucked my apple from my lunch bag and casually tossed it into the air in front of me. *Whoops! Too high!* The apple came down right on top of my head with a soft thunk.

    So much for casual. It worked, though. After retrieving my apple from beneath my chair, I sat up and found myself looking directly at her perfect face. Her eyes lit up, her lips spread into a wide grin, and she waved in my direction! Without hesitating, I waved back, beckoning her to sit with me.

    But, wait. Something was off. We weren't *quite* making eye contact. In fact, she was looking just above my head. *Oh, no.* With a sense of rising dread, I turned around and saw that her best friend was at a table behind me, grinning and waving at Jules. Slowly, I sank lower in my chair, trying to disappear before I could embarrass myself even further.

    Main idea: _____

    Purpose: _____

On your own, read the passage and identify the main idea and purpose.

2. You might think the idea of "good" music is subjective. Everyone has their own opinions and preferences. But why are some songs so much more popular than others? It doesn't come down to the lyrics, instruments, or vocals. There's a scientific reason why pop songs are so popular. It's all about the chords. The same four chords. When repeated in a song, in order, the music becomes exceptionally pleasing to the ear, triggering a part of the brain that makes the listener want to hear the pattern again and again. Our ears begin to crave the song.

    And this isn't a new pattern in music, either. These magical four chords appear in music dating back to the late 1600s, when Pachelbel wrote his famous *Canon in D.* So, the next time you find yourself tapping and singing along to the radio, know that it's not your fault. Your ears just love those chords too much.

    Main idea: _____

    Purpose: _____

Foundation

Work with your teacher to underline the evidence that supports the purpose of each passage.

3. The Olympic Games are the pinnacle of humanity's physical achievement. Time and again, Olympic athletes prove that they are the strongest, fastest, and most competitive individuals on the planet. But are they really? Though the swimmers, gymnasts, rowers, and other competitors are exceptional athletes, they lack a certain sense of daring that those who compete in extreme sports have. Extreme athletes constantly push themselves to the limits of physics and human potential as they perform difficult combinations on a half-pipe or parkour their way through an obstacle course. Can you imagine how much more entertaining it would be to watch an Olympic event featuring rock climbing or base jumping instead of downhill skiing? The Olympics need these extreme sports because, without them, the Olympics simply don't represent the best of humanity's physical and competitive achievements.

    Purpose: *to argue that extreme sports should be included in the Olympic Games*

Work on your own to underline the evidence that supports the purpose of each passage.

4. There are a number of stereotypes that surround people who have multiple tattoos. In fact, one stereotype is that the more covered a person's skin is, the more intimidating they seem. But it's what's lurking beneath that ink that is catching the attention of the medical community.

    Recent studies have shown that greater quantities of tattoos lead to a stronger immune system. Medical researchers studied blood samples from male and female individuals with varying amounts of tattooed skin. Their focus was on analyzing the amount of immunoglobulin A, which is an antibody that helps people ward off illness and infection, in each individual's body both before and after getting a tattoo. Those who had just gotten their first tattoo showed a lowered level of immunoglobulin A, but those who had been through the process before showed elevated levels of the antibody. In addition, the longer the individual spent enduring the tattoo process, the higher their levels seemed to climb. Thus, the researchers were able to conclude that more tattoos are positively correlated with a stronger immune system.

    Purpose: *to present the results of a medical research project*

Practice Set 1 | Complete the practice set. When you have finished, double-check your work.

Questions 1–8 are based on the following passage.

This passage is adapted from Jordan Watts and Frances Davila, "Implications of Digital Learning." ©2019 by MasteryPrep.

In high school classrooms, it is common to find most everyone—teachers and students—utilizing digital technology. Today, approximately 95% of American
Line teenagers own smartphones or tablets. Confident that
5 most students are technologically savvy, educators can use digital innovation for teaching, administering assessments, and providing supplemental instruction. Further, the use of laptops, tablets, or personal devices can engage students in ways that more traditional
10 instruction may not. However, a reliance on the use of electronic devices in the classroom can engender ambivalent feelings among educators. While many relish the chance to embrace the digital age in order to reach students, others worry that a reliance on personal
15 devices in the classroom creates unnecessary distraction, resulting in more harm than good.

Many American students today have never known a world without technology within their reach. As a result, they may underestimate the negative impact of
20 frequent smartphone use on academic performance. According to Barnes (2012), while students generally acknowledge that texting can interfere with learning, this understanding does not seem to impact their texting habits during instruction. In fact, Barnes found
25 that high-volume texters are less apt to believe that this behavior significantly interferes with learning. Students' perceptions are important for educators to consider when making policy decisions, as they reveal the dissonance between student assumptions and reality.

30　Many educators support a movement to ban the use of electronic devices in the classroom. Perhaps because a considerable number of today's teachers remember a time when technology did not prevail, some naturally oppose smartphone use in classrooms and the idea that
35 electronic devices must be available to students at all times. Nevertheless, this point of view can reflect an implied hypocrisy. The expectation that students will reconcile discrepancies between their perceptions about technology and its pitfalls in the classroom does not take
40 into consideration the prevalence of digitization today. Innovation in technology is understood to be advancing rapidly—most people, including adults, are avid consumers—but some educators expect students to learn outside of the context that defines much of their daily
45 lives. As such, a restriction on the use of devices in the classroom could inspire more conflict than obedience.

Is there a balanced approach that would satisfy everyone? This is where "digital learning" enters the conversation. Defined as "learning facilitated by
50 technology that gives students some element of control over time, place, path, and/or pace," it can be used to formally engage students in their own education. Teachers who incorporate digital learning believe that it empowers students to learn through methods that are
55 familiar and relevant while preparing them for the world of work in today's digital society. Likewise, students may be motivated by a teacher's decision to incorporate digital learning into the classroom. Many students find that the use of technology in learning helps to strike a
60 balance between their personal preferences and their educational needs. Such a classroom strategy does not give students free reign over connectivity that some assume is a right, but it does grant them access to online technology in the classroom.

65　In today's America, almost everyone relies on smartphones in order to connect with others, accomplish daily tasks, and gather information, so it is unrealistic to think that students would understand a movement to ban them in the classroom. Most students
70 do not fully comprehend the degree of disruption that personal devices can pose to learning, as they do not consider such distractions abnormal. The crux of the controversy seems to center around whether a classroom environment should mimic daily life—which
75 includes a reliance on technology—or act as an insulated microcosm of its own. Surely a compromise between the two can be reached whereby educators feel confident about the efficacy of digital learning and students recognize the educational value of stepping away from
80 their smartphones from time to time.

1

The authors most likely use the statistic in lines 3–4 of the passage ("Today ... tablets") to highlight the

A) pervasiveness of electronic device usage among students today.

B) recent increase of smartphone use by teenagers.

C) distraction that texting can cause for students.

D) rising popularity of tablets among school-aged children.

Practice Set 1

2

The primary function of the second paragraph (lines 17–29) is to

A) describe teens' misperceptions about the effects of smartphone use during instruction.

B) summarize students' points of view about digital learning in the classroom.

C) illustrate the potential drawbacks of banning personal devices.

D) explain the method Barnes used in his research.

3

In the fourth paragraph (lines 47–64), the definition of "digital learning" primarily functions to

A) emphasize that it is recognized as a formal method of instruction.

B) propose an explanation for why some educators support its use in schools.

C) stress the differences between student and teacher preferences with regard to technology.

D) illustrate the proven effectiveness of the approach.

Approach

<table>
<tr><td colspan="1">Entrance</td></tr>
</table>

Purpose questions can be identified by these features:

- answer choices starting with verbs
- a question asking you about a paragraph or the entire passage

... and by these terms:

- purpose
- functions
- serves
- the author ... to ...

The following questions refer to the passage on page 238. Review question 4 with your teacher. Do not answer the question.

Entrance Evidence and Elimination Exit

4

In the fifth paragraph (lines 65–80), the main purpose of the discussion of distractions caused by personal devices is to

A) suggest that the authors' defense of a smartphone ban is valid.

B) provide further context for why students would likely oppose a ban on devices.

C) imply that students are unaware of basic facts concerning the use of technology.

D) account for why students often have difficulty focusing on a task.

Approach

Review questions 5 and 6 on your own. Circle the part of the question that identifies it is as a purpose question. Do not answer the questions.

5

The main purpose of the first paragraph is to

A) establish an argument regarding teachers' bans on personal electronic devices.

B) provide background information about teenagers' electronics use.

C) introduce varying points of view about the use of electronics in learning.

D) validate assumptions about teenagers and their electronics dependency.

6

The fourth paragraph (lines 47–64) serves mainly to

A) suggest continued research to deal with some of the pitfalls of classroom technology.

B) introduce an educational approach that may balance the preferences of both students and teachers.

C) summarize findings of a study about the impact of frequent technology use in schools.

D) reinforce the importance of re-examining the learning preferences of today's students.

Questions 1–8 are based on the following passage.

This passage is adapted from Jordan Watts and Frances Davila, "Implications of Digital Learning." ©2019 by MasteryPrep.

In high school classrooms, it is common to find most everyone—teachers and students—utilizing digital technology. Today, approximately 95% of American
Line teenagers own smartphones or tablets. Confident that
5 most students are technologically savvy, educators can use digital innovation for teaching, administering assessments, and providing supplemental instruction. Further, the use of laptops, tablets, or personal devices can engage students in ways that more traditional
10 instruction may not. However, a reliance on the use of electronic devices in the classroom can engender ambivalent feelings among educators. While many relish the chance to embrace the digital age in order to reach students, others worry that a reliance on personal
15 devices in the classroom creates unnecessary distraction, resulting in more harm than good.

Many American students today have never known a world without technology within their reach. As a result, they may underestimate the negative impact of
20 frequent smartphone use on academic performance. According to Barnes (2012), while students generally acknowledge that texting can interfere with learning, this understanding does not seem to impact their texting habits during instruction. In fact, Barnes found
25 that high-volume texters are less apt to believe that this behavior significantly interferes with learning. Students' perceptions are important for educators to consider when making policy decisions, as they reveal the dissonance between student assumptions and reality.

30 Many educators support a movement to ban the use of electronic devices in the classroom. Perhaps because a considerable number of today's teachers remember a time when technology did not prevail, some naturally oppose smartphone use in classrooms and the idea that
35 electronic devices must be available to students at all times. Nevertheless, this point of view can reflect an implied hypocrisy. The expectation that students will reconcile discrepancies between their perceptions about technology and its pitfalls in the classroom does not take
40 into consideration the prevalence of digitization today. Innovation in technology is understood to be advancing rapidly—most people, including adults, are avid consumers—but some educators expect students to learn outside of the context that defines much of their daily
45 lives. As such, a restriction on the use of devices in the classroom could inspire more conflict than obedience.

Is there a balanced approach that would satisfy everyone? This is where "digital learning" enters the conversation. Defined as "learning facilitated by
50 technology that gives students some element of control over time, place, path, and/or pace," it can be used to formally engage students in their own education. Teachers who incorporate digital learning believe that it empowers students to learn through methods that are
55 familiar and relevant while preparing them for the world of work in today's digital society. Likewise, students may be motivated by a teacher's decision to incorporate digital learning into the classroom. Many students find that the use of technology in learning helps to strike a
60 balance between their personal preferences and their educational needs. Such a classroom strategy does not give students free reign over connectivity that some assume is a right, but it does grant them access to online technology in the classroom.

65 In today's America, almost everyone relies on smartphones in order to connect with others, accomplish daily tasks, and gather information, so it is unrealistic to think that students would understand a movement to ban them in the classroom. Most students
70 do not fully comprehend the degree of disruption that personal devices can pose to learning, as they do not consider such distractions abnormal. The crux of the controversy seems to center around whether a classroom environment should mimic daily life—which
75 includes a reliance on technology—or act as an insulated microcosm of its own. Surely a compromise between the two can be reached whereby educators feel confident about the efficacy of digital learning and students recognize the educational value of stepping away from
80 their smartphones from time to time.

Approach

Evidence and Elimination

To answer a purpose question, follow these steps:

1. Identify the topic of the text selection.
2. Eliminate off-topic answers.
3. Eliminate answers that don't explain *why* the author wrote that text.

Answer question 4 with your teacher.

Entrance **Evidence and Elimination** Exit

4

In the fifth paragraph (lines 65–80), the main purpose of the discussion of distractions caused by personal devices is to

A) suggest that the authors' defense of a smartphone ban is valid.

B) provide further context for why students would likely oppose a ban on devices.

C) imply that students are unaware of basic facts concerning the use of technology.

D) account for why students often have difficulty focusing on a task.

The following questions refer to the passage on page 242. Answer questions 5 and 6 on your own. Focus on eliminating incorrect answers.

5

The main purpose of the first paragraph is to

A) establish an argument regarding teachers' bans on personal electronic devices.

B) provide background information about teenagers' electronics use.

C) introduce varying points of view about the use of electronics in learning.

D) validate assumptions about teenagers and their electronics dependency.

6

The fourth paragraph (lines 47–64) serves mainly to

A) suggest continued research to deal with some of the pitfalls of classroom technology.

B) introduce an educational approach that may balance the preferences of both students and teachers.

C) summarize findings of a study about the impact of frequent technology use in schools.

D) reinforce the importance of re-examining the learning preferences of today's students.

Exit
If you've found the answer … Verify that your answer has support in the passage and mark your choice.
If you're stuck between two choices … Split each answer in half and check if either part is inaccurate based on evidence in the passage. Select the choice that is most accurate.
If you have no idea what the answer is … Select an answer that uses a verb closest to *review* or *explain*.

Review questions 7 and 8. Work with your teacher to choose the correct answer from the remaining choices.

Entrance 〉 Evidence and Elimination 〉 Exit

7

The primary purpose of the passage is to

A) reveal findings of a research study regarding students.

B) analyze reported data on a social phenomenon.

C) examine conflicting opinions about a key issue in education.

D) question the methods of research involving school environments.

8

The main purpose of the final paragraph is to

A) summarize the passage's opposing ideas about the use of technology in the classroom.

B) speculate on the reason for the results of Barnes' research study.

C) contrast teacher and student assumptions about the best way to learn.

D) emphasize the distractions caused by electronics in the classroom.

Warm-Up 〉 Foundation 〉 **Approach** 〉 Strategy 〉 Mini-Test 〉 Wrap-Up 〉 Review   **245**

Practice Set 2 | Complete the practice set. When you have finished, double-check your work.

Questions 9–11 are based on the following passage.

This passage is adapted from Jordan Watts and Frances Davila, "Implications of Digital Learning." ©2019 by MasteryPrep.

In high school classrooms, it is common to find most everyone—teachers and students—utilizing digital technology. Today, approximately 95% of American
Line teenagers own smartphones or tablets. Confident that
5 most students are technologically savvy, educators can use digital innovation for teaching, administering assessments, and providing supplemental instruction. Further, the use of laptops, tablets, or personal devices can engage students in ways that more traditional
10 instruction may not. However, a reliance on the use of electronic devices in the classroom can engender ambivalent feelings among educators. While many relish the chance to embrace the digital age in order to reach students, others worry that a reliance on personal
15 devices in the classroom creates unnecessary distraction, resulting in more harm than good.

Many American students today have never known a world without technology within their reach. As a result, they may underestimate the negative impact of
20 frequent smartphone use on academic performance. According to Barnes (2012), while students generally acknowledge that texting can interfere with learning, this understanding does not seem to impact their texting habits during instruction. In fact, Barnes found
25 that high-volume texters are less apt to believe that this behavior significantly interferes with learning. Students' perceptions are important for educators to consider when making policy decisions, as they reveal the dissonance between student assumptions and reality.

30 Many educators support a movement to ban the use of electronic devices in the classroom. Perhaps because a considerable number of today's teachers remember a time when technology did not prevail, some naturally oppose smartphone use in classrooms and the idea that
35 electronic devices must be available to students at all times. Nevertheless, this point of view can reflect an implied hypocrisy. The expectation that students will reconcile discrepancies between their perceptions about technology and its pitfalls in the classroom does not take
40 into consideration the prevalence of digitization today. Innovation in technology is understood to be advancing rapidly—most people, including adults, are avid consumers—but some educators expect students to learn outside of the context that defines much of their daily
45 lives. As such, a restriction on the use of devices in the classroom could inspire more conflict than obedience.

Is there a balanced approach that would satisfy everyone? This is where "digital learning" enters the conversation. Defined as "learning facilitated by
50 technology that gives students some element of control over time, place, path, and/or pace," it can be used to formally engage students in their own education. Teachers who incorporate digital learning believe that it empowers students to learn through methods that are
55 familiar and relevant and prepare them for the world of work in today's digital society. Likewise, students may be motivated by a teacher's decision to incorporate digital learning into the classroom. Many students find that the use of technology in learning helps to strike a balance
60 between their personal preferences and their educational needs. Such a classroom strategy does not give students free reign over connectivity that some assume is a right, but it does grant them access to online technology in the classroom.

65 In today's America, almost everyone relies on smartphones in order to connect with others, accomplish daily tasks, and gather information, so it is unrealistic to think that students would understand a movement to ban them in the classroom. Most students
70 do not fully comprehend the degree of disruption that personal devices can pose to learning, as they do not consider such distractions abnormal. The crux of the controversy seems to center around whether a classroom environment should mimic daily life—which
75 includes a reliance on technology—or act as an insulated microcosm of its own. Surely a compromise between the two can be reached whereby educators feel confident about the efficacy of digital learning and students recognize the educational value of stepping away from
80 their smartphones from time to time.

9

The authors most likely cite the study in lines 21–24 of the passage ("According … instruction") to highlight the

A) dissonance between student awareness and texting behavior.

B) latest decrease in students' attention spans as a result of technology.

C) proposed ban of personal devices by some of today's educators.

D) number of students who text during classroom instruction.

10

The third paragraph serves mainly to

A) propose that additional research be conducted to support a ban on devices in the classroom.

B) explain the reasons for and against a ban on technology in the classroom.

C) summarize the point of view of teachers who are hesitant to embrace digital learning.

D) reinforce the importance of examining best practices in education.

11

The authors most likely include a statement about student conflict in lines 45–46 ("As … obedience") to emphasize the

A) negative consequences of imposing a ban on personal devices.

B) recent increase of student uprisings against schools' electronics policies.

C) misconceptions of teachers about the benefits of digital learning.

D) importance of maintaining order and cooperation in the classroom.

Strategy

Questions 12–20 are based on the following passage.

This passage is adapted from Marcus L. Griffin and Susan M. Ridolph, "The Cart Before the Horse: The Challenge and Promise of Restorative Justice Consultation in Schools." ©2019 by MasteryPrep.

Schools have long struggled to identify a disciplinary system that is not only fair and balanced, but also prevents "punishment for punishment's sake." An approach called "restorative justice" has recently seen a rise in popularity, but some educators have found it difficult to find a consistent, formal definition of the approach, as well as reliable data on its implementation and effectiveness.

Restorative justice is a disciplinary strategy that appears to be based in global history; references to its roots and underlying philosophy can be found in longstanding cultural and religious practices across the world. In the late 1960s and early 1970s, the approach took hold in U.S. criminal justice systems as an avenue to help prisoners repair the harm caused by the crimes they committed. Today, school practitioners are attempting to employ restorative justice as an alternative to an overdependence on exclusionary disciplinary actions—such as lengthy school suspensions—while also improving student and school morale. "Restorative justice is about building, strengthening, and repairing relationships," says Troi Bechet, founder and CEO of the Center for Restorative Approaches in New Orleans.

Perhaps because of its indeterminate origins, restorative justice has been difficult to define in absolute terms. Some conceptualize the approach as a step-by-step program, while others consider it to be a philosophy that guides behavior. Even use of the term *restorative justice* has been subject to debate because of its ties to the criminal justice system. As such, variations on the approach's name have emerged, which include *restorative practices*, *restorative strategies*, and *restorative interventions*.

Regardless of the terminology used to define it, the restorative justice approach is intended to create and maintain a stronger sense of community in schools, thereby decreasing discipline issues. Theoretically, through the approach, students begin to understand that when they break a rule, they also "harm relationships in the school community," Bechet says, "and that should engender contrition." The use of dialogue and discussion in response to student offenses and their resulting harm supports the idea that both offenders and victims must work to repair the damage, and conversing about it is part of the process. According to Bechet, "Offenders have an obligation to repair the harm, and victims should be willing to listen."

Although restorative justice is growing in popularity, the research regarding its outcomes and implementation is narrow. For example, formal data about the system are largely limited to single-school evaluations, and the research does not demonstrate a reduction in exclusionary disciplinary actions that restorative justice is meant to replace. Therefore, it is difficult to predict the success or failure of the approach, or even best practices in its implementation.

"There needs to be more systematic research on restorative justice that uses rigorous and innovative methodologies," writes William Martell, associate professor of school psychology at the University of Nevada, Las Vegas. "The important question," he writes, "is does restorative justice work, and how do we use restorative justice well in schools?"

The role of teachers appears to be critical to its success. Research conducted in 2016 (Gregory et al.) illustrated the movement's positive impact on teacher-student relationships, which are also vital to the health of a school community. Redirecting teachers to focus on what can be done *with* students, instead of *to* students, in response to disciplinary offenses is part of the job of Becky McCammon, who advised schools in St. Paul, Minnesota, during their shift to restorative practices. Through teacher-led facilitation, students are ideally led to understand the damage they have done to a personal relationship as well as to the school community, and they are taught effective ways to restore these connections.

As programs of restorative practices become more popular among school administrators, it is critical that their successful implementation be documented. In the future, schools should have access to reliable models of effective restorative justice programs in order to develop their own initiatives. Research must be done that outlines the specific components of such programs that ensure their integrity, as well as methods of teacher training, to bolster the program's success. Through such efforts, schools can attempt to diminish exclusionary disciplinary methods while building character, student morale, and a strong sense of school community.

Convince Yourself

When you answer a purpose question, you're explaining why the author wrote something. If you can't seem to pick an answer, you can get unstuck by asking yourself why you're debating over your remaining options. By analyzing your own thought process, you can catch yourself before you talk yourself into a bad choice. After you've eliminated choices you know are wrong, follow these steps:

❶ Explain to yourself why each remaining answer could be correct.

❷ Select the answer choice that requires the least amount of explanation.

Review question 12 with your teacher. Use the Convince Yourself strategy to answer the question as a class.

12

In the second paragraph (lines 10–24), the description of restorative justice's origins primarily functions to

A) provide context for its evolution and current use in schools.

B) illustrate the use of dialogue and discussion in its implementation.

C) present a description of the environments in which it is intended to be used.

D) compare the restorative justice approach to other disciplinary programs.

The following questions refer to the passage on page 248. Work on your own using the Convince Yourself strategy to answer questions 13 and 14.

13

The main purpose of the seventh paragraph (lines 65–77) is to

A) propose an audit of restorative justice programs to ensure their adherence to the authors' suggestions.

B) describe the process by which teachers are trained and advised when implementing restorative justice.

C) illustrate that educators are a key component of what makes for a successful restorative justice program in schools.

D) recommend a specific training program for administrators who will be implementing a restorative justice program.

14

The main purpose of the passage is to

A) describe how cultures have historically used restorative justice in their religious practices.

B) discuss the effects of discipline on students and teachers.

C) introduce key issues surrounding the definition and implementation of restorative justice.

D) illustrate how students engage in discussions and dialogue with peers.

Strategy

Avoiding Traps

Purpose questions are filled with trap answers that seem convincing and cost you points. Follow these tips to avoid the traps and boost your score:

1. Connect to the main idea.

2. Watch out for half-right/half-wrong answers.

3. Maintain a high standard.

Review question 15 with your teacher. Use the elimination tips to answer the question as a class.

15

The main purpose of the fifth paragraph (lines 49–57) is to

A) question schools on their motivation to implement restorative practices.

B) summarize the main flaws in data reporting on restorative justice.

C) identify a key drawback of current research on restorative justice.

D) challenge practitioners in schools to provide more data for studies.

The following questions refer to the passage on page 248. Work on your own using the elimination tips to answer questions 16 and 17.

16

The primary function of the fourth paragraph (lines 35–48) is to

A) summarize the goals inherent in the approach.

B) establish the need for stronger data.

C) provide details about the foundation of the program.

D) address damaged relationships in schools.

17

The first paragraph serves mainly to

A) explain how punishment is defined.

B) acknowledge a controversy about an issue.

C) introduce an educational approach and a hindrance to its implementation.

D) present a program and summarize its outcomes.

This page intentionally left blank

Practice Set 3 | Complete the practice set. When you have finished, double-check your work.

Questions 12–20 are based on the following passage.

This passage is adapted from Marcus L. Griffin and Susan M. Ridolph, "The Cart Before the Horse: The Challenge and Promise of Restorative Justice Consultation in Schools." ©2019 by MasteryPrep.

Schools have long struggled to identify a disciplinary system that is not only fair and balanced, but also prevents "punishment for punishment's sake." An
5 approach called "restorative justice" has recently seen a rise in popularity, but some educators have found it difficult to find a consistent, formal definition of the approach, as well as reliable data on its implementation and effectiveness.
10 Restorative justice is a disciplinary strategy that appears to be based in global history; references to its roots and underlying philosophy can be found in longstanding cultural and religious practices across the world. In the late 1960s and early 1970s, the approach
15 took hold in U.S. criminal justice systems as an avenue to help prisoners repair the harm caused by the crimes they committed. Today, school practitioners are attempting to employ restorative justice as an alternative to an overdependence on exclusionary disciplinary
20 actions—such as lengthy school suspensions—while also improving student and school morale. "Restorative justice is about building, strengthening, and repairing relationships," says Troi Bechet, founder and CEO of the Center for Restorative Approaches in New Orleans.
25 Perhaps because of its indeterminate origins, restorative justice has been difficult to define in absolute terms. Some conceptualize the approach as a step-by-step program, while others consider it to be a philosophy that guides behavior. Even use of the term *restorative*
30 *justice* has been subject to debate because of its ties to the criminal justice system. As such, variations on the approach's name have emerged, which include *restorative practices, restorative strategies,* and *restorative interventions.*
35 Regardless of the terminology used to define it, the restorative justice approach is intended to create and maintain a stronger sense of community in schools, thereby decreasing discipline issues. Theoretically, through the approach, students begin to understand that
40 when they break a rule, they also "harm relationships in the school community," Bechet says, "and that should engender contrition." The use of dialogue and discussion in response to student offenses and their resulting harm supports the idea that both offenders and victims must

45 work to repair the damage, and conversing about it is part of the process. According to Bechet, "Offenders have an obligation to repair the harm, and victims should be willing to listen."

Although restorative justice is growing in popularity,
50 the research regarding its outcomes and implementation are narrow. For example, formal data about the system are largely limited to single-school evaluations, and the research does not demonstrate a reduction in exclusionary disciplinary actions that restorative justice
55 is meant to replace. Therefore, it is difficult to predict the success or failure of the approach, or even best practices in its implementation.

"There needs to be more systematic research on restorative justice that uses rigorous and innovative
60 methodologies," writes William Martell, associate professor of school psychology at the University of Nevada, Las Vegas. "The important question," he writes, "is does restorative justice work, and how do we use restorative justice well in schools?"
65 The role of teachers appears to be critical to its success. Research conducted in 2016 (Gregory et al.) illustrated the movement's positive impact on teacher-student relationships, which are also vital to the health of a school community. Redirecting teachers to focus on
70 what can be done *with* students, instead of *to* students, in response to disciplinary offenses is part of the job of Becky McCammon, who advised schools in St. Paul, Minnesota, during their shift to restorative practices. Through teacher-led facilitation, students are ideally led
75 to understand the damage they have done to a personal relationship as well as to the school community, and they are taught effective ways to restore these connections.

As programs of restorative practices become more popular among school administrators, it is critical that
80 their successful implementation be documented. In the future, schools should have access to reliable models of effective restorative justice programs in order to develop their own initiatives. Research must be done that outlines the specific components of such programs
85 that ensure their integrity, as well as methods of teacher training, to bolster the program's success. Through such efforts, schools can attempt to diminish exclusionary disciplinary methods while building character, student morale, and a strong sense of school community.

18

The sixth paragraph (lines 58–64) serves mainly to

A) argue that no more schools should implement new programs until more data are provided.

B) provide a call to action for researchers and schools to close a gap in data.

C) summarize the purpose of restorative justice programming in schools.

D) challenge schools to address the problems they have found in their discipline programs.

19

The authors' main purpose for including the information about the approach's alternative names is to

A) create consistency in reference to the program's real-life implementation.

B) propose the use of terms that better describe the approach.

C) present support for the claim that restorative justice is difficult to define for schools.

D) question the confusion regarding restorative justice and its implementation.

20

The last paragraph serves mainly to

A) propose strategies to better implement the program discussed in the passage.

B) introduce actions that will provide necessary data to address gaps reported in the passage.

C) criticize the lack of useful studies conducted into the program.

D) establish the potential utility of social experiments such as restorative justice.

Mini-Test | Complete the mini-test. When you have finished, double-check your work.

Questions 22–32 are based on the following passage.

This passage is adapted from Candace Moore, "The Most Important Meals of the Day." ©2019 by MasteryPrep.

When faced with the option of eating cafeteria food or no food at all, too many teenagers are choosing the latter. Because they claim that they are too busy, are
Line watching their weight, or other justifications, adolescents
5 are more likely than ever to miss or skip meals. However, "your brain runs primarily on glucose," says Kristin Kirkpatrick, manager of wellness nutrition services at the Cleveland Clinic. "So when there isn't enough sugar in your blood to pull from, you lose the ability to focus."
10 Students who routinely miss meals at school are not only jeopardizing their health, but also their learning. Whether breakfast or lunch (or even both) is consistently skipped, adolescents are inadvertently affecting their mental and physical health, and most do not even
15 realize it.

Researchers discovered that existing literature on meal omission among adolescents does not focus on skipping individual meals, nor does it cover the lifestyle and dietary behaviors that typically accompany meal-
20 skipping. To compensate for these research deficiencies, Zewditu Demissie and colleagues conducted a cross-sectional study to investigate multiple aspects of meal omission among adolescents, including how often students skip meals and coexisting factors. They studied
25 the eating habits and characteristics of over 11,000 high school students across the United States, and the results were somewhat surprising.

One might assume that adolescents skip dinner most often, since breakfast and lunch are usually available
30 at school. On the contrary, the aforementioned study found that teens were more likely to skip breakfast than any other meal. Alison Eldridge of the Nestlé Research Center in Lausanne, Switzerland, conducted an additional study and found that a surprising number
35 of children and adolescents were also regularly skipping lunch.

Demissie's team consulted the National Youth Physical Activity and Nutrition Study from the Centers for Disease Control and Prevention to collect
40 information on the dietary habits and behaviors of students who skipped meals. The researchers also investigated both the physical and sedentary activity of these students. Their aim was to identify correlations between meal omission and the prevalence of certain
45 behaviors.

Students were asked about physical activity and sports participation over the previous seven days and over the previous 12 months, respectively, as well as television watching and video game playing
50 on an average school day. The participants were also asked about their dietary habits, including their fruit and vegetable intake, as well as their consumption of sugar-sweetened beverages. Once collected, the data were compared to the nutritional recommendations
55 published by the Healthy People initiative in order to assess a possible link between behaviors, dietary habits, and meal skipping. Researchers suspected that routine meal omission would be linked to unfavorable physical behaviors and outcomes.

60 The results of the study proved their suspicions. Students who missed meals were more likely to spend an average of five or more hours on the computer or playing video games on school days. When cross-tabulated with height and weight measurements, both
65 ends of the spectrum were represented: students who were underweight were more likely to miss meals, as were students who were overweight. The data led to further correlations between missing meals and unhealthy behaviors. The students who missed breakfast,
70 specifically, were found to be less likely to eat healthy foods throughout the day and more likely to drink soft drinks. Likewise, the Nestlé study found that teens who regularly skipped lunch were not consuming enough protein, fiber, and healthy fats. Similar levels of sugar
75 intake, however, were reported among students who regularly eat lunch and those who skip it consistently. There are psychological factors to consider as well. "Skipping meals is not only one of the biggest predictors of overeating and unhealthy weight gain," says
80 psychiatrist Kimberli McCallum. "It's also a gateway to the development of eating disorders."

The researchers hope that their findings will be used in schools to promote healthy nutritional habits. Experts in the field recommend that schools target
85 those students who are likely to skip meals on a regular basis. In particular, the data suggest that students who routinely skip breakfast should be encouraged to change this behavior. While students are most likely to skip their first meal, a healthy breakfast has been shown to set the
90 tone for a physically and mentally productive day.

1   1

22

The primary purpose of the passage is to

A) explain the reasons underlying a scientific hypothesis.

B) describe the purpose and outcomes of research on a specific topic.

C) present and analyze conflicting data about a trend.

D) emphasize the innovative nature of a research study.

23

As presented in the passage, the research conducted in the studies primarily relied on which type of evidence?

A) Random sampling

B) Direct observation

C) Historical data

D) Expert testimony

24

Which statement about students and daily physical activity can most reasonably be inferred from the passage?

A) Students who eat three meals a day consume more sugar than those who skip meals.

B) Students who engage in daily physical activity are healthier than those who do not.

C) Students who do not play video games regularly are more likely to exercise.

D) Students who regularly skip meals are more likely to be sedentary.

25

The main purpose of the last paragraph is to

A) develop a counterargument to the claim that missing meals correlates with other unhealthy behaviors.

B) speculate on the reason for the outcome of the research study.

C) propose further action on the part of schools based on the outcome of the study.

D) identify key study findings regarding students who miss meals.

26

The main purpose of the sixth paragraph (lines 60–81) is to

A) compare the findings of two similar studies of eating habits.

B) provide recommendations for applying the results of the study.

C) transition from a summary of the study's research methods to a description of the study's findings.

D) illustrate that students are most likely to skip meals during adolescence.

27

The author's main purpose of including the information about sedentary and active behaviors is to

A) establish that students involved in gaming are more likely to be sedentary.

B) present an opposing hypothesis about specific adolescents who miss meals.

C) demonstrate the relationship between certain behaviors and meal omission.

D) support the author's claims about the overriding benefits of physical activity.

28

In lines 32–36, the author mentions the results of an additional nutritional study primarily to

A) compare the differences between two related research studies.

B) support the author's claim that many students are routinely skipping meals.

C) report the drawbacks of some research on meal omission in children.

D) highlight the need for more research to be conducted regarding skipping meals.

29

The primary function of the second paragraph (lines 16–27) is to

A) introduce why and how researchers conducted a study.

B) illustrate the researchers' hypotheses about a lack of solid data.

C) explain the research methods used in an individual study.

D) describe the outcomes of a long-term study.

30

As used in line 90, "tone" most nearly means

A) mood.

B) quality.

C) tenor.

D) character.

31

According to the passage, the research offers an answer to which of the following questions?

A) How often does the average student skip a meal during the school week?

B) What other behaviors are found in students who regularly skip meals?

C) Why are students missing meals when food is available at school?

D) What behaviors are parents exhibiting that cause students to miss meals?

32

Which choice provides the best evidence for the answer to the previous question?

A) Lines 53–57 ("Once ... skipping")

B) Lines 61–63 ("Students ... day")

C) Lines 72–74 ("Likewise ... fats")

D) Line 77 ("There are ... well")

STOP

**If you finish before time is called, you may check your work on this section only.
Do not turn to any other section.**

This page intentionally left blank

Wrap-Up

Complete the wrap-up. When you have finished, double-check your work.

Questions 4–6 are based on the following passage.

This passage is adapted from Daniel Kroeper, "School Bells and Sleep Debt." ©2019 by MasteryPrep.

A combination of school start times and heavy academic loads is causing chronic sleep debt for adolescents across America. Those with extracurricular
Line activities and/or part-time jobs are at an even bigger
5 disadvantage. Combining the necessity to "burn the midnight oil" to complete homework and the need to wake early for school the following day, many adolescents are simply not getting the sleep they need. Numerous reports have shown that delaying school start
10 times can improve sleep patterns and help adolescents live healthier, more balanced lives. However, many school districts are reticent to adjust their operations. Therefore, parent advocacy is a must. Parents must understand the effect of sleep deprivation on their
15 children; further, if they understand that later school start times can alleviate the problem, they may be willing to help convince school administrators.

Sleep debt is accrued like financial debt. When a teen does not get the recommended nine-plus hours of sleep
20 per night (maintain a positive bank balance), a sleep deficit (insufficient funds) is created. As consecutive days of insufficient sleep are accrued, the greater the sleep debt grows. Unlike financial debt, however, sleep debt is not recovered; deficits in sleep throughout the
25 week cannot be made up by sleeping in on weekends. Rather, the body needs adequate and consistent sleep throughout the week. Chronic sleep deprivation in adolescents leads to mental and physical fatigue, which can drastically affect academic performance.

30 In 2017, experts created a study based on the hypothesis that many parents either misperceived their teen's sleep needs or misunderstood the correlation between early school start times and health and academic performance. The resulting National Poll
35 on Children's Health revealed that some parents indeed supported shifting school hours to allow their adolescents adequate sleep. In fact, parents whose child had a school start time at or before 7:30 a.m. were three times more likely to support delaying the
40 start bell. Other parents did not support delaying school start times, perceiving negative outcomes such as interference with family schedules, after-school activities, and transportation to and from school. Many of these parents also misunderstood the sleep needs
45 of adolescents, reporting the belief that approximately seven hours of sleep per night is sufficient.

Parent education on the importance of sleep (particularly in adolescence) along with the effect of sleep deprivation on student performance may
50 encourage advocacy for delayed school hours. Research has shown that shifting school start times to after 8:30 a.m. can have positive effects on students' mental and physical health, academic performance, and even attitude. Increased parental pressure on schools to
55 accommodate the sleep needs of teens is a simple and effective solution to chronic adolescent sleep debt in America.

4

The author's main purpose of including the results of the National Poll on Children's Health is to

A) establish that many school administrators are misinformed about the needs of their children as they grow.

B) present an alternative hypothesis about how sleep needs vary within families.

C) provide support for the idea that parents differ in their awareness of how early school start times may impact their children.

D) confirm the relationship between sleep deprivation in adolescents and early school start times.

5

The main purpose of the first paragraph is to

A) convey the passage's focus by showing how adolescents spend their time on a typical day.

B) indicate how sleep needs shift as children progress through elementary and high school.

C) introduce the passage's main idea by explaining why many adolescents are unable to get the sleep they need.

D) foreshadow an outcome that is described in detail later in the passage.

6

The primary purpose of the passage is to

A) explain adolescent sleep debt caused by early school start times and encourage parental involvement.

B) present research suggesting that that school administrators are largely unaware of adolescent sleep needs.

C) identify the process by which high school students accomplish their daily responsibilities.

D) provide an overview of adolescent behavior and how it affects their overall health.

Review

Entrance

Purpose questions can be identified by these features:

- answer choices starting with verbs
- a question asking you about a paragraph or the entire passage

... and by these terms:

- purpose
- functions
- serves
- the author ... to ...

Evidence and Elimination

To answer a purpose question, follow these steps:

1. Identify the topic of the text selection.
2. Eliminate off-topic answers.
3. Eliminate answers that don't explain *why* the author wrote that text.

Exit

If you've found the answer ...

Verify that your answer has support in the passage and mark your choice.

If you're stuck between two choices ...

Split each answer in half and check if either part is inaccurate based on evidence in the passage. Select the choice that is most accurate.

If you have no idea what the answer is ...

Select an answer that uses a verb closest to *review* or *explain*.

9

Chapter

Point of View

LEARNING TARGETS

1. Identify and interpret an author's point of view.

2. Implement the basic approach for point of view questions.

3. Apply the *Keep It Simple* strategy and use attention to detail and reasoning to eliminate answer choices for point of view questions.

Warm-Up

Complete the warm-up. When you have finished, double-check your work.

Questions 1–3 are based on the following passage.

This passage is adapted from Kevin O'Brien, "What's Charging Tech Advances in the Battery Industry?" ©2018 by MasteryPrep.

Battery usage has skyrocketed in concurrence with technological advances, but the battery manufacturing industry has not kept pace with this increase in
Line demand. However, the slow innovation process may be
5 undergoing a reboot, and inventors are excited; judging by the way scientists at the BAIO Thermodynamics Scholars Convention in Denver, Colorado reacted, people in the industry feel positive that overdue change is sure to come.
10 Many in the quantum battery industry, including Marcus Grey, professor at the University of British Columbia and one of the top quantum battery researchers, are confident that quantum batteries are on the horizon. Soon to be introduced to the commercial
15 market, quantum batteries may offer big improvements over current lithium-ion technology. Grey contends that quantum batteries can be made from current solid-state technology but with improved performance. Grey's lab built a prototype in 2016 that showed a record charging
20 time for its quantum batteries—a record that continues to improve. Studies suggest that Grey's charging techniques could dramatically improve quantum battery life, whereby they could generate enough power to run an electric car or laptop all day—but at much lower costs
25 than lithium-ion batteries can offer.

Meanwhile, experts at the National Innovative Technology Laboratory have begun work on a sodium-ion battery, which uses sodium in place of lithium. This type of battery is the top competitor in the energy
30 storage industry in terms of cost-effective production. However, the batteries are limited in that they can be used only for stationary equipment because of their weight.

One of Grey's former interns and colleagues,
35 Niànzhēn Thao, founder of the ion battery manufacturer China Energetics, announced this month that he is creating a test manufacturing line for a lithium-sulfur battery that may reduce or even eliminate battery waste. The basic concept is that while it charges, the lithium-
40 sulfur battery may consume active materials while emitting energy and expelling waste. The discharge is consumed and recycled for later use. This technology is particularly well-suited to the aviation and space flight industries. This is because batteries made with
45 lithium-sulfur are lighter than those made with lithium or sodium ions. Thao also notes that lithium-sulfur

batteries produce two to four times more power than their leading competitors.

Looking long term, Grey is placing his bets on
50 quantum technology, hoping to take advantage of the solid-state technology already available. Some companies are already utilizing quantum computers to optimize solid state batteries. Grey hopes the future will bring dramatic improvements in the efficiency of portable
55 power through a combination of high-endurance quantum battery life and quick charging effects. It's estimated that replacing just one device's battery could reduce home power costs by up to 15 percent. Additional replacements could decrease costs as much
60 as 30 percent, which would cut almost a third from the country's overall power utilization. The difficulty arises in encouraging consumers to pay a bit more for these cutting-edge alternatives, which is more challenging in times of economic stress.

1

Which choice best reflects the perspective of the "scientists" (line 6) on the field of battery development?

A) It is undergoing much-needed change, and the field is likely to see innovation soon.

B) It is a stagnant field and is unlikely to develop into anything worthwhile in the near future.

C) It is financially limited in its ability to create long-term power solutions.

D) It hasn't kept pace with changing technology but is expected to soon outpace other technology.

2

Which choice best reflects the perspectives of the "experts" (line 26) on the potential of new sodium-ion batteries?

A) They provide a more affordable option due to the materials used but are not good options for portability.

B) They are a bit more costly but will be more user-friendly as a result.

C) They will provide long-term power storage solutions for many communities.

D) Their performance is equivalent to lithium-ion batteries and is likely to take over the industry.

3

The author's attitude toward the quantum battery industry is best described as one of

A) appreciation.

B) optimism.

C) reverence.

D) astonishment.

Foundation

Read paragraph 1 with your teacher. As you read, decide whether the author has a positive or negative attitude toward the topic. Underline the information that supports your analysis of the narrator's feelings.

Paragraph 1

Dear Journal,

I've been thinking about Hollywood a lot lately. Random, I know, but bear with me: I just bought *Hercules* from Amazon, but I'm probably gonna skip the remake. That movie was my all-time favorite. I loved the music, and Pegasus was the horse of my dreams. And now they're doing a live-action remake. Hollywood needs to get a grip. They keep remaking all these old movies, trying to make money off of our nostalgia. It must be sad to be all out of ideas and have to recycle the old stuff.

The author has a _____ attitude toward this subject.

Key Terms

Tone: the author's attitude toward a subject or topic.

Read paragraphs 2 and 3 with your partner. As you read, decide whether the author has a positive or negative attitude toward the subject. Underline the information that supports your analysis of the narrator's feelings.

Paragraph 2

The gentle snow falls, like a sinister blanket slowly suffocating the world and everything in it. The temperatures drop, and the flowers that flourished all summer are but a memory. It's winter. The barren land is not lacking in opportunity, though; it offers the humiliation of an ice-patch-induced fall that will undoubtedly happen in front of a crowd. Or, better yet, the wind chill will slip right through the material of your jacket, nipping at your skin and making your teeth chatter. Perhaps you'll even need to visit a dentist for repair work, you think. The winter just keeps on giving, doesn't it?

The author has a _____ attitude toward this subject.

Paragraph 3

Chore time. I fill the sink with satisfyingly hot water, so hot that my hands turn a bit pink each time they dip below the surface. I make sure to add soap, too. I use that blue kind that smells a little like daffodils and clean laundry. Then, the dance begins. I reach for a cup near the edge of the sink, and I swiftly rinse the pomegranate juice from the very bottom. It takes a quick plunge into the soapy pool, and I bring my sponge, so well-worn that it fits my palm beautifully, to the cup's surface. Once I've decided that it's to my liking, it does another quick dip into the soapy side before the waterfall of fresh water rinses it to a perfect sheen. On to the next!

The author has a _____ attitude toward this subject.

Work with your teacher to review the passage and answer questions 4–6.

So many students in today's society think of Shakespeare as a pompous, overrated author who wrote a bunch of plays in such a complicated style that only Ivy League literature students can understand. But, that's not actually the case. When you really dig into the details, Shakespeare was amazing, and his stories were actually written for the general public. He also went against the typical style of the time and wrote about *real* characters, who had their own values, opinions, and flaws. Plus, he was a writing rebel. If he didn't have a word that fit what he wanted to say, he made up a new one! He was a true artist who wove his personal knowledge and experience into his stories, and he was never one to shy away from showing the truth about humanity, regardless of who might be offended. In essence, it's not the fancy words that make Shakespeare so amazing; it's his creation of stories and themes that feel relevant to anyone, no matter what time period they might live in.

4. The author's point of view in this passage is that Shakespeare is _____

5. The author includes an alternative perspective in this passage. Who has the other point of view?

   _____

6. Which side would *most likely agree* with the idea that reading a Shakespeare play is too hard to even try?

   _____

With a partner, read the passage and answer questions 7–9.

Who does a school belong to? The community and its taxpayers? The school district? The teachers? It doesn't really matter who actually owns the school; what matters is how the students feel while they're in class and learning. And one of the best ways to help students feel good in school is to give them a little bit of ownership. Teachers might say that since it's their assigned classroom, they should be the ones to decorate and cover the walls. However, if students are given the opportunity to improve their own environments, they'll be much happier and better prepared to learn. This doesn't mean letting students tag the walls. By utilizing disposable posters, wall papers, or other similar mediums, students can create art and inspiration to fill the classrooms and halls. And by giving them this little bit of ownership of their campus, they become more invested in keeping the school a wonderful place.

7. The author's point of view in the passage is that _____ should be given ownership of the school.

8. The author includes an alternative perspective in the passage. Who has the other point of view?

   _____

9. Which side would *most likely* agree with the idea that the extra cost of art supplies is well worth the investment?

   _____

Read the following passage. Underline the words that indicate a positive perspective on autumn. Circle the words that indicate a negative perspective on autumn.

Autumn: A Rant

Don't get me wrong—autumn isn't the worst season we get to experience. The ridiculously hot weather starts to fade to the point where I think, "Yay, I can breathe again!" Plus, all the bugs go back to wherever they came from, leaving me mosquito-bite-free and happier than ever. But, autumn is absolutely loathsome. In a lot of ways.

Let me break it down for you.

Three words: pumpkin … spice … everything. Pumpkin spice drinks, pumpkin spice air fresheners, pumpkin spice-colored walls. Seriously, people. It's a vegetable! Who goes nuts for a vegetable? Because that's what a pumpkin is. That giant orange veggie just has too much power in this world once September hits.

But what's worse is that it's basically the law to go on one of those hayrides while you pick out said vegetable. You sit, bobble around as the driver hits every pothole he can find, and watch parents cling to their offspring so they don't go overboard. Then, when you get home, the allergies hit! Who here isn't a little allergic to hay? I mean, seriously?

Have you noticed the squirrels, too? It's like they know they're running out of time to store all their acorns, so they get extra angry. I lost a bagel, two bags of chips, and a shoe to them just last week! Would a spring squirrel do this? NOPE! Only the autumn squirrels get this crazy.

On top of all that is awful about autumn, the colors are the worst thing this horrendous season has to offer. Orange? Yellow? Brown? It's all bright and neon plus a "blah" color, which ends up looking like one of those old afghan blankets that everyone in the 1980s had draped over their couches. Yuck.

Finally, let's talk boots. They're not comfortable, they're not helpful, and they completely turn on you if the top isn't tight enough. Ever get a splash of water down the top of your boot? It's like having a smelly, dead fish slapped up against your calf, all cold and slick. Gives me goosebumps just thinking about it.

Okay, maybe autumn isn't as bad as it could be. Maybe it's got a good side. I don't know. I just can't see it.

According to this passage, what is the worst offense the autumn season has to offer?

_____

Practice Set 1

Complete the practice set. When you have finished, double-check your work.

Questions 1–8 are based on the following passages.

Passage 1 is adapted from Tanger et al, *Report on Military Personnel*. Originally published in 1917. Passage 2 is adapted from Holly Warelock, *The Affirmation of Women in the Military*. Originally published in 1918. Tanger was a U.S. diplomat; the report was a strategy for military training. Warelock, an American novelist and sociology writer, wrote *The Affirmation* in response to Tanger.

Passage 1

To see one half of the human population prevented by the other half from enlistment in the military; that they are equal by birth but lesser by law in the same country
Line where they were raised; and that they are American
5 citizens yet have no inherent authority or autonomy: are all societal phenomena apparently inexplicable in contemporary American life.

But what I fail to understand is why women are so determined to give up their particular way of life. Who
10 prefers a soldier's life? What value is there in it? Can you trade it? Will it lift you from poverty to success like an elevator? The American politicians have explained from their perspectives that enlistment in military fields is dangerous to a person's physical well-being, or so I read
15 in a report.

It is unclear why this topic is the subject of debate, especially since a war is something violent and gruesome to endure but that nevertheless transpires, because man is determined to seek out and attain justice whether or
20 not the end result includes his death.

It seems incontrovertible that our common welfare, above all that of women, stipulates that they never aspire to an involvement in military action and careers. Here we must accept their shortcomings as the will of nature.
25 It is rather glaring that their fragile constitutions, their compassionate tendencies, and the many responsibilities of motherhood make them unfit for combative activities and arduous lifestyles and invite them to uncomplicated duties and the tasks of a homemaker. Of course, that's
30 also how most military leaders might regard female soldiers, if they were to exist. They have confirmed male soldiers as superior in their physicality—and intellectually and emotionally, as well—to these women following their own foolish aspirations. This
35 is acceptable; we need not initiate questions that are irrelevant to the debate. Let us not create competition between life's allies. You must, you truly must forget the dreams of a life that no training, no experience, can possibly prepare you for. Realize that the harmony of
40 mankind begs this of you.

Passage 2

Advocating for the rights of women, my central idea is based on a simple premise, that if we shall not permit by law and policy to allow the enlistment of women, we shall limit the power of our military and country;
45 for enemies are common to all, and to exclude women would be injudicious with respect to the country's safety. Bid farewell to this world of "manpower," in which gendered exclusion creates armies from limited pools. Moreover, the military does acknowledge the
50 fact that there is something formidable about today's generation of women—something that could result in an even stronger military. The question, they ask, is whether American policies will evolve to embrace the potential. Will old traditions created with closed minds
55 be a guidepost for a bounded future, or will we allow a gender-equal scenario in which female and male soldiers, with open-minded attitudes, collaborate to bring about a peaceful world?

Consider, sir, impartially, these conclusions—
60 for a glimpse of reason seemed to appear before as you concluded, "that to see one half of the human population prevented by the other from any enlistment in military . . . is a societal phenomenon inexplicable in contemporary American life." If so, on what does
65 your policy rest? If time-honored customs do not bear scrutiny and investigation, the evolution of man, by a parity of reasoning, will not withstand the same test: thus, a double standard reigns, held up by the weak evidence that you use to justify the veneration of man—
70 superiority.

However, this is not how many individuals (both male and female) regard the human race. They wholeheartedly agree that we are capable of change— and optimistic and progressive, as well—rather than
75 holding fast to outdated misgivings. This is despite your belief that you are acting in a manner best considered to maintain our safety. Who named man the autonomous judge, if women partake with him in the art of reasoning?
80 Is it not clear that their sharp intellectual skills, their fierce loyalty, and their ability to conquer childbirth classify them as superior to their male counterparts and simplistic duties, demanding that they take on leadership roles in the support of the country? Do you not show
85 an inability to evolve, when you limit our country, by withholding women's civil and patriotic freedom, enforcing their resignation into obscurity and falling in line?

1

Which choice best reflects the perspective of the "military leaders" (line 30) on female soldiers in Passage 1?

A) They are inferior physically and mentally to their male counterparts.

B) They are efficient and reduce the need for excessive recruiting techniques.

C) Their involvement could be good for the military only in the short term.

D) They consume critical resources but offer varying skill sets.

2

Which choice best describes how the narrator of Passage 1 views women joining the military?

A) Acceptable but immoral

B) Promoted by some but undesirable

C) Socially beneficial but misunderstood

D) Socially important but atypical

3

It can be inferred that the author of Passage 1 believes that raising children and running a household

A) are rewarding activities for men as well as for women.

B) offer fewer benefits for society than the actions of the military.

C) include very few tasks that are difficult or demanding in nature.

D) require discipline and skills similar to those necessary in war.

Approach

Entrance

Point of view questions can be identified by these terms:

- perspective/point of view
- attitude
- believe
- likely to describe/agree/disagree

The following questions refer to the passage on page 270. Review question 4 with your teacher. Do not answer the question.

Entrance ⟩ Evidence and Elimination ⟩ Exit

4

In Passage 1, the author's attitude toward female soldiers is best described as one of

A) resolution.

B) uncertainty.

C) approval.

D) amazement.

Approach

Review questions 5 and 6 on your own. Circle the part of the question that identifies it as a point of view question. Do not answer the questions.

5

Which of the following best characterizes the perspective of members of the military on "American policies" and their ability to "embrace the potential" (lines 52–54) in Passage 2?

A) They are shocked by the country's inability to consider the future progress of gender rights.

B) They are uninterested in the idea of changing public policy for the benefit of women.

C) They are uncertain whether the country will be able to accept women in the military.

D) They are optimistic that Americans will approve female enlistment for the first time in the history of the country.

6

The author of Passage 2 would most likely describe women as

A) physically resilient.

B) emotionally volatile.

C) spiritually evolved.

D) academically superior.

Questions 1–8 are based on the following passages.

Passage 1 is adapted from Tanger et al, *Report on Military Personnel*. Originally published in 1917. Passage 2 is adapted from Holly Warelock, *The Affirmation of Women in the Military*. Originally published in 1918. Tanger was a U.S. diplomat; the report was a strategy for military training. Warelock, an American novelist and sociology writer, wrote *The Affirmation* in response to Tanger.

Passage 1

To see one half of the human population prevented by the other half from enlistment in the military; that they are equal by birth but lesser by law in the same country
Line where they were raised; and that they are American
5 citizens yet have no inherent authority or autonomy: are all societal phenomena apparently inexplicable in contemporary American life.

But what I fail to understand is why women are so determined to give up their particular way of life. Who
10 prefers a soldier's life? What value is there in it? Can you trade it? Will it lift you from poverty to success like an elevator? The American politicians have explained from their perspectives that enlistment in military fields is dangerous to a person's physical well-being, or so I read
15 in a report.

It is unclear why this topic is the subject of debate, especially since a war is something violent and gruesome to endure but that nevertheless transpires, because man is determined to seek out and attain justice whether or
20 not the end result includes his death.

It seems incontrovertible that our common welfare, above all that of women, stipulates that they never aspire to an involvement in military action and careers. Here we must accept their shortcomings as the will of nature.
25 It is rather glaring that their fragile constitutions, their compassionate tendencies, and the many responsibilities of motherhood make them unfit for combative activities and arduous lifestyles and invite them to uncomplicated duties and the tasks of a homemaker. Of course, that's
30 also how most military leaders might regard female soldiers, if they were to exist. They have confirmed male soldiers as superior in their physicality—and intellectually and emotionally, as well—to these women following their own foolish aspirations. This
35 is acceptable; we need not initiate questions that are irrelevant to the debate. Let us not create competition between life's allies. You must, you truly must forget the dreams of a life that no training, no experience, can possibly prepare you for. Realize that the harmony of
40 mankind begs this of you.

Passage 2

Advocating for the rights of women, my central idea is based on a simple premise, that if we shall not permit by law and policy to allow the enlistment of women, we shall limit the power of our military and country;
45 for enemies are common to all, and to exclude women would be injudicious with respect to the country's safety. Bid farewell to this world of "manpower," in which gendered exclusion creates armies from limited pools. Moreover, the military does acknowledge the
50 fact that there is something formidable about today's generation of women—something that could result in an even stronger military. The question, they ask, is whether American policies will evolve to embrace the potential. Will old traditions created with closed minds
55 be a guidepost for a bounded future, or will we allow a gender-equal scenario in which female and male soldiers, with open-minded attitudes, collaborate to bring about a peaceful world?

Consider, sir, impartially, these conclusions—
60 for a glimpse of reason seemed to appear before as you concluded, "that to see one half of the human population prevented by the other from any enlistment in military . . . is a societal phenomenon inexplicable in contemporary American life." If so, on what does
65 your policy rest? If time-honored customs do not bear scrutiny and investigation, the evolution of man, by a parity of reasoning, will not withstand the same test: thus, a double standard reigns, held up by the weak evidence that you use to justify the veneration of man—
70 superiority.

However, this is not how many individuals (both male and female) regard the human race. They wholeheartedly agree that we are capable of change— and optimistic and progressive, as well—rather than
75 holding fast to outdated misgivings. This is despite your belief that you are acting in a manner best considered to maintain our safety. Who named man the autonomous judge, if women partake with him in the art of reasoning?
80 Is it not clear that their sharp intellectual skills, their fierce loyalty, and their ability to conquer childbirth classify them as superior to their male counterparts and simplistic duties, demanding that they take on leadership roles in the support of the country? Do you not show
85 an inability to evolve, when you limit our country, by withholding women's civil and patriotic freedom, enforcing their resignation into obscurity and falling in line?

Approach

Evidence and Elimination

To answer a point of view question, follow these steps:

1. Identify the point of view in the question.
2. Find the section of the passage that describes the question's topic.
3. Eliminate answers that describe the wrong point of view.
4. Eliminate answers that are not supported by evidence.

Answer question 4 with your teacher.

Entrance **Evidence and Elimination** Exit

4

In Passage 1, the author's attitude toward female soldiers is best described as one of

A) resolution.

B) uncertainty.

C) approval.

D) amazement.

The following questions refer to the passages on page 274. Answer questions 5 and 6 on your own. Focus on eliminating incorrect answers.

5

Which of the following best characterizes the perspective of members of the military on "American policies" and their ability to "embrace the potential" (lines 52–54) in Passage 2?

A) They are shocked by the country's inability to consider future progress of gender rights.

B) They are uninterested in the idea of changing public policy for the benefit of women.

C) They are uncertain whether the country will be able to accept women in the military.

D) They are optimistic that Americans will approve female enlistment for the first time in the history of the country.

6

The author of Passage 2 would most likely describe women as

A) physically resilient.

B) emotionally volatile.

C) spiritually evolved.

D) academically superior.

Approach

Exit

If you've found the answer ...

Check the passage for evidence and confirm that it aligns with your answer. Mark your answer and continue to the next question.

If you're stuck between two choices ...

Compare the two answers to find the difference in tone and pick the one that best matches the tone of the passage.

If you have no idea what the answer is ...

Go with your gut. Skim the passage quickly and select the answer that best matches your overall understanding of the information.

Review questions 7 and 8. Work with your teacher to choose the correct answer from the remaining choices.

Entrance > Evidence and Elimination > Exit

7

Which choice best reflects the perspective of the "individuals" (line 71) on the human race?

A) They collectively agree that people are capable of change and evolution.

B) ~~They remain stubbornly convinced that their misgivings are true.~~

C) ~~They are certain that people are capable of change only in the short term.~~

D) They believe people can change but cannot actually give up old beliefs.

8

It can be inferred that the author of Passage 2 believes that filling leadership roles and serving the country

A) ~~are responsibilities that are not meant for both men and women.~~

B) ~~offer fewer rewards for the overall community when women are involved.~~

C) include responsibilities that require hard work and loyalty.

D) require skills similar to ones needed to command and succeed in politics or business.

Practice Set 2 | Complete the practice set. When you have finished, double-check your work.

Questions 9–11 are based on the following passage.

This passage is from Diego Ruiz Sanchez, *A Satch Game* ©2019 by MasteryPrep. The narrator, a writer, recalls his childhood in mid-20th century Madrid, Spain.

All my life, my only companions were made of sheet music and notes. Yet again, I feel there is borne upon me the realization of what I have told to many over my

Line 25 years: that my obsession with melody is not based on
5 reason. Chords and the allure of their hidden science hypnotized me, and I found in them a door through which I could reach a limitless world, a refuge from my father, that house, and those fearful days during which I would almost believe that never a joyful moment would
10 come again. My father didn't want to hear music in our house. There was something about it—apart from the rhythms that he could never detect—that aggravated him. He would often tell me that the moment I turned 12 he would shove me off to work and that I'd better drop
15 all of my empty-headed ideas if I wanted to avoid being a deadbeat, a failure. I would hide my sheet music deep in my closet and await the time he'd leave or go to sleep so that I could sing. Once he heard me singing outside and launched into a fury. He grabbed me by my shirt and
20 brought his face close to mine.

"If I catch you wailing this nonsense again, acting like a fool, you'll be sorry."

My father wasn't an evil man, and regardless of our financial hardships, if he could spare it, he'd give me
25 some coins so that I could buy something for myself. He was sure that I spent it on saltwater taffy, poppyseed muffins, or chocolate, but I would stash it in a wooden box below a floorboard, and once I'd accumulated five or six *pesetas*, I'd quietly sneak out to get myself some sheet
30 music.

The best spot in the whole town was the Santiago & Sons record shop on Calle Los Féliz. It smelled of greasy food and vinyl, and it became my hideaway, my oasis. The owner would let me sit on a cushion in the corner
35 and listen with headphones until my heart sang. He almost never let me pay for the sheet music I took home, so when he was busy, I'd drop the money I'd been able to save by the register as I left. It was barely anything—if I'd had to pay for music with that measly amount, I doubt
40 I would have been able to buy even a single page. When the time came for me to head home, I would do so with a heavy heart, a wound to my spirit. This daily occurence was a sad sight to other regular customers.

One year, Santiago gave me the greatest birthday
45 present ever. It was an old record, dusty and clearly well loved.

"'Ella and Louis'" by Louis Armstrong, I read across the label.

I had heard that Santiago knew a few musicians who
50 visited his establishment, and, based on the caution with which he carried the record, I wondered if possibly this Mr. Armstrong was one of them.

"Is he a friend?"

"A true friend. And now, he can be your friend too."
55 What I was on the verge of understanding, I now know, was not a crescendoing musical love, but myself. That winter was bleak, with weeks as cold as ice, and I listened to "Ella and Louis" a million times, partly because I didn't have other music on hand, but mostly
60 because I didn't think there was a better record in the entire world. I was starting to believe that Mr. Armstrong had composed it just for me. Eventually, I felt sure that I didn't want to become anything else but a master in what Mr. Armstrong had created.

9

With which of the following statements about his father would the narrator most likely agree?

A) He showed no kindness toward the narrator.

B) He disapproved of spending unnecessarily.

C) He would have disapproved of Santiago's gift.

D) He particularly disapproved of Louis Armstrong.

10

The "regular customers" mentioned in paragraph 4 (lines 43–44) would most likely describe the "daily occurence" of the narrator going home as

A) depressing.

B) inevitable.

C) alarming.

D) anticipated.

11

Over the course of the passage, the narrator's attitude shifts from

A) anxiety about his obsession with music to excitement about it.

B) worry about his talents to confidence in his skills as a musician.

C) captivated by music to determination to follow his dream.

D) disdain for musical activities to appreciation of good musical talent.

Strategy

Questions 12–20 are based on the following passages.

These passages are based on the Fulkerth–Singh debates. Passage 1 is from a speech by Adam Fulkerth. Passage 2 is from a statement made by Ajit Singh. Fulkerth and Singh participated in a series of debates regarding the "Deny India" movement in 1942.

Passage 1

Mr. Singh compares the bond of the Indian democracy, blending Hindu and Muslim people together, to a struggle for freedom, and says that the common struggle will eliminate differences and the bond will become stronger. Why does he believe, and from what delusion has he awoken, to think that their government will forget religious differences and become a cooperative unit? Welcome to a dream world of "idealism," in which long-fought battles between two warring groups will simply cease to even exist. Throughout the past, we have settled disputes between Hindu and Muslim people, though I think our intentions when asserting our influence weren't completely selfless; we have offered our wisdom and greatly improved their economy, their trade, and their political system more than anyone could have foreseen; we have guided them from a needy and ineffective country to becoming a contender and authority within the civilized world; if ever there has been contact between the religious groups, and that contact is without a doubt an inevitable occurrence, we've settled the conflict. A democracy consisting of Hindu and Muslim citizens cannot stand because of inherent differences, which Mr. Singh does not accept. Hopefully, Mr. Singh is a smarter man than those who demand to be given control of something they have no experience with, thus refusing British help. ...

I'd like to address this question: why can't this cooperation exist eventually, combining the Hindu and Muslim people, as any man would hope for? It can surely exist if Muslims will live by the guidelines upon which their religion was based; to explain, the practice of each person to live an honorable life, without disobeying their deity or his commandments. But what's worrisome to British officials is the fact that Muslims, whose religious beliefs "demand absolute loyalty," refuse to allow the practice of differing religions. We need to keep in mind that the Hindu and Muslim people are long-time adversaries, fighting due to fundamentally divergent values at the core of their beliefs, that their religious groups are devout, and that an alliance between the two is implausible, requiring us to mediate and settle disputes from time to time, so that we give our Indian friends a safe place to live. If we remove our influence on Indian soil and colonial efforts, these groups become subject to a conflict between the past and present. What we are on the brink of seeing, it is clear, is not a nonviolent democratic success but chaos. ...

Passage 2

In criticism of the speech I gave to the National Indian Congress, in which he claims I declared my leadership for the "Deny India" movement ... he mentions a part in which I say that "you will forget the differences ... in the common struggle for independence." I would like to address this matter. He attempts to argue that we must have an authority in the interactions between the Hindus and Muslims; that their authority saves us from the occurrence of conflict, civil war, from the downfall of our government, and the reigniting of the historical struggle of our religions. I disagree with that. If British influence disappears, who can say what will happen? We don't know. But why should we not be given the chance to work together in a government designed to promote the cooperation that previously had not been achieved? Welcome to the future of a "combined state," in which simple political policies help citizens become cooperative, interdependent individuals. Are we capable of this achievement? We don't know. Our uncertainty is apparent to British politicians. They don't realize they are the enemy in "the common struggle." They'll be the match that ignites our fire and solidifies our cooperation.

If the British lose their foothold, how will they remain a stable country? Have they not always piggybacked on our successful trade? And how will they make up for that loss? Lost revenue is lost revenue. It is clear that their intentions are not actually for our benefit or for civil peace, and that they are really worried about their own well-being in their efforts to keep their influence intact. Whenever it has been beneficial for them to intervene, and there were clear consequences for us, they always pushed forward. All this struggle and suffering is thanks to their efforts to maintain their own prosperity. It has been so since the start of the Dutch colonialism. It was true with the rivalry with the Netherlands; true during the established trade post of the French; and it is true now. If ever there was an effort to resist it, there has been domination and oppression. ... Do we believe that the success of India is dependent on them, that the same powers who enforced oppression so many times will really have our best interests at heart?

Keep It Simple

If you find yourself struggling to find an answer that describes someone else's point of view, focus only on the topics in the passage to eliminate answer choices that don't match.

1. Find the part of the text that discusses the opinion.

2. Find the topics of that text.

3. Eliminate choices that don't line up with those topics.

Review question 12 with your teacher. Use the Keep It Simple strategy to answer the question as a class.

12

Based on Passage 1, with which of the following hypothetical situations would British officials be most concerned?

A) A Muslim leader who attempts to go against the doctrine of his religion.

B) A Muslim leader who refuses to allow citizens to practice a different religion.

C) A Muslim leader who fails to prioritize members of his own religious group.

D) A Muslim leader who improves relations among different religious groups.

The following questions refer to the passages on page 280. Work on your own using the Keep It Simple strategy to answer questions 13 and 14.

13

Over the course of Passage 1, the narrator's attitude shifts from

A) worry about British influence on religious groups to certainty of it.

B) doubt about Muslim and Hindu cooperation to confidence it will happen.

C) hesitation about a Hindu and Muslim partnership to support of British involvement.

D) contempt for Indian civilians to consideration for their troubles.

14

Based on Passage 1, Fulkerth would be most likely to agree with which claim about the controversy over Hindu and Muslim conflicts?

A) They can be avoided only if contact between the two groups is limited to little or no interaction.

B) They can be settled if the British are allowed the opportunity to mediate their conflicts.

C) They have made solidifying trade and economic prosperity almost impossible.

D) They are fueled by the differences between the Indian and British cultural practices in each country.

Strategy

A New Perspective

Point of view questions can be challenging because they force you to view the passage from someone else's perspective. Use these tips to help you find that perspective and eliminate answers more efficiently.

1 Author or other?

2 Fact check.

3 Make the perspective your own.

Review question 15 with your teacher. Use the elimination tips to answer the question as a class.

15

In Passage 1, the author's attitude toward idealism is best described as

A) uncertainty.

B) amazement.

C) skepticism.

D) eagerness.

Strategy

The following questions refer to the passages on page 280. **Work on your own to use the elimination tips to answer questions 16 and 17.**

16

Which of the following best characterizes Singh's attitude toward the disappearance of "British influence" (lines 59–60)?

A) He is skeptical about the country's dependence on the British.

B) He is unconcerned about whether or not their influence will remain.

C) He is uncertain about the future of the country and its success.

D) He is optimistic that the country will overcome this loss of influence.

17

In Passage 2, the author's attitude toward a "combined state" is best described as one of

A) worry.

B) doubt.

C) hope.

D) alarm.

This page intentionally left blank

Practice Set 3 | Complete the practice set. When you have finished, double-check your work.

Questions 12–20 are based on the following passages.

These passages are based on the Fulkerth–Singh debates. Passage 1 is from a speech by Adam Fulkerth. Passage 2 is from a statement made by Ajit Singh. Fulkerth and Singh participated in a series of debates regarding the "Deny India" movement in 1942.

Passage 1

Mr. Singh compares the bond of the Indian democracy, blending Hindu and Muslim people together, to a struggle for freedom, and says that the common struggle will eliminate differences and the bond will become stronger. Why does he believe, and from what delusion has he awoken, to think that their government will forget religious differences and become a cooperative unit? Welcome to a dream world of "idealism," in which long-fought battles between two warring groups will simply cease to even exist. Throughout the past, we have settled disputes between Hindu and Muslim people, though I think our intentions when asserting our influence weren't completely selfless; we have offered our wisdom and greatly improved their economy, their trade, and their political system more than anyone could have foreseen; we have guided them from a needy and ineffective country to becoming a contender and authority within the civilized world; if ever there has been contact between the religious groups, and that contact is without a doubt an inevitable occurrence, we've settled the conflict. A democracy consisting of Hindu and Muslim citizens, cannot stand because of inherent differences, which Mr. Singh does not accept. Hopefully, Mr. Singh is a smarter man than those who demand to be given control of something they have no experience with, thus refusing British help. ...

I'd like to address this question: why can't this cooperation exist eventually, combining the Hindu and Muslim people, as any man would hope for? It can surely exist if Muslims will live by the guidelines upon which their religion was based; to explain, the practice of each person to live an honorable life, without disobeying their deity or his commandments. But what's worrisome to British officials is the fact that Muslims, whose religious beliefs "demand absolute loyalty," refuse to allow the practice of differing religions. We need to keep in mind that the Hindu and Muslim people are long-time adversaries, fighting due to fundamentally divergent values at the core of their beliefs, that their religious groups are devout, and that an alliance between the two is implausible, requiring us to mediate and settle disputes from time to time, so that we give our Indian friends a safe place to live. If we remove our influence on Indian soil and colonial efforts, these groups become subject to a conflict between the past and present. What we are on the brink of seeing, it is clear, is not a nonviolent democratic success but chaos. ...

Passage 2

In criticism of the speech I gave to the National Indian Congress, in which he claims I declared my leadership for the "Deny India" movement ... he mentions a part in which I say that "you will forget the differences ... in the common struggle for independence." I would like to address this matter. He attempts to argue that we must have an authority in the interactions between the Hindus and Muslims; that their authority saves us from the occurrence of conflict, civil war, from the downfall of our government, and the reigniting of the historical struggle of our religions. I disagree with that. If British influence disappears, who can say what will happen? We don't know. But why should we not be given the chance to work together in a government designed to promote the cooperation that previously had not been achieved? Welcome to the future of a "combined state," in which simple political policies help citizens become cooperative, interdependent individuals. Are we capable of this achievement? We don't know. Our uncertainty is apparent to British politicians. They don't realize they are the enemy in "the common struggle." They'll be the match that ignites our fire and solidifies our cooperation.

If the British lose their foothold, how will they remain a stable country? Have they not always piggybacked on our successful trade? And how will they make up for that loss? Lost revenue is lost revenue. It is clear that their intentions are not actually for our benefit or for civil peace, and that they are really worried about their own well-being in their efforts to keep their influence intact. Whenever it has been beneficial for them to intervene, and there were clear consequences for us, they always pushed forward. All this struggle and suffering is thanks to their efforts to maintain their own prosperity. It has been so since the start of the Dutch colonialism. It was true with the rivalry with the Netherlands; true during the established trade post of the French; and it is true now. If ever there was an effort to resist it, there has been domination and oppression. ... Do we believe that the success of India is dependent on them, that the same powers who enforced oppression so many times will really have our best interests at heart?

18

The "British politicians" mentioned in Passage 2 (line 68) would likely describe the "achievement" of cooperation between Hindus and Muslims as

A) uncertain.

B) ensured.

C) menacing.

D) extraordinary.

19

Which of the following best characterizes Singh's attitude toward the British losing their "foothold" in India (lines 71–72)?

A) He is doubtful that the loss will have any lasting impact on Britain.

B) He is ambivalent about whether or not he would like to see it happen.

C) He is confident it would have negative effect on Britain as a country.

D) He is positive that Britain will persevere and maintain its prosperity.

20

Based on Passage 2, Singh would most likely agree with which claim about the controversy over British colonialism?

A) It can be ended only if the Indian people band together and work with other countries to defeat the British.

B) It has been proven time and again that the British have only their own interests in mind and do not care about the Indian people.

C) It would have less influence if the government were better able to manage its own trade routes and agreements.

D) It is enflamed in part by the differences between the Hindu and Muslim religions and cultural practices.

Mini-Test

Complete the mini-test. When you have finished, double-check your work.

Questions 11–20 are based on the following passages.

This passage is adapted from Dorothy J. DeSantis and Anna S. Smythe, "It's Not the Cost that Counts: Asymmetry in Gift Giving." ©2013 by MasteryPrep.

Each year as the holidays approach, hoards of shoppers embark on the hunt for the "perfect gift," digging deep into their wallets with family and friends in
Line mind. Last December alone, shoppers spent an average
5 of over one thousand dollars on gifts—both online and in stores. And it doesn't stop with annual holidays; well-meaning shoppers routinely purchase gifts for special occasions—including birthdays, weddings, and retirements—all year long. For some, in fact, gift-giving
10 is something of a sport. However, while many delight in the chance to purchase gifts, the mere thought of gift-giving calls up equivocal feelings in others; they fear that their choices will disappoint, rather than please.

Gift-giving is defined by social psychologists as a
15 universal process that integrates a society. Some financial experts, however, have a less encouraging opinion about the matter. According to Franks (1995), gift-giving is an objective waste of money that results when people make choices for others. He purports that most gift-givers seek
20 to purchase items that they think the recipient would like but would not be inclined to buy for themselves. However, gift-givers fail to consider the perceived value of a gift. That is, just because the recipient might like to have an item does not mean that they consider
25 it valuable. This, according to Franks, is the critical error made by many gift-givers as they exchange their earnings for what they consider a "perfect gift."

For example, a gift-giver might spend $50 on a bottle of perfume that the recipient believes is worth much
30 less. As such, the giver's financial loss outweighs the recipient's gain. This phenomenon suggests that people are generally unskilled at predicting what others will appreciate, a conclusion that is not surprising to social psychologists. Research has shown that gift-givers often
35 struggle to understand the perspectives of others; their insights are subject to social projection (the tendency to expect similarities between oneself and others) and egocentrism (the inability to understand that another's view may be different from one's own).
40 We have proposed an explanation for why many gift-givers overspend on what they consider to be a "worthwhile" gift. We believe that people typically equate the price of a gift with how much they believe the recipient will appreciate it. That is, people assume

45 that the more an item costs, the more positively it will be received. In reality, however, a connection between the cost of a gift and how much it is appreciated may be baseless; at the very least, the link is less viable than most gift-givers conclude.
50 What is the basis for the assumption that a higher price tag will engender greater feelings of appreciation? According to anthropologists, gift-giving is a symbolic ritual whereby people attempt to convey positivity toward others through their willingness to invest in
55 the future of the relationship. Therefore, people may be inclined to invest in a bigger, more expensive gift in order to impart a stronger sense of thoughtfulness to the recipient. The receiver, on the other hand, may not equate the magnitude of a gift with the giver's levels of
60 effort and sensitivity.

That people continue to misconstrue the perspective of others when it comes to gift-giving leaves us puzzled. We know that the exchange of gifts is deeply rooted in society and culture. Further, most people have
65 experienced both the roles of gift-giver and gift-receiver. Yet, it appears that shoppers fail to utilize their own experiences when it comes to purchasing gifts. As shopping malls and online vendors stock their shelves for the holiday rush, the average person continues to
70 waste hundreds to thousands of dollars on gifts.

1   1

11

As used in line 12, "equivocal" most nearly means

A) conflicted.

B) imaginative.

C) supportive.

D) opposing.

12

Which of the following best characterizes a typical person's attitude toward gift-giving according to Franks?

A) They are alarmed at the thought of shopping for a meaningful gift.

B) They are optimistic that the recipient will express appreciation for the gift.

C) They are concerned with choosing a gift that the recipient would want.

D) They are uncertain whether their gift will be appreciated by the recipient.

13

Which choice best reflects the perspective of Franks (line 17) on gift giving?

A) It results in wasteful spending and a relative loss for the gift giver.

B) It is key to the integration of society and promotes thoughtfulness.

C) It is good for the economy but only at certain times of the year.

D) It depletes financial resources but strengthens relationships.

14

The authors' attitude toward the notion that people fail to discern the perceptions of others when it comes to gift giving is best described as one of

A) wonder.

B) ambivalence.

C) confusion.

D) astonishment.

15

The "social psychologists" mentioned in paragraph three (lines 34–35) would most likely describe the phenomenon mentioned as

A) foreseeable.

B) controversial.

C) disconcerting.

D) unexpected.

16

The authors indicate that people value gift-giving because they feel it

A) is a simple way to show appreciation.

B) represents social and cultural conformity.

C) acts as a valuable form of self-expression.

D) can serve to strengthen a relationship.

1 | Warm-Up > Foundation > Approach > Strategy > Mini-Test > Wrap-Up > Review | **1**

17

Which choice provides the best evidence for the answer to the previous question?

A) Lines 14–15 ("Gift-giving . . . society")

B) Lines 19–21 ("He purports . . . themselves")

C) Lines 32–34 ("This phenomenon . . . psychologists")

D) Lines 53–56 ("According . . . relationship")

18

In line 58, "impart" most nearly means

A) carry.

B) imply.

C) exchange.

D) communicate.

19

The passage is written from the point of view of

A) psychologists explaining the nature of social projection.

B) journalists comparing research methods within the social sciences.

C) researchers defining and explaining a social phenomenon.

D) economists evaluating the impact of gift-giving in the retail industry.

20

Which choice best describes the authors' view of gift giving?

A) Moral but unnecessary

B) Well-intentioned but misguided

C) Socially beneficial but hazardous

D) Economically beneficial but wasteful

STOP

**If you finish before time is called, you may check your work on this section only.
Do not turn to any other section.**

This page intentionally left blank

Wrap-Up

Complete the wrap-up. When you have finished, double-check your work.

Questions 4–6 are based on the following passage.

This passage is adapted from Kevin O'Brien, "What's Charging Tech Advances in the Battery Industry?" ©2018 by MasteryPrep.

Battery usage has skyrocketed in concurrence with technological advances, but the battery manufacturing industry has not kept pace with this increase in
Line demand. However, the slow innovation process may be
5 undergoing a reboot, and inventors are excited; judging by the way scientists at the BAIO Thermodynamics Scholars Convention in Denver, Colorado, reacted, people in the industry feel positive that overdue change is sure to come.
10 Many in the quantum battery industry, including Marcus Grey, professor at the University of British Columbia and one of the top quantum battery researchers, are confident that quantum batteries are on the horizon. Soon to be introduced to the commercial
15 market, quantum batteries may offer big improvements over current lithium-ion technology. Grey contends that quantum batteries can be made from current solid-state technology but with improved performance. Grey's lab built a prototype in 2016 that showed a record charging
20 time for its quantum batteries—a record that continues to improve. Studies suggest that Grey's charging techniques could dramatically improve quantum battery life, whereby they could generate enough power to run an electric car or laptop all day—but at much lower costs
25 than lithium-ion batteries can offer.
Meanwhile, experts at the National Innovative Technology Laboratory have begun work on a sodium-ion battery, which uses sodium in place of lithium. This type of battery is the top competitor in the energy
30 storage industry in terms of cost-effective production. However, the batteries are limited in that they can be used only for stationary equipment because of their weight.
One of Grey's former interns and colleagues,
35 Niànzhēn Thao, founder of the ion battery manufacturer China Energetics, announced this month that he is creating a test manufacturing line for a lithium-sulfur battery that may reduce or even eliminate battery waste. The basic concept is that while it charges, the lithium-
40 sulfur battery may consume active materials while emitting energy and expelling waste. The discharge is consumed and recycled for later use. This technology is particularly well-suited to the aviation and space flight industries. This is because batteries made with
45 lithium-sulfur are lighter than those made with lithium or sodium ions. Thao also notes that lithium-sulfur

batteries produce two to four times more power than their leading competitors.
Looking long term, Grey is placing his bets on
50 quantum technology, hoping to take advantage of the solid-state technology already available. Some companies are already utilizing quantum computers to optimize solid state batteries. Grey hopes the future will bring dramatic improvements in the efficiency of portable
55 power through a combination of high-endurance quantum battery life and quick charging effects. It's estimated that replacing just one device's battery could reduce home power costs by up to 15 percent. Additional replacements could decrease costs as much
60 as 30 percent, which would cut almost a third from the country's overall power utilization. The difficulty arises in encouraging consumers to pay a bit more for these cutting-edge alternatives, which is more challenging in times of economic stress.

4

This passage is written from the point of view of a

A) consumer evaluating a number of options.

B) scientist researching competitors in his industry.

C) journalist summarizing changes in a field.

D) hobbyist describing the characteristics of new technology.

5

Which choice best describes the author's view of the potential improvements in the battery industry?

A) Necessary but wasteful

B) Promising but still evolving

C) Important but unsupported

D) Scientifically important but hazardous

6

With which of the following statements about lithium-sulfur batteries would Thao most likely agree?

A) They will fully eradicate battery waste.

B) They are more cost-efficient than batteries made with lithium or sodium-ions.

C) They are significantly more powerful than other kinds of batteries.

D) They have the potential to significantly lower energy costs at home.

Review

Point of view questions can be identified by these terms:

- perspective/point of view
- attitude
- believe
- likely to describe/agree/disagree

Evidence and Elimination

To answer a point of view question, follow these steps:

1. Identify the point of view in the question.
2. Find the section of the passage that describes the question's topic.
3. Eliminate answers that describe the wrong point of view.
4. Eliminate answers that are not supported by evidence.

Exit

If you've found the answer ...

Check the passage for evidence and confirm that it aligns with your answer. Mark your answer and continue to the next question.

If you're stuck between two choices ...

Compare the two answers to find the difference in tone and pick the one that best matches the tone of the passage.

If you have no idea what the answer is ...

Go with your gut. Skim the passage quickly and select the answer that best matches your overall understanding of the information.

Arguments

LEARNING TARGETS

1. Identify and interpret an author's argument.

2. Implement the basic approach for arguments questions.

3. Apply the *Convince Yourself* and *Negation Test* strategies to arguments questions.

Warm-Up

Complete the warm-up. When you have finished, double-check your work.

Questions 1–3 are based on the following passage.

This passage is adapted from Lonnie Carpenter, "A Virtuous Economy." © 2019 by MasteryPrep.

Is it possible to develop an economic system that's inherently fair? The question of how virtue aligns with money is old, and every new generation seems to revive
Line it. A pressing concern about today's economy is the
5 extent of government intervention. The U.S. operates under a capitalist economic system, characterized by private ownership of assets and business. Through capitalism, the prices of goods and services are determined by the free market, which in turn affects
10 income and wealth. In other words, assets are owned by private firms and individuals, with little regulation by the government.

The historic debates between Alexander Hamilton and Thomas Jefferson played an important role in the
15 creation of our modern economic system. Hamilton, the first Secretary of the Treasury, succeeded in giving the government power and oversight over currency when he established the First Bank of the United States in 1791. At the time, many felt that Hamilton gave the
20 government too much direct power over commerce.

Secretary of State Thomas Jefferson, on the other hand, strongly opposed Hamilton's idea of a national bank, advocating for the establishment of independent banks. He believed in a decentralized banking system
25 with a widespread, regional power base, whereby the power to issue currency would be in the hands of the people.

Jefferson's proposed economic system began to take hold when, in 1833, President Andrew Jackson
30 dismantled the country's national bank. The reformed system, which balanced many independent banks against a centralized treasury, seemed to provide stability and flexibility, giving power to private commerce as well as to the government.

35 Over recent years, this sense of balance has shifted. In the current capitalist economy, mergers of private banks have resulted in mega-banks that have been referred to as "too big to fail." This centralized wealth has resulted in a new economic aristocracy, challenging our very
40 democracy. Some feel we should change laws, reverting back to our former economic and commercial balance. Others advocate for more forceful remedies, such as breaking up large banks and redistributing wealth to create a new, just economic system to replace capitalism.
45 Various forms of socialism, by contrast, use government centralization as a tool to balance the

incomes of the general population. Socialism also allows economists to make clear decisions about what should be regulated by the government (medical systems, for
50 example) and what forms of commerce should remain under private management. Hybrid socialist systems that intertwine multiple methods of regulation can be created, serving as a flexible approach to economic policy-making. A limited form of socialism is appealing
55 to many Americans who strive for an optimized, stable, and efficient economy.

1

The author claims that Americans have historically

A) sought to develop a fair economic system.

B) been opposed to governmental power over commerce.

C) preferred a decentralized banking system.

D) thought Jefferson's economic philosophy was flawed.

2

A student claims that conflicting beliefs about the country's most suitable economic system surfaced for the first time in recent years. Which of the following best contradicts the student's claim?

A) Lines 4–5 ("A pressing … intervention")

B) Lines 5–7 ("The U.S. … business")

C) Lines 13–15 ("The historic … system")

D) Lines 15–19 ("Hamilton … 1791")

3

In the passage, the author makes which point about Hamilton's philosophy relative to that of Jefferson?

A) Hamilton proposed an intricate tax system, but Jefferson opposed it.

B) Hamilton wanted policies that gave the government more control over commerce, but Jefferson believed that the people should have control.

C) Hamilton believed in a centralized treasury, but Jefferson wanted to abolish the National Treasury.

D) Hamilton thought the economy should be decentralized, but Jefferson believed in private commerce.

Foundation

Work with a partner to fill in the table below using points for and against the following prompt:

Listening to music helps you complete homework more quickly.

Defense	Criticism

Foundation

Read the following paragraph. Follow along with your teacher to complete the table below, identifying which points from the paragraph belong in each section.

Teachers are constantly competing for their students' attention today. Why? Cellphones. Cellphones limit student learning for various reasons. For example, if notifications are continuously erupting from their phones, students are anxious to check those notifications, so they're completely ignoring what their teacher is saying. Cyberbullying is also on the rise in today's schools. With all the social media apps available to the average student, the opportunities to bully or be bullied are plentiful, leading to depression and failing grades. Some may say that the cellphone can be a valuable learning tool in the classroom. However, when it comes to using cellphones in school, the consequences far outweigh the benefits.

Claim	Evidence	Assumption	Criticism
Cell phones are the reason for lack of attention in school	Notifications, cyberbullying, social media		

Practice Set 1 | Complete the practice set. When you have finished, double-check your work.

Questions 1–11 are based on the following passage.

This passage is adapted from Dr. Leah Lovett, "Wolves in the Park." © 2019 by MasteryPrep.

In 1995, a research team led by Dr. James McCoy arranged for a small pack of gray wolves to be relocated to Yellowstone National Park. The aim of the team's study
Line was to reintroduce these natural predators back into
5 their native region and examine the outcome. Wolves had been hunted out of the park in 1926 by ranchers invested in protecting their livestock. Researchers observed that the elk population had subsequently risen to problematic levels. McCoy's team hypothesized
10 that the reintroduction of the gray wolves would help reduce the size of the elk herds. McCoy says, "Elk had taken over, flourishing not only in their own niche, but overflowing into other niches, including that of the beaver. In fact, by the early 1990s, the park held only one
15 surviving beaver colony. However, broader implications of reintroducing the wolves had yet to be understood, as few were focusing on the big picture—what the return of an apex predator could accomplish on a large scale."

Many ecological changes took place in Yellowstone
20 National Park between 1920 and the 1995 release of the gray wolves, though many did not understand how the loss of a primary predatory species had contributed to these changes. While the absence of the wolves in the park seemed to directly lead to a dramatic rise in
25 the numbers of large animals such as elk and buffalo, justification for the resulting decrease in beavers and beaver ponds seemed less clear. Through the 1995 experiment, McCoy and his team primarily hoped to see a reduction in the number of elk in the park, as the
30 animals were overgrazing their territory, multiplying beyond the bearing capacity of the range.

The return of the wolves indeed led to a reduction in the park's elk population. What the scientists had not predicted, or even considered, however, was how
35 a diminished elk population in the region would lead to the establishment of new beaver colonies. While the researchers did not quantify the beaver population, their arrival into the newly vacated territory led to an intricate system of restored dams and renewed ponds.
40 These, in turn, led to the conversion of overstressed meadows into rich wetlands and the regrowth of prairie pasture. Unexpectedly, the wolf-induced reduction of the overgrazing elk population had also led to a wealth of positive ecological developments. The "gray wolf
45 project" ultimately provided a valuable lesson on the interconnectivity of species in a landscape as well as the animals' effect on their own ecosystems.

The return of one key species—gray wolves—caused a ripple effect that resulted in a rejuvenation of the park's
50 wetlands, which encouraged the return of many more species and reduced erosion and ecological damage. McCoy, having observed these changes, stated, "The domino effect of damage to the system was reversed with a cascade of ecological improvements after the wolves
55 returned. Today, the region of Yellowstone National Park that the wolves inhabit has recovered remarkably—with greater biodiversity and overall ecological health." In addition, the gray wolves are thriving; in less than 20 years since their reintroduction to the park, Yellowstone's
60 wolf population has grown to over 100 wolves in 11 packs. Further, they are protected by law within the park's boundaries.

There are some who object to the return of predatory animals to a territory shared with humans—campers,
65 day-trippers, ranchers, and others who live in range of Yellowstone. Some argue that serious culling by human hunters would be a safer way to control the elk herds while providing income from hunting licenses and small, hunting-related businesses. Others cite the
70 dangers posed by the wolves to local livestock. But the counterargument is that Yellowstone National Park is set aside as a natural preserve where predation among species should naturally occur. By protecting the gray wolves, officials are helping to maintain a region of
75 Yellowstone that demonstrates an undisturbed ecology at work.

Practice Set 1

1

Which statement best captures Dr. McCoy's central assumption in setting up his research?

A) The reintroduction of a native predator to an environment will lead to a reduction in the herd sizes of its prey.

B) The tendency of certain predators to prey on larger animals such as elk is a somewhat recently evolved behavior.

C) The population of a certain predator is more likely to thrive in a protected ecological setting than in the wild.

D) The return of a native predator to a natural area will result in a renewed ecosystem.

2

What did McCoy and his team learn as part of their study that most directly allowed McCoy to reason that "the region of Yellowstone National Park that the wolves inhabit has recovered remarkably" (lines 55–56)?

A) They discerned that the elks' overgrazing had led to the erosion of the park's wetlands and prairie pasture.

B) They learned that by protecting the wolves through legislation, the number of wolf packs had grown.

C) They found that the lack of an apex predator in Yellowstone allowed elk to overgraze their territory and grow in number.

D) They discovered that the reduction of elk enabled beavers to reinhabit the region, inadvertently improving the condition of the wetlands.

3

Which action would best address a concern some raise about the introduction of predatory wolves into Yellowstone National Park?

A) Providing maps indicating the location of protected dams and ponds

B) Using physical barriers to separate the wolves from people and livestock

C) Requiring hunters to secure a license to cull elk during hunting season

D) Informing visitors about the history of the gray wolves' existence in the park

Approach

Arguments questions can be identified by these terms:

- claim
- point
- criticism
- assumption
- reason
- evidence

The following questions refer to the passage on page 300. Review question 4 with your teacher. Do not answer the question.

Entrance ❯ Evidence and Elimination ❯ Exit

4

Lovett makes which point about gray wolves relative to elk in Yellowstone National Park?

A) Gray wolves depend on elk for survival, but elk do not prey on wolves.

B) Gray wolves can impact the elk population, while elk can impact the beaver population.

C) Gray wolves prey on elk, but elk destroy the wolves' habitat.

D) Gray wolves do not pose a threat to livestock, but elk do.

Approach

Review questions 5 and 6 on your own. Circle the part of the question that identifies it as an arguments question. Do not answer the questions.

5

A student claims the gray wolves in Yellowstone National Park rely primarily on elk for survival. Which of the following statements in the passage contradicts the student's claim?

A) Lines 23–27 ("While . . . clear")

B) Lines 42–44 ("Unexpectedly . . . developments")

C) Lines 61–62 ("Further . . . boundaries")

D) Lines 66–69 ("Some . . . businesses")

6

Based on the passage, what potential criticism might be made of McCoy's conclusions about the gray wolves' reintroduction to Yellowstone National Park?

A) McCoy's understanding of the relationship between the wolves and the elk was incorrect.

B) McCoy's study did not measure the difference in the beaver population before and after the wolves were reintroduced.

C) McCoy's observations failed to take into account the loss of other large animals such as buffalo.

D) McCoy's research outcomes were not made available to the general public.

Questions 1–11 are based on the following passage.

This passage is adapted from Dr. Leah Lovett, "Wolves in the Park." © 2019 by MasteryPrep.

In 1995, a research team led by Dr. James McCoy arranged for a small pack of gray wolves to be relocated to Yellowstone National Park. The aim of the team's study
Line was to reintroduce these natural predators back into
5 their native region and examine the outcome. Wolves had been hunted out of the park in 1926 by ranchers invested in protecting their livestock. Researchers observed that the elk population had subsequently risen to problematic levels. McCoy's team hypothesized
10 that the reintroduction of the gray wolves would help reduce the size of the elk herds. McCoy says, "Elk had taken over, flourishing not only in their own niche, but overflowing into other niches, including that of the beaver. In fact, by the early 1990s, the park held only one
15 surviving beaver colony. However, broader implications of reintroducing the wolves had yet to be understood, as few were focusing on the big picture—what the return of an apex predator could accomplish on a large scale."

Many ecological changes took place in Yellowstone
20 National Park between 1920 and the 1995 release of the gray wolves, though many did not understand how the loss of a primary predatory species had contributed to these changes. While the absence of the wolves in the park seemed to directly lead to a dramatic rise in
25 the numbers of large animals such as elk and buffalo, justification for the resulting decrease in beavers and beaver ponds seemed less clear. Through the 1995 experiment, McCoy and his team primarily hoped to see a reduction in the number of elk in the park, as the
30 animals were overgrazing their territory, multiplying beyond the bearing capacity of the range.

The return of the wolves indeed led to a reduction in the park's elk population. What the scientists had not predicted, or even considered, however, was how
35 a diminished elk population in the region would lead to the establishment of new beaver colonies. While the researchers did not quantify the beaver population, their arrival into the newly vacated territory led to an intricate system of restored dams and renewed ponds.
40 These, in turn, led to the conversion of overstressed meadows into rich wetlands and the regrowth of prairie pasture. Unexpectedly, the wolf-induced reduction of the overgrazing elk population had also led to a wealth of positive ecological developments. The "gray wolf
45 project" ultimately provided a valuable lesson on the interconnectivity of species in a landscape as well as the animals' effect on their own ecosystems.

The return of one key species—gray wolves—caused a ripple effect that resulted in a rejuvenation of the park's
50 wetlands, which encouraged the return of many more species and reduced erosion and ecological damage. McCoy, having observed these changes, stated, "The domino effect of damage to the system was reversed with a cascade of ecological improvements after the wolves
55 returned. Today, the region of Yellowstone National Park that the wolves inhabit has recovered remarkably—with greater biodiversity and overall ecological health." In addition, the gray wolves are thriving; in less than 20 years since their reintroduction to the park, Yellowstone's
60 wolf population has grown to over 100 wolves in 11 packs. Further, they are protected by law within the park's boundaries.

There are some who object to the return of predatory animals to a territory shared with humans—campers,
65 day-trippers, ranchers, and others who live in range of Yellowstone. Some argue that serious culling by human hunters would be a safer way to control the elk herds while providing income from hunting licenses and small, hunting-related businesses. Others cite the
70 dangers posed by the wolves to local livestock. But the counterargument is that Yellowstone National Park is set aside as a natural preserve where predation among species should naturally occur. By protecting the gray wolves, officials are helping to maintain a region of
75 Yellowstone that demonstrates an undisturbed ecology at work.

Approach

Evidence and Elimination

To answer an arguments question, follow these steps:

1. Find evidence in the passage that relates to the question topic.
   - For specific points, look in the middle paragraphs.
   - For claims and assumptions, look in the first and last paragraph.
2. Eliminate choices that are unsupported or contradicted by the evidence.
3. Compare the remaining choices and select the answer that best aligns with the passage.

Answer question 4 with your teacher.

Entrance | **Evidence and Elimination** | Exit

4

Lovett makes which point about gray wolves relative to elk in Yellowstone National Park?

A) Gray wolves depend on elk for survival, but elk do not prey on wolves.

B) Gray wolves can impact the elk population, while elk can impact the beaver population.

C) Gray wolves prey on elk, but elk destroy the wolves' habitat.

D) Gray wolves do not pose a threat to livestock, but elk do.

The following questions refer to the passage on page 304. Answer questions 5 and 6 on your own. Focus on eliminating incorrect answers.

5

A student claims the gray wolves in Yellowstone National Park rely primarily on elk for survival. Which of the following statements in the passage contradicts the student's claim?

A) Lines 23–27 ("While . . . clear")

B) Lines 42–44 ("Unexpectedly . . . developments")

C) Lines 61–62 ("Further . . . boundaries")

D) Lines 66–69 ("Some . . . businesses")

6

Based on the passage, what potential criticism might be made of McCoy's conclusions about the gray wolves' reintroduction to Yellowstone National Park?

A) McCoy's understanding of the relationship between the wolves and the elk was incorrect.

B) McCoy's study did not measure the difference in the beaver population before and after the wolves were reintroduced.

C) McCoy's observations failed to take into account the loss of other large animals such as buffalo.

D) McCoy's research outcomes were not made available to the general public.

Arguments

Approach

<table>
<tr><td colspan="2">Exit</td></tr>
</table>

If you've found the answer ...

Double-check that your answer is supported by evidence. Mark your choice and continue working.

If you're stuck between two choices ...

The best choice for an assumption strengthens the argument when you insert it somewhere into the passage. The best choice for a claim can replace an explicit claim in the passage.

If you have no idea what the answer is ...

Go with your gut. Select the answer that avoids complicated words and that makes the most sense to you.

Review questions 7 and 8. Work with your teacher to choose the correct answer from the remaining choices.

Entrance > Evidence and Elimination > **Exit**

7

An unstated assumption made by the author about the elk is that they

A) contributed to the decline of the beaver population.

B) had multiplied beyond the range's capacity.

C) are predominately located in western regions of the United States.

D) will not be a good food source for wolves moving forward.

8

The author claims that maintaining the gray wolf population in Yellowstone National Park has

A) resulted in an ecological landscape that exists in its natural state.

B) provided protection to an endangered species.

C) caused arguments between environmentalists and ranchers.

D) ensured the protection of the park's beaver colonies.

Practice Set 2

Complete the practice set. When you have finished, double-check your work.

Questions 1–11 are based on the following passage.

This passage is adapted from Dr. Leah Lovett, "Wolves in the Park." © 2019 by MasteryPrep.

In 1995, a research team led by Dr. James McCoy arranged for a small pack of gray wolves to be relocated to Yellowstone National Park. The aim of the team's study
Line was to reintroduce these natural predators back into
5 their native region and examine the outcome. Wolves had been hunted out of the park in 1926 by ranchers invested in protecting their livestock. Researchers observed that the elk population had subsequently risen to problematic levels. McCoy's team hypothesized
10 that the reintroduction of the gray wolves would help reduce the size of the elk herds. McCoy says, "Elk had taken over, flourishing not only in their own niche, but overflowing into other niches, including that of the beaver. In fact, by the early 1990s, the park held only one
15 surviving beaver colony. However, broader implications of reintroducing the wolves had yet to be understood, as few were focusing on the big picture—what the return of an apex predator could accomplish on a large scale."

Many ecological changes took place in Yellowstone
20 National Park between 1920 and the 1995 release of the gray wolves, though many did not understand how the loss of a primary predatory species had contributed to these changes. While the absence of the wolves in the park seemed to directly lead to a dramatic rise in
25 the numbers of large animals such as elk and buffalo, justification for the resulting decrease in beavers and beaver ponds seemed less clear. Through the 1995 experiment, McCoy and his team primarily hoped to see a reduction in the number of elk in the park, as the
30 animals were overgrazing their territory, multiplying beyond the bearing capacity of the range.

The return of the wolves indeed led to a reduction in the park's elk population. What the scientists had not predicted, or even considered, however, was how
35 a diminished elk population in the region would lead to the establishment of new beaver colonies. While the researchers did not quantify the beaver population, their arrival into the newly vacated territory led to an intricate system of restored dams and renewed ponds.
40 These, in turn, led to the conversion of overstressed meadows into rich wetlands and the regrowth of prairie pasture. Unexpectedly, the wolf-induced reduction of the overgrazing elk population had also led to a wealth of positive ecological developments. The "gray wolf
45 project" ultimately provided a valuable lesson on the interconnectivity of species in a landscape as well as the animals' effect on their own ecosystems.

The return of one key species—gray wolves—caused a ripple effect that resulted in a rejuvenation of the park's
50 wetlands, which encouraged the return of many more species and reduced erosion and ecological damage. McCoy, having observed these changes, stated, "The domino effect of damage to the system was reversed with a cascade of ecological improvements after the wolves
55 returned. Today, the region of Yellowstone National Park that the wolves inhabit has recovered remarkably—with greater biodiversity and overall ecological health." In addition, the gray wolves are thriving; in less than 20 years since their reintroduction to the park, Yellowstone's
60 wolf population has grown to over 100 wolves in 11 packs. Further, they are protected by law within the park's boundaries.

There are some who object to the return of predatory animals to a territory shared with humans—campers,
65 day-trippers, ranchers, and others who live in range of Yellowstone. Some argue that serious culling by human hunters would be a safer way to control the elk herds while providing income from hunting licenses and small, hunting-related businesses. Others cite the
70 dangers posed by the wolves to local livestock. But the counterargument is that Yellowstone National Park is set aside as a natural preserve where predation among species should naturally occur. By protecting the gray wolves, officials are helping to maintain a region of
75 Yellowstone that demonstrates an undisturbed ecology at work.

9

Based on the passage, in studying the effect of predator reintroduction, McCoy and his colleagues made the most extensive use of which type of evidence?

A) Mathematical models to predict the number of wolves required to minimize the elk population

B) Analysis of data collected from previous researchers' work involving the gray wolves' interaction with elk

C) Numerical data demonstrating changes in the size of the elk herd in response to the reintroduction of the wolves

D) Published theories by scientists who had developed previous models of predator reintroduction

10

A student claims that the number of elk in Yellowstone National Park had no bearing on the health of the area's wetlands. Which of the following statements from the passage contradicts the student's claim?

A) Lines 23–27 ("While ... clear")

B) Lines 27–31 ("Through ... range")

C) Lines 33–36 ("What ... colonies")

D) Lines 48–51 ("The return ... damage")

11

In the passage, the author anticipates which of the following objections to restoring the gray wolf population in Yellowstone National Park?

A) The wolves will jeopardize Yellowstone's tourism dollars.

B) Elk will reach endangered status given the wolf invasion.

C) Ranchers will vacate the area rather than risk extensive losses to their livestock.

D) Guests of the park will not be safe if wolves are free to roam.

Strategy

Questions 12–20 are based on the following passages.

Passage 1 is adapted from Emily Howell, "Views on Abolition." Originally published in 1837. Passage 2 is adapted from Amelia Gartside, "Letter to Emily Howell." Originally published in 1838. Gartside encouraged Southern women to oppose slavery. Passage 1 is Howell's response to Gartside's views. Passage 2 is Gartside's response to Howell.

Passage 1

Nature has appointed one gender the dominant, and to the other gender the inferior role, and has done so without consideration of the behavior or character of
Line either. As a result, it is as much for the respect as it is
5 for the interest of women, in all matters, to concede to the duties of her station … But while women hold an inferior place in society to men, it is not because she was born with less important duties or a lack of influence on society. Nature dictates that the female sex indeed holds
10 influence and power, but that she should exert them in unique and different ways.

Men may interact in society through the colliding of intellectual ideas, in open discourse; they may foment their ideas by belittling others, through fear and through
15 personal investment; they may persuade through the rhetoric of public opinion; they may urge by physical force, and they stay within the boundaries of their identity. But all the influence and the battles that are permissible for women, are those that align with the
20 principles of kindness, hospitality, peace, and goodwill.

Women are to win through extolling peace and love; by making themselves so respected, revered, and loved, so that to yield to her opinions and to satisfy her requests is done through kindness and free will. However, such
25 transactions are only to take place in the home and in social circles. Let every woman become so informed and refined in intellect, that her opinions and outlook will be respected; so generous in emotion and action, that her motives will be respected—so unassuming and humble,
30 that discourse and competition will not exist—so "gentle and agreeable," that others will be at ease in her presence; then, the patriarchs, the husbands, and the boys will absorb her influence, to which they will yield not only willfully but also proudly.
35 A woman may seek the collaboration and cooperation of other women, to assist her in her suitable posts of piety, endowment, maternal and domestic obligations; but whatever, under any circumstance, shifts a woman into the role of combatant, either for herself or
40 those around her—whatever embroils her in conflict— whatever obliges her to exert persuasive influence, places

her outside her natural identity. If these constructs are correct, they are in direct opposition to any notion of involving females in abolitionist actions of any kind.

Passage 2

45 A detailed look into the rights of the slave has brought me to a better awareness of my own. I have found the Anti-Slavery movement to be the highest example of morals in this country—the example through which human rights are more fully examined, and
50 better understood and conveyed, than anywhere else. Here a tremendous but basic principle is extolled and illuminated, and from this beacon, light radiates in all directions.

All people have *rights* because they are *ethical* beings:
55 the rights of all human beings are grown out of their ethical nature; and because all people have the same ethical nature, they essentially have identical rights. The rights may be usurped from slaves, but they cannot be fully removed: their claims to themselves are as perfect
60 now as those of Emily Howell: their rights are stamped on their ethical beings, and are, as such, enduring. Further, if rights are established by the nature of our ethical being, then the mere identity of gender does not give to men greater rights and obligations than women.
65 To assume that it does, would be to rebut the undeniable truth, that humans, by their nature, are instruments of morality. To assume that it does, would be to destroy the relationship between the two entities, and to reverse their roles, glorifying animalism into sovereignty, and
70 reducing emperors to slaves, making the former an owner, and the latter its property.

When people are viewed as ethical beings, gender, instead of being seated at the highest peak of the land, managing upon rights and responsibilities, sinks into
75 insignificance and worthlessness. My belief then is that whatever is ethically right for men is ethically right for women. Our responsibilities originate, not from gender differences, but from the diversity of our roles in life, the various charges and talents committed to our
80 guardianship, and the different eras in which we breathe.

Strategy

Convince Yourself

After making eliminations, if you still have choices remaining, start a debate with yourself. Argue in favor of each answer choice. The simplest, easiest argument wins.

❶ Explain to yourself why each remaining answer could be correct.

❷ Select the answer choice that requires the least amount of explanation.

Review question 12 with your teacher. Use the Convince Yourself strategy to answer the question as a class.

12

In Passage 2, the author claims that the ethical nature of all people should

A) result in indistinguishable rights.

B) privilege some groups over others.

C) provoke arguments about gender roles.

D) allow fairness to both owners and slaves.

The following questions refer to the passages on page 310. Work on your own using the Convince Yourself strategy to answer questions 13 and 14.

13

A student claims that the roles of men and women have remained constant throughout the course of history. Which of the following statements in Passage 2 contradicts the student's claim?

A) Lines 57–61 ("The rights … enduring")

B) Lines 62–64 ("Further… women")

C) Lines 65–67 ("To assume … morality")

D) Lines 77–80 ("Our responsibilities … breathe")

14

In Passage 1, the author claims that a woman's influence

A) is powerful in a unique way.

B) should be asserted publicly.

C) is displayed through aggression.

D) has a significant impact on her daughters.

Strategy

Negation Test
Every argument on the SAT will contain some unstated assumptions. Because the author agrees with their own assumptions, the author should always disagree with the opposite of the assumption. You can use this to test out an assumption answer choice. Here's how ...   **1** Find the opposite of the answer choice.   **2** Ask yourself, "Does this hurt what the author said?"   • If the opposite hurts the author's argument, it is an assumption.   • If it is irrelevant to the author's argument, eliminate it.

Review question 15 with your teacher. Use the Negation Test strategy to answer the question as a class.

15

An unstated assumption made by the author of Passage 1 about men is that they

A) are not as naturally compassionate as women.

B) utilize aggression when interacting with women on important matters.

C) are primarily focused on providing for family.

D) are proud of the role women have in society.

Strategy

The following questions refer to the passages on page 310. Work on your own using the Negation Test strategy to answer questions 16 and 17.

16

The author of Passage 1 makes which of the following assumptions about a woman's nature?

A) A woman's nature is incompatible with power and influence.

B) A woman will never use physical force to satisfy her goals.

C) Conflict is inconsistent with a woman's identity.

D) Kindness and hospitality come naturally to all women.

17

An unstated assumption made by the author of Passage 2 about slaves is that

A) they should enjoy the same rights as do women.

B) they do not belong in the company of white men.

C) their cause is not as important as the cause for women.

D) their rights in society should not be fully examined.

This page intentionally left blank

Practice Set 3 | Complete the practice set. When you have finished, double-check your work.

Questions 12–20 are based on the following passages.

Passage 1 is adapted from Emily Howell, "Views on Abolition." Originally published in 1837. Passage 2 is adapted from Amelia Gartside, "Letter to Emily Howell." Originally published in 1838. Gartside encouraged Southern women to oppose slavery. Passage 1 is Howell's response to Gartside's views. Passage 2 is Gartside's response to Howell.

Passage 1

Nature has appointed one gender the dominant, and to the other gender the inferior role, and has done so without consideration of the behavior or character of
Line either. As a result, it is as much for the respect as it is
5 for the interest of women, in all matters, to concede to the duties of her station … But while women hold an inferior place in society to men, it is not because she was born with less important duties or a lack of influence on society. Nature dictates that the female sex indeed holds
10 influence and power, but that she should exert them in unique and different ways.

Men may interact in society through the colliding of intellectual ideas, in open discourse; they may foment their ideas by belittling others, through fear and through
15 personal investment; they may persuade through the rhetoric of public opinion; they may urge by physical force, and they stay within the boundaries of their identity. But all the influence and the battles that are permissible for women, are those that align with the
20 principles of kindness, hospitality, peace, and goodwill.

Women are to win through extolling peace and love; by making themselves so respected, revered, and loved, so that to yield to her opinions and to satisfy her requests is done through kindness and free will. However, such
25 transactions are only to take place in the home and in social circles. Let every woman become so informed and refined in intellect, that her opinions and outlook will be respected; so generous in emotion and action, that her motives will be respected—so unassuming and humble,
30 that discourse and competition will not exist—so "gentle and agreeable," that others will be at ease in her presence; then, the patriarchs, the husbands, and the boys will absorb her influence, to which they will yield not only willfully but also proudly.

35 A woman may seek the collaboration and cooperation of other women, to assist her in her suitable posts of piety, endowment, maternal and domestic obligations; but whatever, under any circumstance, shifts a woman into the role of combatant, either for herself or
40 those around her—whatever embroils her in conflict— whatever obliges her to exert persuasive influence, places

her outside her natural identity. If these constructs are correct, they are in direct opposition to any notion of involving females in abolitionist actions of any kind.

Passage 2

45 A detailed look into the rights of the slave has brought me to a better awareness of my own. I have found the Anti-Slavery movement to be the highest example of morals in this country—the example through which human rights are more fully examined, and
50 better understood and conveyed, than anywhere else. Here a tremendous but basic principle is extolled and illuminated, and from this beacon, light radiates in all directions.

All people have *rights* because they are *ethical* beings:
55 the rights of all human beings are grown out of their ethical nature; and because all people have the same ethical nature, they essentially have identical rights. The rights may be usurped from slaves, but they cannot be fully removed: their claims to themselves are as perfect
60 now as those of Emily Howell: their rights are stamped on their ethical beings, and are, as such, enduring. Further, if rights are established by the nature of our ethical being, then the mere identity of gender does not give to men greater rights and obligations than women.
65 To assume that it does, would be to rebut the undeniable truth, that humans, by their nature, are instruments of morality. To assume that it does, would be to destroy the relationship between the two entities, and to reverse their roles, glorifying animalism into sovereignty, and
70 reducing emperors to slaves, making the former an owner, and the latter its property.

When people are viewed as ethical beings, gender, instead of being seated at the highest peak of the land, managing upon rights and responsibilities, sinks into
75 insignificance and worthlessness. My belief then is that whatever is ethically right for men is ethically right for women. Our responsibilities originate, not from gender differences, but from the diversity of our roles in life, the various charges and talents committed to our
80 guardianship, and the different eras in which we breathe.

18

In Passage 1, which point does Howell make about the status of men relative to the status of women?

A) Women are largely separate from men, but women depend on men for their well-being and security.

B) Women play a role as significant as that of men, but women are viewed as subordinate.

C) Women have fewer responsibilities than men, but they also have fewer rights.

D) Women are superior to men, but history requires women to be submissive to men.

19

A student claims that both men and women shape society in identical ways. Which of the following statements in Passage 1 contradicts the student's claim?

A) Lines 6–9 ("But … society")

B) Lines 9–11 ("Nature … ways")

C) Lines 12–18 ("Men … identity")

D) Lines 21–24 ("Women … will")

20

What is Gartside's central claim in Passage 2?

A) The rights of human beings are not determined by race or gender.

B) Men and women must learn to work together to improve society.

C) Ethical rights are the most important distinction between people and animals.

D) Men and women should have equal opportunities outside of the home.

Mini-Test

Complete the mini-test. When you have finished, double-check your work.

Questions 42–52 are based on the following passages.

Passage 1 is adapted from Bellamy Bright, "New Horizons for the Human Race." ©2019 by MasteryPrep. Passage 2 is adapted from John Palmer Rhodes, "The Skeptic's Philosophy." ©2019 by MasteryPrep.

Passage 1

If you're placing a bet, gamble on radical change. Wager on a new kind of humanity that is so far from its roots that we no longer recognize it. That's the takeaway
Line from a recently held forum on transhumanism.
5   Hosted by Humanity 2.0, a group advocating transhuman advances, the purpose of the conference was to bring issues surrounding augmented humanity and transhumanism to public awareness. Experts in the field urged participants to develop plans, policies,
10 and strategies for dealing with the looming impact of technology on the very nature of human existence.

A recent flood of research on the topic suggests that, along with advances in biotechnology, medicine, and nanotechnology, the ability to alter humans is likely
15 to become a reality—perhaps within the next century. However, the current buffers in place to moderate the field (such as penalties for those who attempt to take humanity into the realm of the dangerous or "unnatural") are flimsy at best.
20   The capacity to augment the human species as we know it is becoming increasingly realistic. If we consider the degree of disruption that has come from historical advancements—the ability to vaccinate against diseases, for example—we can begin to foresee the impact of the
25 ability to tailor our offspring, augment our intellectual abilities, or "cure" old age. These are only a few of the radical innovations facing the human race. Humans do not resist the opportunity to explore scientific possibilities, and a plan to regulate subversive experimentation is
30 essential.

"Humanity is at a crossroads, and the time has come for us not just to think collaboratively, but to put our thoughts into action," states Matthew Sanders, CEO of Humanity 2.0. "This forum assembles thought leaders
35 from around the world to act on providing global oversight over augmented humanity—and to do so sooner rather than later."

Both the costs and the benefits of such technology are staggering. Potential "advancements" range from the
40 genetic removal of birth defects to the augmentation of the human mind with artificial intelligence. But with such innovation, say critics, will come inevitable consequences. It's impossible to foresee the moral and ethical fallout from

our co-existence with living, breathing "superhumans"
45 who are not bound by natural evolution.

Passage 2

In spite of immediate concerns facing the future of our species, scientists, philosophers, and techno-warriors seem to think it's time we start to consider the possibility that "humans," as we define them, may soon
50 be obsolete. Oxford University Professor Nick Bostrom believes that we, as a species, are very close to becoming a "lesser human subspecies," and how we handle this radical change may make a huge difference in what the future holds.
55   Bostrom is one of many people considering the challenges that lie ahead as we become increasingly able to alter humanity itself. We are rapidly gaining the ability to modify core human traits, but our society has dealt with this capability by suggesting moral and ethical
60 boundaries that are unlikely to be universally honored. We are already living in the world of genetically mutated organisms (GMOs), human cloning, stem-cell experimentation, artificial intelligence (AI), and the creation of superhuman prosthetics. In other words,
65 the era of "mere humanity" is quickly passing … and we are not ready. Bostrom yearns for proper evaluation, prioritization, and regulation before our "reality" becomes undefinable.

Many people have already exceeded their capacity for
70 enduring radical notions about the technology to come, a phenomenon that experts call "future shock." Recently, pressure has emerged from some to resist the urge to engineer humans and return to a simpler time. Such initiatives suggest that some would prefer to just shout
75 "no" to innovations that tamper with nature.

Then there are those who believe that a focus on human alteration is misguided when the longevity of our natural world is in jeopardy. Many think we have more pressing issues to contend with, including
80 climate change and the potential for mass extinction. Perhaps, they believe, we should focus on reducing the severity of the planet's current problems, not on creating "superhumans." Ironically, a counterargument to this notion is that humans have been unable to
85 mitigate problems such as global warming thus far, which makes a case for the use of artificial intelligence in the environmental arena. Regardless, a new version of humanity as we know it is at our threshold, the door has been opened, and we are ill-prepared.

1   1

42

Which statement best captures Humanity 2.0's central assumption in setting up the forum on transhumanism?

A) Transhumanism is an issue that will be hotly contested by leaders of religious organizations.

B) If left unchecked, the pursuit of transhumanism will lead to unfavorable outcomes.

C) The general public is unaware of the moral and ethical issues surrounding the field of transhumanism.

D) A select group of people will be in charge of creating policies on transhumanism and augmented humanity.

43

As used in line 16, "buffers" most nearly means

A) tools.

B) railways.

C) defenses.

D) cushions.

44

Which action would best address an issue raised by the hosts of the forum on transhumanism in Passage 1?

A) Developing a long-range plan to protect future generations from disease

B) Making laws against tailoring human physiology through genetic engineering

C) Establishing a comprehensive system of governance over transhumanistic practices

D) Educating the public about the costs and benefits of augmented humanity

45

A student claims that augmented humanity is unlikely to become a reality within our lifetime. Which of the following statements in Passage 1 contradicts the student's claim?

A) Lines 2–3 ("Wager … recognize it")

B) Lines 5–8 ("Hosted … awareness")

C) Lines 12–15 ("A recent … century")

D) Lines 20–21 ("The capacity … realistic")

46

What is Rhodes' central claim in Passage 2?

A) Artificial intelligence is the answer to many global concerns we currently face.

B) Transhumanism is a fictional concept being pursued by fantasists and dreamers.

C) Society at large is unprepared for the radical changes that will result from transhumanism.

D) Widespread research and experimentation on augmented humanity should take top priority.

47

Based on Passage 2, what potential criticism might be made of the notion that addressing climate change should take priority over the advancement of transhumanism?

A) Environmental issues will not be relevant as transhumanism takes hold.

B) Research in the field of global warming is already over-funded.

C) Climate change has yet to be proven with reliable scientific data.

D) Transhumanism and environmental protection may go hand in hand.

48

Which choice best supports Rhodes' claim that we must prepare for the radical challenges that lie ahead?

A) Lines 46–50 ("In spite … obsolete")

B) Lines 57–60 ("We … honored")

C) Lines 66–68 ("Bostrom … undefinable")

D) Lines 81–83 ("Perhaps … superhumans")

49

What does the author of Passage 1 do that most directly allows the reader to conceptualize the impact that transhumanism is likely to have on the human race?

A) He provides specific examples of the negative consequences of such radical technology.

B) He quotes a leading expert in the field of transhumanism who urges people to act.

C) He refers to research suggesting that society is not prepared for the radical changes to come.

D) He highlights the social disruption that resulted from the development of vaccines.

50

As used in line 85, "mitigate" most nearly means

A) alleviate.

B) soften.

C) quiet.

D) weaken.

51

The author of Passage 2 would probably respond to the discussion of transhumanism in Passage 1 by claiming that such a future

A) is chronologically inconsistent with the projections of experts.

B) may result in a backlash in the absence of regulations.

C) cannot be attained without technologies that do not exist.

D) seems certain to affect climate change in a negative way.

52

Which point about the challenges of transhumanism are explicit in Passage 1, and implicit in Passage 2?

A) It may result in forms of human life that pose a danger to society.

B) It will only become a reality if executed through funding from private sources.

C) It is likely to make research on the cause of genetic mutations unnecessary.

D) It may displace efforts to reduce climate change and the possibility of mass extinction.

STOP

**If you finish before time is called, you may check your work on this section only.
Do not turn to any other section.**

Wrap-Up

Complete the wrap-up. When you have finished, double-check your work.

Questions 4–6 are based on the following passage.

This passage is adapted from Lonnie Carpenter, "A Virtuous Economy." © 2019 by MasteryPrep.

Is it possible to develop an economic system that's inherently fair? The question of how virtue aligns with money is old, and every new generation seems to revive
Line it. A pressing concern about today's economy is the
5 extent of government intervention. The U.S. operates under a capitalist economic system, characterized by private ownership of assets and business. Through capitalism, the prices of goods and services are determined by the free market, which in turn affects
10 income and wealth. In other words, assets are owned by private firms and individuals, with little regulation by the government.

The historic debates between Alexander Hamilton and Thomas Jefferson played an important role in the
15 creation of our modern economic system. Hamilton, the first Secretary of the Treasury, succeeded in giving the government power and oversight over currency when he established the First Bank of the United States in 1791. At the time, many felt that Hamilton gave the
20 government too much direct power over commerce.

Secretary of State Thomas Jefferson, on the other hand, strongly opposed Hamilton's idea of a national bank, advocating for the establishment of independent banks. He believed in a decentralized banking system
25 with a widespread, regional power base, whereby the power to issue currency would be in the hands of the people.

Jefferson's proposed economic system began to take hold when, in 1833, President Andrew Jackson
30 dismantled the country's national bank. The reformed system, which balanced many independent banks against a centralized treasury, seemed to provide stability and flexibility, giving power to private commerce as well as to the government.
35 Over recent years, this sense of balance has shifted. In the current capitalist economy, mergers of private banks have resulted in mega-banks that have been referred to as "too big to fail." This centralized wealth has resulted in a new economic aristocracy, challenging our very
40 democracy. Some feel we should change laws, reverting back to our former economic and commercial balance. Others advocate for more forceful remedies, such as breaking up large banks and redistributing wealth to create a new, just economic system to replace capitalism.
45 Various forms of socialism, by contrast, use government centralization as a tool to balance the
incomes of the general population. Socialism also allows economists to make clear decisions about what should be regulated by the government (medical systems, for
50 example) and what forms of commerce should remain under private management. Hybrid socialist systems that intertwine multiple methods of regulation can be created, serving as a flexible approach to economic policy-making. A limited form of socialism is appealing
55 to many Americans who strive for an optimized, stable, and efficient economy.

4

The author claims that the establishment of socialism may allow for

A) a more flexible and stabilized economy.

B) the destruction of mega-banks.

C) a return to Jefferson's economic philosophy.

D) a system of commerce regulated solely by the government.

5

Which choice best supports the author's claim that the current American economic system is flawed?

A) Lines 30–34 ("The reformed … government")

B) Line 35 ("Over … shifted")

C) Lines 38–40 ("This centralized … democracy")

D) Lines 45–47 ("Various … population")

6

An unstated assumption made by the author about democracy is that it

A) is incompatible with economic aristocracy.

B) is threatened by some forms of socialism.

C) is not the best form of government.

D) is an unethical system of government.

This page intentionally left blank

Review

Arguments questions can be identified by these terms:

- claim
- point
- criticism
- assumption
- reason
- evidence

Evidence and Elimination

To answer an arguments question, follow these steps:

1 Find evidence in the passage that relates to the question topic.

- For specific points, look in the middle paragraphs.
- For claims and assumptions, look in the first and last paragraph.

2 Eliminate choices that are unsupported or contradicted by the evidence.

3 Compare the remaining choices and select the answer that best aligns with the passage.

Exit

If you've found the answer ...

Double-check that your answer is supported by evidence. Mark your choice and continue working.

If you're stuck between two choices ...

The best choice for an assumption strengthens the argument when you insert it somewhere into the passage. The best choice for a claim can replace an explicit claim in the passage.

If you have no idea what the answer is ...

Go with your gut. Select the answer that avoids complicated words and that makes the most sense to you.

11

Chapter

Multiple Texts

LEARNING TARGETS

1. Compare and contrast information and points of view from paired passages.

2. Implement the basic approach for multiple texts questions.

3. Apply the *Diagram the Margins* and *Bare Bones* strategies to multiple texts questions.

Warm-Up

Complete the warm-up. When you have finished, double-check your work.

Questions 1–3 are based on the following passages.

Passage 1 is adapted from Abraham Lincoln, "Address to the Young Men's Lyceum of Springfield, Illinois." Originally delivered in 1838. Passage 2 is from Henry David Thoreau, "Resistance to Civil Government." Originally published in 1849.

Passage 1

For the sake of future generations, let all citizens swear by the blood of the Revolution never to violate the laws of the country in any way or tolerate their violation
Line by others. As the patriots of 1776 did to the support of
5 the Declaration of Independence, so to the support of the Constitution and laws let every American pledge his life, his property, and his sacred honor; let every man remember that to violate the law is to trample on the blood of his father, to mar his own character,
10 and to threaten his children's liberty. Let reverence for laws be imparted by every American mother; let it be taught in schools, in seminaries, and in colleges; let it be preached from the pulpit, proclaimed in legislative halls, and enforced in courts of justice. And, in short,
15 let it become the *political doctrine* of the nation; and let the old and the young, the rich and the poor of all genders and colors yield unceasingly upon its altar. While this sentiment prevails throughout the nation, let it be known that efforts to subvert our national freedom
20 would be fruitless.

While I so pressingly urge a strict observance of all laws, I am not suggesting that unjust laws do not exist or that grievances may not arise for which there is no legal recourse; I mean to say no such thing. What I do mean
25 to say is that, if unjust laws exist, they should be repealed as soon as possible; but until that time, for the sake of example, all laws should be religiously observed.

There is no grievance that justifies protest by the masses. In any case that arises, such as a pledge of
30 abolitionism, one of two positions is true: the condition is right within itself, and therefore deserves protection by law, or it is wrong, and therefore should be prohibited by legal enactments. In neither case is intervention by the populace necessary, justifiable, or excusable.

Passage 2

35 Unjust laws exist; shall we be content to obey them, or shall we set out to amend them until we have succeeded? Within our government, men think that they should wait to speak out against wrongful laws until they have persuaded the majority. They think that if they
40 protest, the outcome will be worse than the injustice. But this is the government's fault. Why does it not anticipate and provide for legal reform? Why does it not listen to the minority?

If the injustice is part of the debate within
45 government, let it pass; perhaps it will fade naturally. But if the injustice is a policy, a command, or a strategy that only serves itself, then perhaps you should consider rising up. However, if the breach requires you to be an agent of corruption, then I say, break the law. Let
50 your voice erode authority. I cannot lend myself to the wrongdoing that I condemn.

As for legal procedures to remedy such offenses, I am not aware of any such measures. They would take too much time, and a man's life will be wasted. I have
55 other affairs to attend to. I did not come into this world to make it a good place to live in, but to live in it, be it good or bad. Men cannot do everything but must do something.

I do not hesitate to say that those who call themselves
60 Abolitionists should immediately withdraw their support from the government … and not wait until they constitute a majority of one. I think that with God on their side, they must not wait for others. Moreover, a man whose views are more sound than his neighbors
65 already constitues a majority of one.

1

Which choice best states the relationship between the two passages?

A) Passage 2 challenges the primary argument of Passage 1.

B) Passage 2 advocates a measured approach to a problem discussed in Passage 1.

C) Passage 2 provides further evidence to support an idea introduced in Passage 1.

D) Passage 2 exemplifies an attitude promoted in Passage 1.

2

How would Thoreau most likely respond to Lincoln's statement in lines 24–27, Passage 1 ("What … observed")?

A) He would claim that using proper procedures to counter legal injustice is less likely to be successful during times of war.

B) He would contend that there are no legal procedures that rectify injustices quickly enough to be worthwhile.

C) He would question the likelihood that a civilian population would rally to protest a legal injustice.

D) He would point out that we cannot predict the kinds of injustices that civilians would consider intolerable.

3

Based on the passages, both Lincoln and Thoreau would agree with which of the following claims?

A) Unjust laws at the hands of the government are not acceptable.

B) U.S. loyalists fought courageously on behalf of the country.

C) The ethical obligations of citizens are often undervalued.

D) Political activism is as important for leaders as it is for citizens.

Foundation

Work with your teacher to review the following character cards and speech excerpts.

Senior Class President Candidate #1: Rachel McMiller

- Valedictorian of class
- Favorite subjects: science, math
- Notable character traits: mature, respectful, kind

Excerpts from speech:

"High school is preparing us for the world beyond, and I believe we should do all we can to reach our potential. As such, I propose we do away with unnecessary extracurricular activities and focus on the subjects that will lead to future success. For instance, instead of gym class, we should have an extra study hall where students can be tutored in assignments they are struggling with or practice standardized tests in preparation for college. We can and should do more to realize our highest academic potential. I want to support that goal."

"As your class president, I will do all I can to ensure we receive the best instruction, advice, and opportunities to learn in the most effective ways. I want to see all of us reach our goals. So, vote for me, and let's see what we're made of!"

Senior Class President Candidate #2: Kenny Springleaf

- Class clown
- Favorite subjects: gym, history
- Notable character traits: outgoing, athletic, good with puns

Excerpts from speech:

"Who else thinks school is boring? High school should be the best experience of our lives! Why do we have so many homework assignments? Why do we have to learn so many things that we aren't going to need later on in life? I propose we balance our class schedules a little more with extracurricular activities. We should have a period where we just get to relax, like in elementary school where kids get to take a nap. I'd be able to focus better on my studies if I was given a break once in a while. Furthermore, we need to be conscious of our health, so let's make gym class longer. And what ever happened to recess? We should have more time to relax and enjoy our childhood; I want to make sure we can, so that we don't all collapse from anxiety and academic stress."

"As your class president, I am going to make high school fun. So, vote for me, and say goodbye to homework!"

Foundation

Work with your teacher to fill in the Venn diagram below using the changes suggested by Rachel and Kenny.

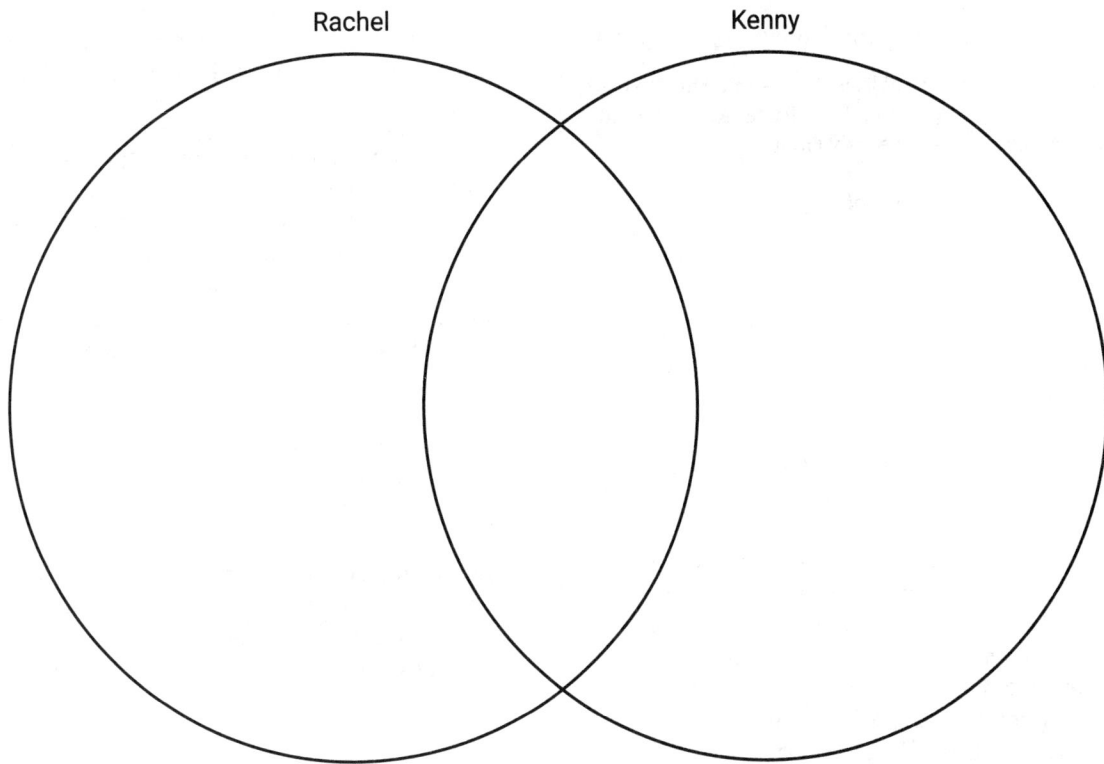

Rachel   Kenny

Using your assigned candidate's position, work on your own to write a 3–5 sentence response to your opponent's speech.

Response:

_____

_____

_____

_____

_____

Venn diagram: a visual aid used to organize similarities and differences between two topics.

Practice Set 1 | Complete the practice set. When you have finished, double-check your work.

Questions 1–8 are based on the following passages.

Passage 1 is adapted from John Bickle, "Space Tourism: The Next Luxury Industry?" ©2019 by MasteryPrep. Passage 2 is adapted from Sarah Campell, "Touring the Final Frontier." ©2019 by MasteryPrep. Both articles are responses to a recent conference held to facilitate the collaboration of various entrepreneurial space companies.

Passage 1

World travelers may eventually be able to go to space. That's the stance taken at an unparalleled conference on tourism beyond Earth.

Line Gathered in San Francisco by the Gateway
5 Foundation for Space Exploration, aerospace engineers, robotics experts, and scientists from NASA teamed up to help make space tourism an industry.

The conference directly followed the 2008 unveiling of two luxury space companies. Virgin Galactic of
10 California will operate a zero-gravity atmospheric flight for travelers, whereas World View of Arizona hopes to send tourists to the edge of space under a massive, balloon-like aircraft. A third company that launched in 2010, Space Adventures of Virginia, plans to offer orbital
15 spaceflights to tourists, even allowing some to float outside the spacecraft.

In a few short decades, these companies could be leaders in space exploration, offering travelers unmatched views of space and giving them the
20 opportunity to experience zero gravity. But unlike commercial airlines, which were the first to open the door to tourism through flight, these travel companies also hope to enrich the scientific community. One company is designing an anti-gravity orbital spaceport
25 where NASA vehicles could dock and refuel: scientists could also conduct long-term experiments there.

Furthermore, as private travel companies venture into space, the scientific community may be able to expand its efforts in space mining. "NASA has been impeded by
30 insufficient funding," explains NASA engineer, Connor Zusck. "But with private companies sending people to space, we could finally make better use of what exists beyond the atmosphere." The extraction of rare minerals from space by private companies could lead to a number
35 of unprecedented scientific projects, which would be a win-win for both the scientific community and the space tourism industry.

While space tourism companies are primarily focused on developing efficient launch methods in order
40 to market "luxury travel into outer space," the scientific community is eager to expand its research and continue to explore space's infinite mysteries. By working together,

both the space tourism industry and the scientific community hope to expand Earth's horizon.

Passage 2

45 The motivation behind outer space travel is shifting from exploration to profit. In recent years, a number of private companies have jumped into the space race marketed for the ultrarich. This will certainly give millionaires even more options for indulgent
50 entertainment, but we may all benefit: potentially valuable resources harvested from space, along with the travel industry's technological advancements, may enrich a host of scientific fields.

But before these companies ramp up their rocket
55 power, we should think carefully. On the surface, space touring endeavors seem to bypass some environmental concerns; for example, they aim to use efficient launching methods in order to minimize carbon emissions. But the consequences—both in space and on
60 Earth—warrant scrutiny.

Consider the principles behind the industry. One might argue that launching tourists into space could interfere with scientific exploration, just as one might argue that some habitats on Earth should remain off-
65 limits to the general public for the sake of research. Others might advise that expending precious, limited resources on entertaining the super-wealthy is not a wise choice.

Historically, however, business ambitions have
70 overruled the conservation of nature, and it may be hard to convince the world that the vast emptiness of space is worth protecting. After all, space is limitless, and there are very few people who have experienced—or will ever experience it.

75 But there's also the potential for companies to compete for monopolies on some of the materials extracted from space. For example, some resources are more valuable and more abundant in space than they are on Earth. Discussions of their ownership haven't even
80 begun—and appropriate governmental regulations on the industry are altogether nonexistent, to put it bluntly.

Space tourism companies, like most private businesses, have been hesitant to discuss such concerns. One speaker from the space tourism conference in San
85 Francisco spoke out with an appeal to limit regulations on luxury space travel at all costs. But it benefits those in the industry to reach a general agreement on the utilization of space. Without it, those in the space tourism industry are subject to challenge, lost
90 investments, and uncertain gains. It's time a consensus is reached.

1

Which statement best describes the relationship between the passages?

A) Passage 2 refutes the central claim advanced in Passage 1.

B) Passage 2 details a phenomenon discussed more generally in Passage 1.

C) Passage 2 disputes the practicality of the plans described in Passage 1.

D) Passage 2 expresses reservations about developments discussed in Passage 1.

2

The author of Passage 2 would most likely respond to the discussion of the future of space exploration in lines 27–37, Passage 1, by suggesting that such a future

A) is unrealistic given the limited resources available for space travel.

B) could be challenging to carry out without formal oversight and regulation.

C) cannot be realized because the technologies have not been developed.

D) appears likely to affect Earth's economy in a harmful manner.

3

On which of the following points would the authors of both passages most likely agree?

A) Space companies will be able to mine precious minerals in space more easily than companies can mine previous resources on Earth.

B) Those who wish to protect natural environments tend to be overruled by industry.

C) The resources mined and technologies developed by space tourism companies could benefit the scientific community.

D) Space tourism companies are unlikely to support space mining and exploration.

Approach

Entrance

Multiple texts questions can be identified by these features:

- two passages
- a question that asks you to compare or contrast the passages or the authors' ideas

The following questions refer to the passages on page 330. Review question 4 with your teacher. Do not answer the question.

Entrance › Evidence and Elimination › Exit

4

The main purpose of both passages is to

A) suggest a strategy to address Earth's depleting resources.

B) discuss the potential effects of the space tourism industry.

C) describe the latest proposals from entrepreneurial space companies.

D) analyze the responsibilities space companies have to humanity.

Review questions 5 and 6 on your own. Circle the parts of the questions that identify them as multiple texts questions. Do not answer the questions.

5

Which point regarding the resources attainable in space is implicit in Passage 1 and explicit in Passage 2?

A) They may be more valuable and more abundant in space than they are on Earth.

B) They will only be valuable if they can be mined effectively.

C) They will primarily be useful for scientific experiments conducted in space.

D) They will become more valuable as those same resources become less scarce on Earth.

6

Which choice best describes how the two authors regard the developing space tourism economy?

A) Bickle believes that the developing space tourism economy is leading the way for scientific endeavors to develop, while Campell believes that the developing space tourism economy warrants some careful consideration before it develops further.

B) Bickle believes that the developing space tourism economy should pursue the economic gains from resources mined in space, while Campell believes that the economic gains from mining in space are overblown.

C) Bickle believes that scientists should not be involved with the developing space tourism economy, while Campell believes that scientists could benefit from an expanding space tourism industry.

D) Bickle believes that the developing space tourism industry should be regulated for the sake of what is most beneficial for humanity, while Campell believes it should be regulated for the sake of preserving the beauty of space.

Questions 1–8 are based on the following passages.

Passage 1 is adapted from John Bickle, "Space Tourism: The Next Luxury Industry?" ©2019 by MasteryPrep. Passage 2 is adapted from Sarah Campell, "Touring the Final Frontier." ©2019 by MasteryPrep. Both articles are responses to a recent conference held to facilitate the collaboration of various entrepreneurial space companies.

Passage 1

World travelers may eventually be able to go to space. That's the stance taken at an unparalleled conference on tourism beyond Earth.

Line
5 Gathered in San Francisco by the Gateway Foundation for Space Exploration, aerospace engineers, robotics experts, and scientists from NASA teamed up to help make space tourism an industry.

The conference directly followed the 2008 unveiling of two luxury space companies. Virgin Galactic of
10 California will operate a zero-gravity atmospheric flight for travelers, whereas World View of Arizona hopes to send tourists to the edge of space under a massive, balloon-like aircraft. A third company that launched in 2010, Space Adventures of Virginia, plans to offer orbital
15 spaceflights to tourists, even allowing some to float outside the spacecraft.

In a few short decades, these companies could be leaders in space exploration, offering travelers unmatched views of space and giving them the
20 opportunity to experience zero gravity. But unlike commercial airlines, which were the first to open the door to tourism through flight, these travel companies also hope to enrich the scientific community. One company is designing an anti-gravity orbital spaceport
25 where NASA vehicles could dock and refuel: scientists could also conduct long-term experiments there.

Furthermore, as private travel companies venture into space, the scientific community may be able to expand its efforts in space mining. "NASA has been impeded by
30 insufficient funding," explains NASA engineer, Connor Zusck. "But with private companies sending people to space, we could finally make better use of what exists beyond the atmosphere." The extraction of rare minerals from space by private companies could lead to a number
35 of unprecedented scientific projects, which would be a win-win for both the scientific community and the space tourism industry.

While space tourism companies are primarily focused on developing efficient launch methods in order
40 to market "luxury travel into outer space," the scientific community is eager to expand its research and continue to explore space's infinite mysteries. By working together, both the space tourism industry and the scientific community hope to expand Earth's horizon.

Passage 2

45 The motivation behind outer space travel is shifting from exploration to profit. In recent years, a number of private companies have jumped into the space race marketed for the ultrarich. This will certainly give millionaires even more options for indulgent
50 entertainment, but we may all benefit: potentially valuable resources harvested from space, along with the travel industry's technological advancements, may enrich a host of scientific fields.

But before these companies ramp up their rocket
55 power, we should think carefully. On the surface, space touring endeavors seem to bypass some environmental concerns; for example, they aim to use efficient launching methods in order to minimize carbon emissions. But the consequences—both in space and on
60 Earth—warrant scrutiny.

Consider the principles behind the industry. One might argue that launching tourists into space could interfere with scientific exploration, just as one might argue that some habitats on Earth should remain off-
65 limits to the general public for the sake of research. Others might advise that expending precious, limited resources on entertaining the super-wealthy is not a wise choice.

Historically, however, business ambitions have
70 overruled the conservation of nature, and it may be hard to convince the world that the vast emptiness of space is worth protecting. After all, space is limitless, and there are very few people who have experienced—or will ever experience it.

75 But there's also the potential for companies to compete for monopolies on some of the materials extracted from space. For example, some resources are more valuable and more abundant in space than they are on Earth. Discussions of their ownership haven't even
80 begun—and appropriate governmental regulations on the industry are altogether nonexistent, to put it bluntly.

Space tourism companies, like most private businesses, have been hesitant to discuss such concerns. One speaker from the space tourism conference in San
85 Francisco spoke out with an appeal to limit regulations on luxury space travel at all costs. But it benefits those in the industry to reach a general agreement on the utilization of space. Without it, those in the space tourism industry are subject to challenge, lost
90 investments, and uncertain gains. It's time a consensus is reached.

Approach

Evidence and Elimination

To answer a multiple texts question, follow these steps:

1. Determine how the question relates to both passages.
2. Eliminate any choice that fails to accurately describe both passages or doesn't relate them correctly.

Answer question 4 with your teacher.

Entrance **Evidence and Elimination** Exit

4

The main purpose of both passages is to

A) suggest a strategy to address Earth's depleting resources.

B) discuss the potential effects of the space tourism industry.

C) describe the latest proposals from entrepreneurial space companies.

D) analyze the responsibilities space companies have to humanity.

The following questions refer to the passages on page 334. Answer questions 5 and 6 on your own. Focus on eliminating incorrect answers.

5

Which point regarding the resources attainable in space is implicit in Passage 1 and explicit in Passage 2?

A) They may be more valuable and more abundant in space than they are on Earth.

B) They will only be valuable if they can be mined effectively.

C) They will primarily be useful for scientific experiments conducted in space.

D) They will become more valuable as those same resources become less scarce on Earth.

6

Which choice best describes how the two authors regard the developing space tourism economy?

A) Bickle believes that the developing space tourism economy is leading the way for scientific endeavors to develop, while Campell believes that the developing space tourism economy warrants some careful consideration before it develops further.

B) Bickle believes that the developing space tourism economy should pursue the economic gains from resources mined in space, while Campell believes that the economic gains from mining in space are overblown.

C) Bickle believes that scientists should not be involved with the developing space tourism economy, while Campell believes that scientists could benefit from an expanding space tourism industry.

D) Bickle believes that the developing space tourism industry should be regulated for the sake of what is most beneficial for humanity, while Campell believes it should be regulated for the sake of preserving the beauty of space.

Multiple Texts

Approach

Exit

If you've found the answer …

Verify that it is supported with textual evidence. If so, mark your answer and continue to the next question.

If you're stuck between two choices …

Use your pencil to mark how well each choice fits with each passage. Put a check if a choice agrees with a passage, an "X" if the choice disagrees with the passage, and a dash if it is somewhere in the middle. Compare your marks to select the better choice.

If you have no idea what the answer is …

Use the title and opening paragraph of each passage to get a general idea of the central argument, and select the choice that is most consistent.

Review questions 7 and 8. Work with your teacher to choose the correct answer from the remaining choices.

Entrance 〉 Evidence and Elimination 〉 **Exit**

7

Which choice best describes how Bickle would most likely have reacted to Campell's remarks in the third paragraph of Passage 2?

A) ~~With agreement, because preserving the beauty of space from industry may enhance space tourism attraction.~~

B) With hesitation, because exploring the vastness of space should be a universal right.

C) ~~With skepticism, because Campell does not support her argument with examples of how humanity is better off for preserving environments on Earth.~~

D) With disagreement, because the space tourism industry and the scientific community both stand to benefit from each other.

8

Based on the passages, one commonality in the viewpoints that Bickle and Campell take toward the scientific community is that

A) ~~neither author expects the scientific community to benefit from space tourism.~~

B) neither author embraces the scientific community as his or her own.

C) ~~both authors consider themselves as future leaders in the scientific community.~~

D) both authors view the scientific community as central to their arguments.

Practice Set 2 | Complete the practice set. When you have finished, double-check your work.

Questions 9–14 are based on the following passages.

Passage 1 is adapted from Charles Parson, *Ponderings on the Economy of Europe.* Originally published in 1852. Passage 2 is adapted from Philip Barker, *Occupations of Men,* written in response to Parson's article. Originally published in 1853.

Passage 1

To escape … the evils of ambivalence and adaptability, ten hundred times more dangerous than those of arrogance and the strongest preconception,
Line those of arrogance and the strongest preconception,
5 we have established feudalism; and no man should consider looking into its flaws or vices but with due respect; he should never think of reforming it by rebellion; he should handle the defects of this economic system as he would handle a wounded father, with
10 reverent admiration and timid concern. By this wise preconception, we are instructed to behold with horror those descendants of their nation who are provoked hastily to ruin that elderly father and dump him into the cauldron of witches, dreaming that by their toxic herbs,
15 and wild incantations, they may resurrect the founding economic institution, and restore their father's breath.

Feudalism should be wholly regarded as an economic system. Subordinate economic activities of an inconsequential nature may be conducted at whim—but
20 the feudal system should not be regarded as nothing more than a basic contract in a trade of salt and wheat, coffee or tobacco, or some other related minor thing, to be considered with little, fleeting interest, and to be suspended by the impulse of those involved. It should be
25 approached with pious awe; it is not a system of things subordinate only to the perishing, temporary existence of a gross and animalistic nature. It is a system in all social ranks, a system in all commerce, a system in every occupation, and for all people. As the means of such
30 a system cannot be sustained in just one generation, it becomes a system not just between the living, but also the dead, and those who have yet to be born … The economic parties of this collective partnership are not ethically free to completely dissolve and disband
35 the ties of their subordinate society, reducing it into a chaotic, disunified, unsophisticated mess of rudimentary principles.

Passage 2

Men of all generations must be as free to decide for
40 themselves, *in all instances*, as the men of preceding generations. The foolishness and presupposition of the feudal system dictating occupation from birth is the most absurd and impudent of all cruelties.

Man has no ownership of man; nor does any
45 generation have ownership of subsequent generations. The government and landlords of the early 1600s, or any other time period, are no more entitled to organize the present population or to regulate it in any way whatsoever, than the government and landlords of today
50 are to organize, force, or regulate those who will live hundreds or thousands of years from now.

Every generation is, and ought to be, capable of doing all things that circumstances require. It is the living, and not the deceased, that contain the potential. When a man
55 ceases to exist, his potential and his drive cease with him; and no longer having any interest in the commerce of the world, he no longer has any ambition to participate in business, or in industry, or in innovating …

Men who have left the world, and men who have
60 yet to be born into it, are as distant from each other as the maximum extent of human imagination can comprehend. How, then, can any obligation exist between them; what law or agreement can be reached between two men who, one no longer present, and one
65 not yet present, can not encounter each other, that one man should dictate the other's occupation for all time?

The conditions of the world are always shifting, and the desires of men also shift; and as business is conducted by those who are alive, and not by those
70 who are dead, it is only the living that have any say in it. That which one man may choose as the right and best occupation may be found restricting and unsuitable by his descendants. In this scenario, who should decide, the dead, or the living?

9

In lines 62–66, the author of Passage 2 refers to an idea introduced in Passage 1 in order to

A) question the credentials of the author of Passage 1 to discuss economic theory.

B) refute the statement made about feudalism in the first sentence of Passage 1.

C) further his argument by highlighting the flawed reasoning he sees in Passage 1.

D) endorse the concluding assertion made by the author of Passage 1 regarding the rights of economic parties.

10

How would Barker most likely respond to Parson's statement in lines 18–24, Passage 1 ("Subordinate … involved")?

A) He would state that the concept of feudalism should be adaptable as economic conditions change.

B) He would contend that feudalism is an unreasonable system that should be subject to reform.

C) He would doubt the possibility that significant reforms to feudalism would be achievable even if the system was widely opposed.

D) He would mention that history shows the value of the feudalistic system.

11

Which choice best describes how Parson would most likely have reacted to the remarks made in the final paragraph of Passage 2?

A) With agreement, because adjusting to new economic developments may strengthen existing partnerships.

B) With passivity, because the stability of society is not guaranteed.

C) With doubt, because Barker does not support his argument with examples of people who are better off when deciding their occupations for themselves.

D) With disagreement, because shifting desires are not sufficient reason to justify changing the economic system.

Strategy

The Diagram the Margins strategy is a great way to organize information as you compare and contrast the arguments made in paired passages.

Use this strategy on multiple texts questions when you are asked to identify how the passages or authors' ideas compare or contrast.

1. Use the margins to create a Venn diagram.

2. "Fill" your diagram with evidence from the passage as you read. Similarities go in the center, differences in the margins.

3. Use your Venn diagram to select the best answer.

The following questions refer to the passages on page 338. Review question 12 with your teacher. Use the Diagram the Margins strategy to answer the question as a class.

12

The main purpose of both passages is to

A) recommend a way to address a particular economic hardship.

B) discuss the responsibilities of people to their economic system.

C) analyze the effects of changing the economic system.

D) identify the ways that feudalism organizes society.

Strategy

Work on your own using the Diagram the Margins strategy to answer questions 13 and 14.

13

Which choice best states the relationship between the two passages?

A) Passage 2 opposes the main argument of Passage 1.

B) Passage 2 supports a similar resolution to an issue discussed in Passage 1.

C) Passage 2 gives additional evidence to support a concept introduced in Passage 1.

D) Passage 2 illustrates an idea promoted in Passage 1.

14

Both passages discuss the system of feudalism in relation to

A) the economic functions of people.

B) trade regulations.

C) paternal reverence.

D) questions of ownership.

Questions 15–20 are based on the following passages.

Passage 1 is adapted from Truskowski et al., *Findings on Racial Segregation*. Originally published in 1924. Passage 2 is adapted from Sarah Williams, *A Plea for the Equality of All*. Originally published in 1925. Truskowski was an American politician; *Findings* was an essay in support of racial segregation laws in the South. Williams, an American writer, wrote *A Plea* in response to Truskowski.

Passage 1

That the entire population of a particular race is barred by another from partaking in any public function together; that they are united as humans but segregated
Line by law within the same spaces they live and share;
5 and that they are entitled to the same provisions yet cannot receive them together: are all social phenomena supposedly impossible to rationalize on theoretical principle. But when looking at it in a different way, a logical answer emerges and is easily determined. The
10 goal of these social intrusions is the greatest possible amount of happiness. Anything that hinders this objective is wrong; anything that promotes it is right. If segregating the man of color from the white man advances the mutual happiness of the two races, then
15 this should be recognized and endorsed as the law of the land.

Any other endeavor would be in opposition to our inherent rights of happiness; and so it would never benefit men of color to change their position or the
20 status quo.

It seems indisputable to us that our mutual happiness, not just the contentment of men of color, requires that we never join together in any public place or function. We must pursue our interests in the confines of nature.
25 Is it not obvious that our different complexions, mentalities, and cultural traits prevent us from bonding together in work or recreation and demand that we segregate from each other in public spheres? And is it not obvious that the harmony of society, which
30 transforms the segregation of race into a means of conservation, has been exemplified and shown in nature itself when it created the essences of the two races in such a clearly dissimilar manner? This is enough; we do not need to summon concerns that are irrelevant to the
35 situation. Let us not create bad blood between fellow humans. You must, you absolutely must permit the continuation of a separation that no idea, no emotion, can possibly breach. Realize that the happiness of everyone requires this of you.

Passage 2

40 Vying for the equality of men of color, my primary argument is founded on this basic principle, that if he is not allowed by law to associate with white men, he will never progress into full citizenship; for they are "separate but equal," but they are not equal and never will be until
45 joined together. And how can men of color be equal if the law that segregates them is written by the white man? Unless men of color are present when the law is written, what verification is there that they will receive an equal share? If men of color are to be considered equal in all
50 things to white men, they must be desegregated; and the equality of mankind, which our constitution dictates is an inherent right of all, can only be achieved by removing the corrupted and disadvantaging lines that segregate us; but the social and political station of men
55 of color, currently, prevents them from investigating such things …

Contemplate, sir, objectively, these observations—for a trace of this reality was hinted at when you suggested, "that the entire population of a particular race is barred
60 by another is a social phenomena supposedly impossible to rationalize." If so, on what does your argument stand? If the theoretical rights of white men undergo deliberate thought and reasoning, those of men of color, by the same principle, should undergo the same process:
65 however, the prevailing opinion in this nation differs; founded on the same argument you use to justify the segregation of men of color—prescription.

Consider—I write you as a politician—whether, when white men struggle for their liberty and are permitted to
70 decide for themselves regarding their own happiness, is it not illogical and unfair to exclude men of color, even if you confidently believe you are dictating the principles best estimated to elevate their happiness? Who made white men the only judges, if men of color share with
75 them the ability to reason?

In a similar manner, contend dictators of every fashion, from the weak head of state to the weak head of family; they all eagerly suppress reason; yet always maintain that they take its mantle only to be helpful. Do
80 you not play a similar role, when you force all men of color, by preventing them from participating publicly with white men, to remain locked behind lines and to submit in silence?

Strategy

Bare Bones

When the answer choices use complicated vocabulary, it can make the process of elimination difficult. However, by cutting the choices down to their "bare bones," you can better evaluate each option to eliminate incorrect answers.

Use this strategy on multiple texts questions that ask you to determine the relationship between the passages or how one author may respond to the other.

❶ Identify the key action phrases and passage labels in the answer choices.

❷ Cross out all remaining words.

❸ Eliminate answer choices that do not reflect the relationship between the passages.

Review question 15 with your teacher. Use the Bare Bones strategy to answer the question as a class.

15

Which best describes the overall relationship between Passage 1 and Passage 2?

A) Passage 2 strongly counters the perspective in Passage 1.

B) Passage 2 draws alternate conclusions from the information presented in Passage 1.

C) Passage 2 expands on the viewpoint explained in Passage 1.

D) Passage 2 reiterates the argument made in Passage 1.

The following questions refer to the passages on page 342. Work on your own using the Bare Bones strategy to answer questions 16 and 17.

16

How would Truskowski most likely have reacted to lines 79–83 ("Do you … silence") in Passage 2?

A) He would understand because he believes the principles of nature encourage the different races to function in harmony.

B) He would agree because he believes men of color should not remain confined to a separate social class.

C) He would disagree because he believes men of color have a more difficult role to play in society than white men do.

D) He would oppose this notion because he believes the natures of white men and men of color are fundamentally different.

17

How would Williams most likely respond to Truskowski's statement in lines 21–23, Passage 1 ("It seems … function")?

A) She would claim that the idea of a mutual happiness existing between the races is unlikely as long as the interests of white men differ from the interests of men of color.

B) She would argue that men of color cannot achieve their optimum happiness if they are not allowed to decide for themselves.

C) She would question if mutual happiness between the two races could ever be sustained if they were allowed to associate publicly together.

D) She would point out that we cannot fully understand what would result in societal happiness.

This page intentionally left blank

Practice Set 3 | Complete the practice set. When you have finished, double-check your work.

Questions 15–20 are based on the following passages.

Passage 1 is adapted from Truskowski et al., *Findings on Racial Segregation.* Originally published in 1924. Passage 2 is adapted from Sarah Williams, *A Plea for the Equality of All.* Originally published in 1925. Truskowski was an American politician; *Findings* was an essay in support of racial segregation laws in the South. Williams, an American writer, wrote *A Plea* in response to Truskowski.

Passage 1

That the entire population of a particular race is barred by another from partaking in any public function together; that they are united as humans but segregated
Line by law within the same spaces they live and share;
5 and that they are entitled to the same provisions yet cannot receive them together: are all social phenomena supposedly impossible to rationalize on theoretical principle. But when looking at it in a different way, a logical answer emerges and is easily determined. The
10 goal of these social intrusions is the greatest possible amount of happiness. Anything that hinders this objective is wrong; anything that promotes it is right. If segregating the man of color from the white man advances the mutual happiness of the two races, then
15 this should be recognized and endorsed as the law of the land.

Any other endeavor would be in opposition to our inherent rights of happiness; and so it would never benefit men of color to change their position or the
20 status quo.

It seems indisputable to us that our mutual happiness, not just the contentment of men of color, requires that we never join together in any public place or function. We must pursue our interests in the confines of nature.
25 Is it not obvious that our different complexions, mentalities, and cultural traits prevent us from bonding together in work or recreation and demand that we segregate from each other in public spheres? And is it not obvious that the harmony of society, which
30 transforms the segregation of race into a means of conservation, has been exemplified and shown in nature itself when it created the essences of the two races in such a clearly dissimilar manner? This is enough; we do not need to summon concerns that are irrelevant to the
35 situation. Let us not create bad blood between fellow humans. You must, you absolutely must permit the continuation of a separation that no idea, no emotion, can possibly breach. Realize that the happiness of everyone requires this of you.

Passage 2

40 Vying for the equality of men of color, my primary argument is founded on this basic principle, that if he is not allowed by law to associate with white men, he will never progress into full citizenship; for they are "separate but equal," but they are not equal and never will be until
45 joined together. And how can men of color be equal if the law that segregates them is written by the white man? Unless men of color are present when the law is written, what verification is there that they will receive an equal share? If men of color are to be considered equal in all
50 things to white men, they must be desegregated; and the equality of mankind, which our constitution dictates is an inherent right of all, can only be achieved by removing the corrupted and disadvantaging lines that segregate us; but the social and political station of men
55 of color, currently, prevents them from investigating such things …

Contemplate, sir, objectively, these observations—for a trace of this reality was hinted at when you suggested, "that the entire population of a particular race is barred
60 by another is a social phenomena supposedly impossible to rationalize." If so, on what does your argument stand? If the theoretical rights of white men undergo deliberate thought and reasoning, those of men of color, by the same principle, should undergo the same process;
65 however, the prevailing opinion in this nation differs; founded on the same argument you use to justify the segregation of men of color—prescription.

Consider—I write you as a politician—whether, when white men struggle for their liberty and are permitted to
70 decide for themselves regarding their own happiness, is it not illogical and unfair to exclude men of color, even if you confidently believe you are dictating the principles best estimated to elevate their happiness? Who made white men the only judges, if men of color share with
75 them the ability to reason?

In a similar manner, contend dictators of every fashion, from the weak head of state to the weak head of family; they all eagerly suppress reason; yet always maintain that they take its mantle only to be helpful. Do
80 you not play a similar role, when you force all men of color, by preventing them from participating publicly with white men, to remain locked behind lines and to submit in silence?

18

The authors of both passages would most likely agree with which of the following statements about men of color during their time period?

A) The essence of their personal natures were the same as white men.

B) They needed to be desegregated in order to be equal in society.

C) They were as happy in life as white men were.

D) They were generally prevented from associating with white men in public places.

19

The main purpose of both passages is to

A) suggest a means to resolve a social injustice.

B) discuss the justness of a particular social construct.

C) analyze the effects that segregation has on society.

D) describe the duties that governments have to their citizens.

20

In lines 59–61, the author of Passage 2 refers to a statement made in Passage 1 in order to

A) call into question the credibility of the author of Passage 1 regarding racial issues.

B) offer examples that refute the claim made about men of color in the first sentence of Passage 1.

C) advance her own case by highlighting what she considers illogical reasoning in Passage 1.

D) support the conclusions made by the author of Passage 1 about racial segregation.

Mini-Test

Complete the mini-test. When you have finished, double-check your work.

Questions 32–41 are based on the following passages.

Passage 1 is adapted from Luis DeBois, *Equality in Europe, Volume 1*. Originally published in 1920. Passage 2 is adapted from Heather Mueller, *Empowering All Peoples*. Originally published in 1921. As wealth inequalities in Western democracies soared during the twentieth century, debates arose regarding the impact that wealth inequality was having on society and whether the economic system should address these concerns.

Passage 1

I have demonstrated how socialism destroys or alters the inherent inequalities which propel our society; but is that all? Or does it not also impact the productive
Line inequality between the rich and poor which has been, up
5 to now, eternally grounded in human society? I suspect that the social reforms that render all things equal between the entrepreneur and employee, the innovative and unmotivated, the superiors and inferiors more or less, will exalt the poor and make them ever more equal
10 to the rich. But for this, more than anything else, I feel compelled to make myself abundantly clear; for the crude and unruly whims of our generation have taken no greater liberty than on a matter such as this.

In Europe there are those who, ignoring the great
15 personal driver of wealth, would make the rich and poor not only alike but equal. They would provide to each the same resources, levy on each the same responsibilities, and award to each the same liberties; they would equate them in all things—their stations, their roles, their
20 vocations. Is it not obvious, that by equalizing the rich and the poor, both are demotivated; that so ludicrous a notion set against the natural competitive drive of society could ever result in anything but disheartened rich and idle poor?

25 This is not how the Americans regard the inequalities that exist between the rich and the poor. They believe that because wealth provides such a deep-seated motivator that propels all individuals to be productive, the most efficient society is one that rewards those who
30 strive to work; and they maintain that advancement does not come from leveling the playing field so that everyone can achieve the same living standard, but by motivating each person to achieve their personal standard by working competitively. The Americans have ingrained
35 into their society the great principles of capitalism that have driven the advancements of our generation, by

holding to the inequality between the rich and the poor, in order that both strive to be as productive in society as they can.

Passage 2

40 Until recently, inequality has been embedded into the foundation of society; relations built on equality rarely existed; to be equals was to be competitors; two individuals could barely share in anything, or agree to any good-natured dealing, without the law designating
45 one the superior of the other. Humanity has advanced past this scheme, and most things now tend to utilize, as a starting point in human relations, a fair equality, instead of a ruling by the powerful. But of all relations, the inequality between the rich and poor, being the
50 strongest and most avaricious, and linked to the symbol of elite power, was certain to be the last to throw off the old and reform to the new; for, to the degree that a thing is related to wealth is the degree to which those in power will resist all challenges to their dominion with which
55 they have even accidentally been granted …

… The proper place for all peoples is the greatest and highest they are able to reach. What that is cannot be determined without equality in opportunity … Let every person be given an equal beginning, without bias toward
60 or against any, and riches will begin to be acquired by those people who show by ability to be the most capable and deserving of possessing them. There is no need to fear that the lazy will inherit any occupation that would be better employed by the ambitious who have earned
65 it. Every person will achieve according to their ability, by the only means in which ability can be tested—by working—and society will benefit from employing the best of all its citizens. But to restrict beforehand by an unfair boundary, and hold that whoever is talented,
70 ambitious, intelligent, or able in body—attributes that are developed within individuals from any background or class—should not utilize their potential, or shall only realize it if they can somehow overcome the many obstacles that the wealthy do not know, is unjust to
75 the individual and a loss to society. Furthermore, it is the most effective way of ensuring that, in a society so restricted by income, the potential that is not permitted to be realized is kept at bay.

32

As used in line 9, "exalt" most nearly means

A) praise.

B) revere.

C) intensify.

D) raise.

33

In Passage 1, DeBois implies that making the rich and poor equal in society would have which consequence?

A) Neither population would feel valued.

B) Both populations would be significantly demotivated.

C) The rich would try to reclaim their lost wealth.

D) The rich and the poor would achieve a living standard they do not need.

34

Which choice provides the best evidence for the answer to the previous question?

A) Lines 14–16 ("In Europe … equal")

B) Lines 16–20 ("They … vocations")

C) Lines 20–24 ("Is it … poor")

D) Lines 25–26 ("This is … poor")

35

Which choice best states the relationship between the two passages?

A) Passage 2 explains the practical challenges of a concept proposed in Passage 1.

B) Passage 2 challenges the primary argument of Passage 1.

C) Passage 2 gives additional context to support the viewpoint offered in Passage 1.

D) Passage 2 expands on several ideas suggested in Passage 1.

36

In Passage 2, Mueller most strongly suggests that the rich are resistant to change because they

A) believe they serve as investors in economic growth.

B) wish to maintain their wealth and social power.

C) do not want to work with unmotivated people.

D) think economic inequality is an important construct.

37

Both passages discuss the idea of personal motivation in relationship to

A) individuals' financial resources.

B) personal obstacles to success.

C) humanity's innate competitiveness.

D) governmental provisions.

1   **1**

38

Both authors would most likely agree that the changes to the economic system they describe would be

A) part of a broad shift toward greater equality in society.

B) likely to incur costs that outweigh the benefits.

C) inevitable due to the economic benefits of wealth equality.

D) opposed to the ideals of American capitalism.

39

DeBois in Passage 1 would most likely describe the stance taken by Mueller in lines 58–62 in Passage 2 ("Let every ... them") as

A) less radical about governmental provisions than it might initially seem.

B) convincing on principle but impractical to implement in reality.

C) foolish but consistent with a position held by other proponents of wealth equality.

D) effective in driving economic activity in America but not in Europe.

40

Which choice best describes the factors that the two authors believe are fundamental in an ideal economic system?

A) DeBois believes an ideal economic system would encourage inequalities between the rich and poor, whereas Mueller believes wealth inequalities should be evened out in an ideal economic system.

B) DeBois believes that educational achievement should dictate the position one takes in the economy, whereas Mueller believes education is an irrelevant factor.

C) DeBois believes the government should provide each individual the same economic opportunities, whereas Mueller believes the government should not be involved in providing economic opportunities.

D) DeBois believes people will do what is best for society if they are competitively motivated by the desire for wealth, whereas Mueller believes it is best for society if people are allowed to do what they find most satisfying.

41

Based on Passage 2, Mueller would most likely say that the effect of the "great principles of capitalism" (line 35) on wealth equality has which result?

A) It prevents many people from reaching their highest potential.

B) It makes it hard for people to understand each other's circumstances.

C) It coincidentally promotes income equality.

D) It ensures that qualified people receive suitable employment.

STOP

**If you finish before time is called, you may check your work on this section only.
Do not turn to any other section.**

This page intentionally left blank

Wrap-Up

Complete the wrap-up. When you have finished, double-check your work.

Questions 4–6 are based on the following passages.

Passage 1 is adapted from Abraham Lincoln, "Address to the Young Men's Lyceum of Springfield, Illinois." Originally delivered in 1838. Passage 2 is from Henry David Thoreau, "Resistance to Civil Government." Originally published in 1849.

Passage 1

For the sake of future generations, let all citizens swear by the blood of the Revolution never to violate the laws of the country in any way or tolerate their violation
Line by others. As the patriots of 1776 did to the support of
5 the Declaration of Independence, so to the support of the Constitution and laws let every American pledge his life, his property, and his sacred honor; let every man remember that to violate the law is to trample on the blood of his father, to mar his own character,
10 and to threaten his children's liberty. Let reverence for laws be imparted by every American mother; let it be taught in schools, in seminaries, and in colleges; let it be preached from the pulpit, proclaimed in legislative halls, and enforced in courts of justice. And, in short,
15 let it become the *political doctrine* of the nation; and let the old and the young, the rich and the poor of all genders and colors yield unceasingly upon its altar. While this sentiment prevails throughout the nation, let it be known that efforts to subvert our national freedom
20 would be fruitless.

While I so pressingly urge a strict observance of all laws, I am not suggesting that unjust laws do not exist or that grievances may not arise for which there is no legal recourse; I mean to say no such thing. What I do mean
25 to say is that, if unjust laws exist, they should be repealed as soon as possible; but until that time, for the sake of example, all laws should be religiously observed.

There is no grievance that justifies protest by the masses. In any case that arises, such as a pledge of
30 abolitionism, one of two positions is true: the condition is right within itself, and therefore deserves protection by law, or it is wrong, and therefore should be prohibited by legal enactments. In neither case is intervention by the populace necessary, justifiable, or excusable.

Passage 2

35 Unjust laws exist; shall we be content to obey them, or shall we set out to amend them until we have succeeded? Within our government, men think that they should wait to speak out against wrongful laws until they have persuaded the majority. They think that if they
40 protest, the outcome will be worse than the injustice. But this is the government's fault. Why does it not anticipate and provide for legal reform? Why does it not listen to the minority?

If the injustice is part of the debate within
45 government, let it pass; perhaps it will fade naturally. But if the injustice is a policy, a command, or a strategy that only serves itself, then perhaps you should consider rising up. However, if the breach requires you to be an agent of corruption, then I say, break the law. Let
50 your voice erode authority. I cannot lend myself to the wrongdoing that I condemn.

As for legal procedures to remedy such offenses, I am not aware of any such measures. They would take too much time, and a man's life will be wasted. I have
55 other affairs to attend to. I did not come into this world to make it a good place to live in, but to live in it, be it good or bad. Men cannot do everything but must do something.

I do not hesitate to say that those who call themselves
60 Abolitionists should immediately withdraw their support from the government … and not wait until they constitute a majority of one. I think that with God on their side, they must not wait for others. Moreover, a man whose views are more sound than his neighbors
65 already constitutes a majority of one.

Wrap-Up

4

Which choice identifies a central tension between the two passages?

A) Lincoln proposes changes to policy concerning unjust laws, but Thoreau argues that such changes would not be well-received by civilians.

B) Lincoln expresses concerns about civil uprising against laws, but Thoreau dismisses those concerns as trivial.

C) Lincoln maintains that citizens should observe all laws in every instance, whereas Thoreau argues that citizens should protest if they feel a law is unjust.

D) Lincoln offers a viewpoint about legal injustices that conflicts with Thoreau, and Thoreau states that Lincoln's viewpoint is unfounded.

5

Based on the passages, Lincoln would most likely describe the behavior that Thoreau recommends in lines 48–49 ("However . . . law") as

A) an acceptable reaction to an intolerable situation.

B) a rejection of the country's proper forms of remedy.

C) an honorable response to an unjust law.

D) a misapplication of a core principle of the Constitution.

6

Based on the passages, one commonality in the stances Lincoln and Thoreau take toward abolitionism is that

A) both authors see the cause as warranting drastic action.

B) both authors view the cause as central to their argument.

C) neither author expects the cause to win widespread acceptance.

D) neither author embraces the cause as his own.

Review

Multiple texts questions can be identified by these features:

- two passages
- a question that asks you to compare or contrast the passages or the authors' ideas

Evidence and Elimination

To answer a multiple texts question, follow these steps:

1. Determine how the question relates to both passages.
2. Eliminate any choice that fails to accurately describe both passages or doesn't relate them correctly.

Exit

If you've found the answer ...

Verify that it is supported with textual evidence. If so, mark your answer and continue to the next question.

If you're stuck between two choices ...

Use your pencil to mark how well each choice fits with each passage. Put a check if a choice agrees with a passage, an "X" if the choice disagrees with the passage, and a dash if it is somewhere in the middle. Compare your marks to select the better choice.

If you have no idea what the answer is ...

Use the title and opening paragraph of each passage to get a general idea of the central argument, and select the choice that is most consistent.

Contributors

Publisher
Craig Gehring

Chief Academic Officer
Oliver Pope

Managing Editor
Allison Eskind

Art and Production Director
Jeff Garrett

Lead Instructional Design
Stephanie Constantino

Cover Design
Nicole St. Pierre

Senior Proofreader
Kristin Shirley

Senior Editors
Emily DeYoung
Reeja Geevarghese
Eric Manuel
Nick Pilewski

Senior Slides Designer
Corrine Streff

Content Creation
Alicia Alexander
Christine Benitez
Jennifer Berezewski
Rosa Caraballo
Emily Collins
Lizette Daniel
Emily DeYoung
Carolyn Farricy
Kayla Freeman
Peter Frost
Reeja Geevarghese
Kimberly Haas
James Jones
Danielle Kavc
Aeron Kopriva
Irit Maor
Eric Manuel
Candace Moore
Jennifer Morson
Cheyenne Nicholson
Eboney Pegues
Nick Pilewski
Rebecca Posner
Lauren Pope
Lisa Primeaux-Redmond
Keri Repka
Margaret Robinson
Lindsay Romano
Daniel Romero
Rachel Rorick
Jordan Sermon
Stephanie Stewart
Minrose Straussman
Luke Switzer
Candace Williams
Karmen Williams
Linda Wickersham

Proofreaders
Lauren Brecht
Cassandra Galentine
Ginny Gillikin
June Manuel
Lauren Miklovic
Natalie Mucker
Jillian Musso
Brittany Robertson
Rachel Rorick
Minrose Straussman
Corrine Streff
Luke Switzer
Jackson Thomas

Curriculum Review
Trese Bakker
Kim Blaise
Andrea Broussard
Grace Butler
Khalilah Campfield
Latrisha Jackson
Kamiya Jones
Sarah Kennedy
Shannon Marks
Roland Moore
Keina Nixon
Sarah North
Tabitha Perry
Zola Pollard
Llaina Rash
Kim Redeaux
John Rees
Tia Rutledge
Cathy Tall
Florence Williams
Michelle Wolf

Layout
Elaine Broussard
Haley Herman
Pareesa Khwaja
Karen Kilpatrick
Aeron Kopriva
Kayla Manuel
Hope Oswald
Amanda Pfeil
Jaye Pratt
Lisa Primeaux-Redmond
Julie Snee
Jennifer Taphorn
Eliza Todorova
Elizabeth Turman
Joanna Watkins

Slides
Cheryl Daitch
Chris Davies
Lisa Halem
Karen Kilpatrick
Ryan Streff
Dee Turman